M000113826

KIT CARSON AND HIS THREE WIVES

KIT CARSON

& His Three Wives

A FAMILY HISTORY

◦✕ ⚜ ✕◦

MARC SIMMONS

UNIVERSITY OF NEW MEXICO PRESS ◆ ALBUQUERQUE

A Volume in the Calvin P. Horn Lectures
in Western History and Culture

For Mark L. Gardner,
A True Historian

©2003 by Marc Simmons
First edition
All rights reserved.

First paperbound printing, 2011
Paperbound ISBN: 978-0-8263-3297-4

22 21 20 19 18 17 16   2 3 4 5 6 7 8

Library of Congress Cataloging-in-Publication Data

Simmons, Marc. Kit Carson and his three wives :
a family history / Marc Simmons.—
1st ed.
p.   cm. —
(A volume in the Calvin P. Horn lectures in Western history and culture)
Includes bibliographical references and index.
ISBN 0-8263-3296-X (alk. paper)
1. Carson, Kit, 1809–1868. 2. Carson, Kit, 1809–1868—Family.
3. Pioneers—West (U.S.)—Biography.
4. Pioneers' spouses—West (U.S.)—Biography.
5. Indian women—West (U.S.)—Biography.
6. Hispanic American women—New Mexico—Taos—Biography.
7. Carson family. 8. Frontier and pioneer life—West (U.S.)
9. West (U.S.)—Biography. 10. Taos (N.M.)—Biography.
I. Title. II. Series: Calvin P. Horn lectures in Western history and culture.
F592.C33 S56 2003
978'.02'0922—dc21
2003006702

Design: Mina Yamashita

Contents

Preface

Even before his death in May of 1868, at the relatively young age of 59, Christopher "Kit" Carson had attained the image of a national hero and was well on his way to becoming a symbolic figure, personifying the nineteenth-century ideal of a self-confident man of action.

Carson's career as a frontiersman was magnified by most of his early biographers and shamelessly embellished and exploited by hack authors of dime novels who cast him as a fearless champion and exemplar of the pioneer movement. In the hands of both biographers and novelists Kit Carson glittered as a paragon of virtue.

Beginning in the early 1970s, however, the pendulum swung the other way. Revisionist historians had taken a second look at the prevailing story of the American West and found it wanting. The New Western History that soon emerged aimed at demolishing the "ethnocentric" focus of the old history, which had emphasized "the advancement of white male pioneers across the continent," and substituted in its place a reordered version that extolled the accomplishments of others.[1]

In the process, lionized frontiersmen of old—figures like Daniel Boone, David Crockett, George Armstrong Custer, and Kit Carson—were not merely demoted or banished but in varying degrees were demonized, sometimes with considerable heat. At the same time, some traditional writers continued to produce books about the West and its people that showed respect for objectivity and the rules of evidence.

With the politicizing of much of formal history in the late twentieth century, Carson's reputation became blackened by the hurling of such epithets as genocidal racist, butcher of the Indians, and the western Hitler. Elsewhere, I have termed this negative characterization of him as "Kit's monster image," and noted that it is largely a fabrication of the post-1960s.[2] Unfortunately, it is the image that a majority of Americans now hold of the man, if they can recall him at all.

The widespread perception of "Carson as villain" ironically is exactly the opposite of the view of contemporaries who knew him, and whose eye-witness status lends their judgments credibility. A newspaper correspondent, writing up a profile of Kit that appeared in an 1857 issue of the *Missouri Statesman* attested that: "He is universally beloved, and a favorite with all classes, Indians included."[3] The weight of verifiable evidence establishes that at the time the words were written, they were essentially true.

A statement that has a similar ring was made by a man who in the 1870s had worked for the Kansas Pacific Railroad between Kansas City and Denver. He wrote: "Everyone in this section of the country . . . has a reverence for the memory of Kit Carson . . . He did more toward the civilization of the plains than all other forces, including the army."[4] Few today would be willing to say such a thing, but the important point is that those words reflect the deep-felt sentiments toward Kit Carson by people of his era and immediately afterward.

The answers to Carson's modern critics are readily available and convincingly presented in Harvey Carter's now standard *"Dear Old Kit,' The Historical Christopher Carson* and in Tom Dunlay's comprehensive *Kit Carson & the Indians*. Robert M. Utley's recent survey of the fur trappers' role as explorers, *A Life Wild and Perilous*, includes a fresh treatment of Carson's years as a mountain man, while David Roberts's *A Newer World: Kit Carson, John C. Frémont, and the Claiming of the American West* examines critically the close relationship of the two men and how the evolving friendship influenced each of their careers.[5]

These books, together with earlier biographies, prompt the question: What is there left to say about Kit Carson? In plain fact, a historical figure of his dimensions is in perennial need of renewal by both scholarly and popular writers. In spite of a great deal of past research and publication, there still exist precincts within Carson's life story that remain locked in shadows and surrounded by confusion.

I have been following Kit Carson's trail for more than thirty years, assembling pertinent material from archives and libraries around the country. In this book, meant to be merely the first in a series dealing topically with individual aspects of the Carson saga, I have addressed the subject of his three wives in an attempt to show Kit's struggle to become a settled family man. This is a side of him that has been passed over lightly or even ignored by most previous authors.

For those readers unfamiliar with the outline of Carson's career, the following lean chronology may help to fit my description of his domestic life into the context of all else that swirled about him.

1809–1811	Birth and infancy in Kentucky
1811–1826	Boyhood in the backwoods of central Missouri
1826–1829	His teenage rambles in New Mexico
1829–1832	Apprentice trapper in California with Ewing Young
1831–1841	Kit's decade as a mountain man
1842–1849	Guide for Frémont's expeditions, the Mexican War, and Kit's transcontinental courier missions
1849–1853	Attempts to earn a living and to establish a new residence in Rayado, N.M.
1854–1861	Kit serves as a skilled and effective Indian agent; headquartered in Taos
1861–1867	Military career, Civil War and Indian Wars
1867	Resignation from the Army and the moving of his family to Boggsville, Colo.
1868	Death at Fort Lyon, Colo.

Even a casual reading of the existing Carson biographies suggests that his life was crowded with extraordinary episodes. Destiny appears to have had much in store for this rough-hewn back country boy, when it introduced him as a player in so many of the landmark events that shaped the course of westward expansion.

In 1856, Kit Carson, being illiterate, dictated his personal history up to that point, and the manuscript came to the attention of Army Surgeon DeWitt C. Peters. The doctor decided to use it as the basis for a substantial book about Kit, in part to combat "many erroneous impressions" of him that had been spread by dime novelists and careless journalists.[6]

Carson's memoirs center upon his galaxy of heart-stopping adventures. Dr. Peters, knowing that an eastern audience craved tales of derring-do set in the West, slanted Kit's biography in that direction. Still, it strikes us as strange that the memoirs contain not the slightest mention of the author's two Indian wives and only passing reference to his third wife, Josefa Jaramillo, to whom he had been married for thirteen years, as of 1856.[7]

It is difficult to remember that women in the nineteenth century were, more often than not, largely invisible, a common refrain claiming that the only times their names appeared in the newspapers were upon the occasion of their marriages and deaths.[8] That notwithstanding, Kit had his own reasons for remaining reticent about his spouses, as will be evident from my narrative.

Since the memoirs are the only account of himself, large or small, that Kit ever committed to paper, the failure to say anything about his "love life" must be considered by scholars as a regrettable omission. Working under that handicap, I combed other sources and pulled together available documentary fragments in an effort to sketch profiles of each of the three Carson wives. As much as the thin evidence would allow, I tried to show how they may have affected their husband's attitudes and sentiments and contributed to the legend that enveloped his name.

In the Introduction, readers will find a commentary on some of Carson's personal characteristics that reveal both his assets and deficits when it came to the matter of being a good husband and father. Much mapping of his temperament has already been carried out by historians intent upon revealing the inner man. Kit himself made that task unusually difficult by carefully guarding the privacy of his family and not putting its business and his beliefs on public view.

Introduction

Kit Carson came from a large family. His father, Lindsey Carson, had two wives and sired fifteen children, Kit being eleventh in line. When Lindsey died in a farming accident in 1818 at age 64, his second wife Rebecca was pregnant with their last child, a boy subsequently named Lindsey, Jr.

The Carson farm lay near the village of Franklin, near the Missouri River, in what was known as the Booneslick country of central Missouri. The family had moved there from Kentucky in 1811, when Kit was less than two years old.

Born of Scotch-Irish stock, Lindsey Carson possessed the restlessness said to be characteristic of that people. He had left a prosperous farm in North Carolina in 1793 to take up new land in Kentucky, only to pull stakes as that country became settled and start over again on the Missouri frontier. Kit too was of a restless nature, part of his biological inheritance.

In the wake of Lindsey's untimely death, the Carson family slowly disintegrated. By his early teens Kit had become increasingly troublesome, the more so after his widowed mother married another farmer, Joseph Martin, and started a new household. The boy rebelled against his stepfather, so Rebecca finally placed him in a formal apprenticeship with Franklin saddler and harness-maker David Workman.

Young Kit, shop-bound, suffered miserably. Franklin in those days, the mid 1820s, was teeming with merchants and freighters plying the newly opened trail to Santa Fe within what was then the Republic of Mexico. Buckskin-clad trappers, just in from the Rocky Mountains, also mingled in the streets and sometimes patronized the Workman saddlery. While bent over his leather, Kit listened to the tales of their exotic adventures, built private dreams from them, and plotted his escape to the Far West.

In 1826 Kit Carson ran away under the cover of night, breaking the law by violating his apprentice contract. But having learned in his sixteen years that life could be lived joyously in the wilderness, he had no intention of becoming a farmer like his late father, or remaining confined at a saddler's workbench as his mother wished. Instead, Kit's down-home stubbornness, a trait acquired from his Scotch-Irish forebears, led him westward until he soon caught up with a merchant train bound for Santa Fe. Upon agreeing to help at herding the livestock, he was granted admission to the caravan and passage to New Mexico. Thereby, he took his first steps on a long walk into the history books.

For the next three years, the green Missouri boy ambled around New Mexico, living hand-to-mouth by his wits and gaining experience that seasoned and matured him. Along the way, he acquired fluency in the Spanish language.

Kit gravitated to Taos, the hub of the southern Rockies fur trade. Since 1821, when Mexico won her independence from Spain, far-ranging trappers had found the small adobe-built community 75 miles north of Santa Fe to be a handy supply base and a convenient place to sell their valuable packs of beaver furs. It also served them, between the fall and spring hunts, as a popular winter resort where a man could frolic at lively fandangos and quench his thirst on Taos Lightning, the stout local liquor.

During the winter of 1827–1828, Kit Carson worked in Taos as cook for Ewing Young, a Tennesseean who earlier had been involved in the overland trade with Santa Fe, but was now recognized as a master trapper. Since the night of his hasty departure from Franklin, Kit had yearned to enter the elite ranks of the mountain man fraternity. Yet inasmuch as he lacked knowledge of the trapping trade, no one seemed eager to break him in and give him a chance in the wilds; that is, until Ewing Young reconsidered.

In the summer of 1829, Young assembled his own brigade of forty men, with the intention of crossing the Southwestern deserts to trap the central valley of California. Kit says simply, "I joined the party. We left Taos in August."[1] Following that brief introductory statement in his memoirs, he gives the most detailed account of any of his trapping experiences. With the enthusiasm of youth, he found that long, perilous maiden trip to be exhilarating beyond his wildest imagination.

When the exhausted brigade returned to Taos in April of 1831, Kit rode beside Ewing Young, having earned the role of his most dependable lieutenant. The young man had also mastered the trappers' craft, so that now he could expect a welcome at the campfire of any veteran mountaineer.

Ewing Young paid off the men, several hundred dollars each, and they promptly, in good mountain man fashion, embarked on a headlong spree. Kit, thinking back upon that uproarious occasion, observed sagely: "We passed the time gloriously spending our money freely—never thinking that our lives were risked in gaining it. Our only idea was to get rid of the dross . . . and have as much pleasure and enjoyment as the country would afford."[2]

Those improvident words clearly indicate that the newly fledged Kit Carson was rapidly assimilating the content of mountain man culture, with its distinctive attitudes, customs, and behavior. While the work requirements of fur trapping defined the structure of that way of life, borrowed Indian elements supplied much of its flavor and character.

Kit Carson, therefore, in becoming a mountain man, simultaneously was "Indianized." He learned those Native skills that were most useful in the wilderness, particularly the ones related to survival. Besides sign language, he gained a working knowledge of perhaps a half dozen Indian tongues. And, most significantly, he came to understand the workings of the Indian mind, how and why their thinking ran in seemingly tortured directions. Such knowledge, plus more subtle insights acquired from his Arapaho and Cheyenne wives, would one day stand Kit in good stead when he served as a U.S. Indian agent and led military expeditions against hostile tribes. It also made him a stellar negotiator, for while he could figure out Indians, they could also understand him.

Carson's entering into two Native marriages, in succession, was also typical of the assimilation process. Liaisons between trappers and Indian women invariably were complicated relationships. Sometimes they proved to be serene, almost idyllic, even in the midst of complexity, as with the case of Kit's first marriage to the Northern Arapaho, Waa-nibe. More often, as in his second marriage to an Indian, the conceited Southern Cheyenne named Making-Out-Road, the romance was apt to be tumultuous and short-lived.

At mid point in his life, Kit Carson witnessed the collapse of the fur trade, an event that forced the course of his later career into new channels. As one consequence, he wed in 1843 the captivating Josefa Jaramillo of Taos. They would remain together permanently and have eight children (the first-born dying in infancy). Considering the stresses to which the marriage was subjected, its survival can only be attributed to true love.

By all evidence, Kit was devoted to his Taos family and they to him. His many admirable, even endearing, qualities, however, won the affection of practically all who got to know him. Captain Nelson Thomasson, who marched with Kit in the Navajo campaign, told an assembly of aging veterans at Chicago in 1928 that Carson was often heard to say: "A man should never do anything in day time that would make him repent when the night came." And the captain concluded, "Do you think we [army] youngsters went wrong when we truly idolized this nature's man?"[3]

Even Kit's enemies, the Texan Confederates that he fought against in 1862 at the Civil War battle of Valverde, could not hide their awe of him and their instinctive feeling of attachment. As Southern Private William Davidson expressed their collective sentiments long afterward, Kit Carson was "a man the Texans loved," and our soldiers "who fell into his hands spoke highly of his kindness and say that his heart was really with us, but his judgment as to his duty took him to the Union side."[4]

Carson's unwavering sense of duty and loyalty toward his homeland led him in the years after his trapper period into prolonged tours of government service. His keen admirer Jessie Benton Frémont in 1880, remembering Kit, said that he possessed "a noble devotion to his country ... and a fine and genuinely American character."[5] Similar depictions of Carson were echoed repeatedly by those coming in contact with him. One was a young Army Dragoon, J.H. Coulter, who spoke of Kit's "intense patriotism," adding that, "it was always his ardent desire to do all he could to serve the government."[6]

Unfortunately, such patriotism and service regularly took Kit away from his Taos household, creating inevitable tensions in the marriage and denying him the ability to meet all of his domestic responsibilities. Those circumstances preyed on his mind, notably during the 1860s when he was much absent from home leading campaigns against the Indians.

Yet, even though he knew how much he would miss his wife and children, Carson ever was eager, upon each new assignment, to go once more on the open trail. The wanderlust in his blood, inherited from his father Lindsey, and his own inborn distaste for towns and cities exerted a strong pull toward the wilderness and isolation. As his close friend, Major

Edward Wynkoop once put it: "Kit was always restless in the midst of civilization."[7]

Carson must have wrestled frequently with the demands imposed by a sedentary family life and the conflict created when he attempted to answer the siren call of his restless nature. It was a problem that he never fully resolved, and one dealt with at length in this book.

The author wishes to expresses his sincere gratitude to the many people who over the years have supplied him with fugitive references that specifically speak to the subject of Kit Carson's family life. Foremost among them are the following: Leo and Bonita Oliva, John P. Wilson, Mark L. Gardner, Mel and Mary Cottom, Robert R. White, Joan Phillips, Nasario Garcia, Robert M. Utley, Timothy Messer-Kruse, Louis Serna, Harry Myers, Sandra Jaramillo, Dennis Rowley, José Antonio Esquibel, John M. Pimm, John Carson, Lee Burke, H. Denny Davis, Henry Crawford, William Swagerty, Janet Lecompte, John R. Adams, Tom Dunlay, and Becky Bustamante, Evelyn Vinogradov, and Fay Schiff.

The theme of this book derives from the author's delivery of the Calvin P. Horn Lecture in Western History and Culture at the University of New Mexico, Albuquerque, April 21, 2002. For the invitation, I am particularly indebted to Richard Etulain, formerly of the UNM history department, and David Holtby of the UNM Press.

PART I

Waa-Nibe

In early August, 1835, Kit Carson rode into the sprawling campground on the upper Green River in western Wyoming that was the site in that year of the annual trappers' rendezvous. He was part of a large brigade of mountain men, led by his old friend Jim Bridger, which had just finished a season of beaver hunting in dangerous Blackfeet country, surrounding headwaters of the Missouri River. The previous winter, Kit had suffered a painful shoulder wound in a fight with Blackfeet horse thieves, but the injury had healed nicely during the spring, leaving as a reminder now only an occasional twinge.

The Green at this point, marked by the mouth of Horse Creek, meandered through the broad Bridger Basin, studded with silvery sage. The river's well-grassed floodplain furnished abundant grazing for the herds of saddle horses and pack mules, while stands of cottonwood and willow along the water's edge yielded fuel for the many rendezvous cookfires. To the east loomed the lofty heights of the Wind River Range, in those days bonneted with perpetual snow. Even here at riverside in full summer, the air was uncomfortably cold, or so complained the Rev. Samuel Parker, a missionary on his way to Oregon who reached the camping ground, August 12.[1]

The 1835 rendezvous attracted several hundred white traders and trappers, and some 2,000 Indians who pitched their pale conical tepees for miles up and down the river. The agents for fur trading companies set up large tents stocked with an assortment of goods, luxuries as well as necessities, in demand west of the Rockies. For the trappers, the occasion offered not only an opportunity to resupply for the next hunting season, but also the chance to indulge in an interval of wild roistering. For several weeks, rendezvous provided a venue for horseraces, shooting matches, gambling, fist fighting, and drunken sprees, as the merchants always brought with them from the East, wooden casks of stout liquor to help oil the wheels of their rude frontier commerce.[2]

Carson could have had no inkling as he off-saddled amid the throng there on the banks of the Green that he would soon be facing a test of his courage, one destined to introduce him into the mainstream of Western history. The approaching episode also would prompt his companions in the trapping trade to refer to him thereafter as leading a charmed life and to warn others that the small, ordinarily mild-mannered Kit was emphatically not a man to be crossed.[3]

The theatrical incident, which became one of the best known in Carson's career, involved his "duel" with an arrogant French trapper, referred to in the historical literature as Shunar, but who, according to Rev. Parker, was commonly known by the nickname, "Great Bully of the Mountains."[4]

Dr. Peters in his biography initially applied the terms duel and duello to the Carson/Shunar altercation, a usage continued by later writers. The practice of dueling to settle personal disputes or questions of honor was at its height in the East during the 1830s and had invaded the western frontier. But not unexpectedly, in the rustic West little of the formalized ritual of the code duello survived. Instead, direct challenges were offered, men went for their weapons, and the one left standing when the gunsmoke cleared "gained satisfaction," in the accepted vocabulary of dueling.[5]

The details and outcome of Kit's encounter with Shunar are worth exploring at length, since what followed as a result of that event was his marriage to the Arapaho girl Waa-nibe and in the fullness of time, his first taste of fatherhood. Of equal significance, the duel is worth attention because Kit's conduct in this "affair of honor" reveals aspects of character that governed his behavior later when he played key roles in the ultimate taming of the West.

Considerable mystery has long surrounded the identity of the French bully whom Carson fought on the Green River. Even his true name remained uncertain. The Rev. Parker in his own contemporary account of the duel, the first to see print, wrote down what he heard at the rendezvous, something that sounded like Shunar. It was his best guess at the spelling of the man's French surname, being unfamiliar with that language.[6]

When Carson dictated his memoirs twenty years after publication of Parker's book, he gave no name at all for his opponent, identifying him only as "a large Frenchman." That proved a hindrance for Dr. Peters when shortly afterward he began work on his Carson biography, using the memoirs in manuscript as his chief source of information.

Quite likely, Peters simply asked Kit for the missing name while they were together at Taos, and Kit reaching back over two decades responded with what he could remember: "Shunan." That is close to Parker's Shunar, but plainly not the same. Peters then took the liberty of granting the Frenchman a title, so that throughout his book he indicates that Kit's quarrel was with "Captain Shunan." In fact, the bully had no such title, for as Carson in the memoirs states, his foe was a rank-and-file member of Captain Andrew S. Drips's brigade of trappers for the American Fur Company.[8]

The next two generations of writers blindly used either Shunar or Shunan when referring to the French bully. Finally, Harvey L. Carter in his newly edited version of the Carson memoirs (1968) added a note saying that "'Shunar' was no doubt an Americanized spelling of Chouinard, Chinard or some similar French name."[9]

Carter himself failed to follow up on that reasonable suggestion. And at the time he wrote, no Frenchman with a name resembling Chouinard was known to have been involved in the fur trade.

In 1980, the present writer, pursuing the Carter lead, combed the extensive papers of the American Fur Company in the archives of the Missouri Historical Society at St. Louis. Only a single name was found that met the requirements, that of Joseph Chouinard. On September 17 and 18, 1834, Lucien Fontenelle, a prominent fur man operating out of Bellevue Post on the right bank of the Missouri River below Omaha, wrote a number of orders on the firm of Pratte, Chouteau & Co. of St. Louis (his financial backers), who were successors of the Western Department of the American Fur Company. These orders could be drawn to pay the balances owed to trappers employed by Fontenelle and his associate, Capt. Andrew Drips.[10]

One of Fontenelle's notes, payable in St. Louis for the sum of $911.62 was issued to Joseph Chouinard for his services in the previous year's trapping expedition.[11] Moreover, two months earlier on July 8, 1834, Fontenelle had written another order for $70 in favor of Kit Carson, apparently representing the purchase from him of some twenty beaver skins that Kit as a free trapper had harvested in his spring hunt. This transaction occurred while Fontenelle and Carson were attending the 1834 rendezvous on a fork of the Green River. Chouinard must have been present, too, as an employee in Drips's brigade.[12] This suggests the probability that Carson and Chouinard had met at least a year prior to their duel, and if that was the case, the seeds of bad blood between them may have been sown at that time.

The surname Chouinard (with variant spellings) is a common one to this day in French-speaking Canada. It derives from the name of a village south of Paris. By the 1680s, if not before, settlers named Chouinard appear in the colonial records, and among them the Christian name of Joseph is often found. Neither the direct ancestors of the Joseph Chouinard who provoked Kit to violence, nor the man's personal history prior to 1834 have yet to surface.[13] David L. Brown, who attended the 1837 rendezvous and heard there an account of the duel, described "Shunar" as a "French creole of Lower Canada," while Bernard DeVoto called him "a French half-breed."[14]

Every account agrees, however, on Joseph Chouinard's abrasive nature. He could be arrogant, boastful, insulting and threatening all at once. Roaring drunk, he proved an even greater menace to others. Compounding the danger to anyone who got in his way was the fellow's great size—well over six feet, thick of body, with shoulders as broad as an ax handle. Sir William Drummond Stewart, British adventurer and baronet, who met Chouinard characterized him as "a stupid looking man of great apparent strength." Kit's estimation of his adversary was couched in his usual simple and direct phrasing: "[He was] a large Frenchman, one of those overbearing kind and very strong."[15]

Chouinard chose the height of the rendezvous to go on a day-long rampage. His surly mood, buttressed by "the demon of alcohol," sent him roaming through the camp, picking fights and beating up two or three fellow Frenchmen. No one initially seemed inclined to intervene, a failing that merely encouraged the bully in his barbarous conduct.[16]

By late afternoon, he had turned his attention to denigrating Americans, bellowing to all that he would, "take a switch and switch them," presumably because he thought no more of their fighting prowess than he did that of "mewling school boys." Plainly, Chouinard had the instinct of a brawler and one who enjoyed goading weaker men into rash acts, so he could give them a thrashing.

Then, all at once as evening was almost upon the encampment, a trim fighting rooster of bantam size stepped forward and challenged the blustering giant. Kit Carson at five feet six inches and weighing scarcely 150 pounds, proclaimed that he was the toughest American there and being unafraid, as others were, he told Chouinard to stop such talk or else "he would rip his guts."[17] Both Kit's honor and his patriotism had been offended, and while his blunt and angry words bore scant resemblance to those usually uttered in a formal challenge to a duel, the short speech was understood by everyone within hearing-distance to be just that.

Chouinard, in all likelihood elated, hurried off to his lodge to procure his rifle and saddle his horse. Word of the pending confrontation spread with the speed of a prairie fire, so that trappers and Indians dropped whatever they were doing and hurried to the open circle in front of the company tents.

Kit had rushed off to obtain a firearm for himself, and he grabbed the first loaded weapon that came to hand, a single-shot dragoon pistol. Then he hurried outside the camp circle to the ground where the horses were grazing, caught his own animal, and bridled it. In the heat of the moment, he returned bareback to face down his enemy.[17]

Descendants of the Scotch-Irish, which included a number of the mountain men, were capable, when aroused, of extraordinary feats of energy, violence and bravery. That accurately described Kit Carson. But in addition, he had the presence of mind during moments of crises to remain absolutely cool and focused, able to act in desperate situations that could cause the average man to freeze up, a fact often noted by his contemporaries.[18]

Chouinard and Carson approached the fighting circle from opposite directions, and catching sight of one another dashed forward. They stopped short, but so close that their horses heads were touching. Kit demanded to know whether he was the one Chouinard intended to shoot.

"No," the Frenchman replied, but in the same instant he swung his rifle in line to get a clear shot. Alert, Kit raised his pistol. In his words, "we both fired at the same time; all present said but one report was heard."[19]

On another occasion, however, Kit related that his shot got off a split second in advance of his antagonist.[20] The lead ball struck Chouinard in the right hand, shattering it and entirely tearing away the thumb. Then the ball came out at the wrist and passed through the arm above the elbow. The shot and the wound caused the Frenchman's rifle to jerk upward and his own bullet, instead of penetrating Kit's heart as he had intended, passed by the left side of his head, the powder burning Kit's eye and singeing his hair.[21]

In the 1860s Kit would tell Henry Inman that had Chouinard not been riding a skittish horse, "a Fourth-of-July brute," as he worded it, then in all likelihood his foe would have finished him off, as he was a splendid shot.[22] That the horse's misconduct may have been the ultimate cause of Kit's escaping with his life must be counted as one of the more extraordinary instances of good fortune that seemed to follow him through his trapping years. Still, Inman thought that it was Carson's courage that made the final difference in the fray.

He characterized him as possessing "nerves of steel and an imperturbability in the moment of supreme danger that was marvelous to contemplate." During his subsequent military career, soldiers would comment upon Kit's ability to remain calm and collected under fire. Inman also mentioned in passing that Chouinard's bullet had grazed Kit under the ear, leaving a scar that Inman saw.[23]

Among students of fur trade history, controversy has long existed over whether Joseph Chouinard survived the duel. The highly regarded scholar Dale Morgan declared emphatically that he was not killed.[24] Many have agreed with his conclusion, in the main because no one associated in any way with the episode stated categorically that the bully had died in the exchange of shots. As persuasive as that might appear, on that point we are essentially dealing with negative evidence, which normally is not admissible as valid historical evidence.

Neither of our two most solid accounts, those by Carson and Parker, settle the question. After referring to the gunfire, Kit adds only a single brief sentence to conclude his two paragraphs on the duel. He said, "During our stay in camp we had no more bother with this bully Frenchman."[25] Taken at face value, that sounds as if Chouinard had been defeated and chastened, but not slain. However, Kit, for whatever reason, might well have disguised the outcome in his memoirs by merely claiming that "we had no more bother with [him]." For if Joseph Chouinard was dead, he certainly was no longer a bother.

The Rev. Parker adds an interesting detail to the mix. He informs us that in the wake of both men's shots, Kit went for another pistol. Upon his return, "Shunar" begged that his life be spared. Parker breaks off at that point, leaving the reader to guess the ending. Shortly, nevertheless, he offers the observation that trappers "would see fair play . . . and would not tolerate murder, unless drunkenness or great provocation could be pleaded in extenuation of guilt."[26] We can guess that these represented his own moralizing assumptions rather than the actual sentiments of mountain men. Did the Reverend have his own reasons, moral or religious, for avoiding any statement in his book as to Chouinard's fate?

Harvey Carter believed that had Kit followed through and gunned down Chouinard with his second pistol, it would have been plain murder.[27] But would it, under the code of the time? Kit had not been intoxicated, but Chouinard evidently was. The sight of him drunk and begging for his life would have won no sympathy from the spectators. All knew that Chouinard had provoked the fight, and both men had charged upon the field with the intention of killing the other. That the Frenchman, having failed in his design to shoot Carson through the heart, should turn into a pleading coward did a disservice to the dueling code, which held that a participant disarmed must stand and take the bullet like a man. Any mercy shown under that circumstance was entirely at the discretion of his opponent.

David Brown, from first hand observation, spoke of the mountain men's "reckless indifference to human life, which becomes a mental habitude of those who are constantly exposed to situations of great insecurity and danger."[28] That is, persons who regularly faced death became hardened to its shock. If the crowd witnessing the duel, and Kit Carson, himself, were conditioned in that way, it seems plausible that Kit might well have used his second pistol to fell the contentious and unpopular giant, without fear of public recrimination or personal feelings of guilt. Historians and writers remain about evenly divided over whether he did or did not kill Joseph Chouinard.[29]

Dr. Peters in the revised 1873 edition of his Carson biography is at some pains to justify Kit's performance in the duel. Although in the first edition of 1858, he had ended his narrative of the incident with the firing of shots and a summary statement of both men's injuries, somehow readers were left with the impression that Carson had acted reprehensibly.

Now in 1873, Peters offered a vigorous defense. He wrote that "Kit Carson did not desire to kill his antagonist, but merely to save his own life by disabling [him]." And he offers as sufficient proof that Kit, an excellent marksman, deliberately hit "Shunan" in the arm. Thus, he concludes that "the statement that Kit Carson did not intend to kill his adversary becomes an incontrovertible fact."[30]

All of this is pure balderdash. If Chouinard's horse had shied, as Inman testified, then Kit could have easily hit him in the arm, instead of some lethal spot at which he was aiming. Besides, every other report affirms that both men entered the open arena with fatal intentions.

Dr. Peters added that after the shoot-out, "the wounded man was carried to his quarters and every attention shown him in the power of his companions. His [Chouinard's] punishment had the effect completely to subdue him." If he got that part of the story correct, then we must assume that Kit had not actually used his second single-shot pistol.

"We take leave of this unfortunate scene in his life," concludes the biographer, "feeling confident a just public opinion will see in it no cause to pluck from the brow of Kit Carson any of the laurels which it has been called up to place there."[31] Addressing an eastern audience in his book, Peters not only lapsed into grandiloquent prose, but he also showed no hesitancy in tidying up Kit's behavior to render it more palatable for his effete readership.

One eventuality, seldom considered, is that Chouinard, carried off the field with his ghastly arm wound, could have lingered for days, or even weeks, then succumbed to gangrene or blood poisoning. In that case, it would have still been correct to say that Kit had taken his life.

If Smith H. Simpson, Carson's Taos friend, can be believed, Kit told him in the latter 1850s that "the Frenchman . . . was the only man he ever killed that he was pleased with [him]self for doing it."[32] Jessie Frémont who listened more than once to Kit's telling of the duel avowed that he never finished it without showing on his face deep resentment toward Chouinard.[33] An 1847 Carson interview appearing in the Washington *Daily Union* states that the duel was "the only serious personal quarrel of Kit Carson's life."[34]

This attenuated narration of the duel has been necessary as preparation for considering the true and largely hidden motive that precipitated it. Smith Simpson had it on direct authority from Kit Carson that the fight "was all over this squaw . . . and the Frenchman got mad about it."[35] A reasonable conjecture is that the "squaw" in question was the Northern

Arapaho girl Waa-nibe whom Kit took for his wife, probably soon after the break-up of the rendezvous. Trapper David Brown in speaking of "a feeling of rivalry" between Carson and Chouinard, may well have been referring to the bad blood between them over competition for this girl.[36]

Most of what is known about Waa-nibe at the time of the duel is incorporated in Stanley Vestal's 1928 biography, *Kit Carson, The Happy Warrior of the Old West*. Vestal was close to the Arapaho and Cheyenne of western Oklahoma, and from them gained knowledge and appreciation of their culture and turbulent history. He also came to know George Bent, the half Cheyenne son of William Bent, builder of Bent's Fort in the 1830s and close friend of Kit Carson. From him, and the Indian elders with long memories, Vestal gleaned what he could about Kit Carson's early history.

George Bent told him that he had always heard from the older Cheyenne that Kit had slain "Shunar." But it was from an aged Arapaho named Watan, whose grandfather had been one of Waa-nibe's in-laws, that the author acquired his information about the girl Carson was to marry. The informant indicated that the Arapahoes had regarded Waa-nibe as properly skilled in her domestic duties and pretty.[37] That description coincides with remarks of others who commented upon her appearance and ability to make a good home for Kit in their tepee.

Vestal, drawing upon the memory of Watan and others of his tribe, states that Waa-nibe had a sister, Hisethe (meaning Good Woman) and a brother called Detenin (Short Man). Their mother was an Atsena (sometimes known as the Gros Ventre of the Plains), a people who had split off from the Arapaho and migrated northward to occupy lands stretching from upper Montana into Canada.[38]

Waa-nibe's father had a name that translated from the Arapaho as Running Around, or Running in a Circle. Vestal, who was well-versed in the lore of Plains Indian warfare, thought that name had reference to the custom of Indian scouts riding in a circle on some high point as a signal to their fellow tribesmen that enemies were approaching. He added that Running Around was a member of the Lime Crazy Society, and thus a man of standing among the Arapaho.

Given what is known, it is a safe assumption that Carson had previously met and perhaps already initiated his courtship with Waa-nibe prior to the summer of 1835, conceivably at the 1834 rendezvous.[40]

Now twenty-five years old and having survived a difficult trapping season that included his serious shoulder wound, Kit may have reckoned that it was time to take an Indian wife as so many of his companions had done.

Stanley Vestal has him visiting the detached Arapaho encampment at the beginning of the rendezvous and participating in a social dance along with Chouinard. In the course of this "Soup Dance," as the author identifies it, women select their partners and Waa-nibe chose Kit. At the same time, she rejects and humiliates Chouinard, who later pursues her outside of the camp and attempts to sexually assault her.

When Kit learns of this outrage, he goes looking for the now intoxicated Frenchman who has turned to menacing the entire trappers' camp. The duel follows, the villain is vanquished, and Kit receives the plaudits of all those who observed Chouinard's downfall, a detail Vestal appears to have borrowed from Dr. Peter's biography.[41]

Finally, Vestal's narrative has Carson going to Running Around's lodge, where he proposes marriage to his daughter and is accepted. Waa-nibe then enters to sit beside Kit and her father marries them, according to Arapaho custom, by simply placing a blanket over the pair. For his part, Kit hands over the negotiated "bride price," in this instance amounting to a new gun, three mules, and five blue trade blankets. Relatives are afterward summoned to partake of a wedding feast, and they later join in providing Waa-nibe a new tepee and all the furnishings needed to begin housekeeping.

In conclusion, Vestal, having related the tale of courtship, duel, and marriage in fourteen pages of dense detail, feels compelled to certify its accuracy for his readers, as follows: "This is the true story of Kit Carson's duel with Shunar, as I have got it from the Arapaho Indians in Oklahoma."[42]

The summary just presented attempts to focus upon the main thread of his account, paring away many of what seem to be Vestal embellishments. The so-called "Soup Dance," which he treats at considerable length, for example, does not appear in the modern historical or ethnographic literature on the Arapaho, although it could have just disappeared before scholars came on the scene. Subsequent writers also tell of Carson and the Soup Dance, but they seemingly all rely upon Vestal as their authority.[43]

Stanley Vestal was the pen name of Walter Stanley Campbell (1887–1956), a long-time professor of English at the University of Oklahoma, where he taught creative writing. While he published several novels, he concentrated on histories and biographies about mountain men and Indians. Undeniably, he made a contribution through his extensive interviewing of elderly Plains Indians, including the Sioux, who had participated in inter-tribal warfare, as well as conflicts with the whites. He prided himself on bringing to view their side of the story.

Nevertheless, professional historians criticized him severely as a popularizer who played loose with the facts. Tough-minded Dale L. Morgan condemned him for being willing to work at writing but not at research. And California historian Charles L. Camp, in reviewing Vestal's *Kit Carson,* lambasted it as, "an alluring, colorful mingling of strict fact and highly imaginative fancy." Camp went farther, accusing Vestal of placing too much confidence in those Indian legends of Watan, even assigning some of them precedence over Carson's own recollections.[44]

Vestal's biographer Ray Tassin defended him, claiming that the professor routinely checked his printed sources more thoroughly than other authors. And although he did place greater faith in data secured from Indians than in information coming from whites, it was because the Indian informant usually could produce eye-witnesses to confirm what he said.[45]

Even if only a small part of Vestal's account of the duel is accepted, it might be enough to confirm that the fight indeed occurred over an Indian woman, as Smith Simpson supposedly heard it from Carson. The claim, which Kit vocalized in his memoirs, that Chouinard had offended his sense of honor and patriotism, thus would have to be seen as a smoke screen to hide from the public his true motive. Kit being a Southerner was hypersensitive about his honor and, as his later career demonstrated, he stood tall as a patriot, often sacrificing his own interests when his country called upon him for his services.

Notwithstanding, it seems unlikely that those things could have been sufficient to fuel the anger, even hatred, he displayed toward the Frenchman. On the other hand, a scenario, such as the one sketched by Vestal, in which the Arapaho woman he meant to take for his wife was dishonored by Chouinard could very easily have produced that emotional reaction. It could also reinforce the argument that Kit Carson calculatingly sent his opponent to the grave. But on that point, we may never know conclusively one way or the other.

It has been said that the likelihood of Arapahoes being present at the 1835 rendezvous is small, inasmuch as the site on the Green was within territory of the Shoshones who, along with the Utes, also in attendance, were bitter foes of the Arapahoes. An old practice common in much of Indian America, however, was the honoring of a blanket truce during periodic trade fairs allowing hostile as well as friendly tribes to participate and come and go unhindered. It is possible, but by no means certain, that the familiar Native truce was extended to the whiteman's rendezvous. In any case, Vestal mentioned the presence of an Arapaho tepee camp below the trappers' site.[46]

Marriages between mountain men and Indian women, or what passed for marriages, formed part of the social landscape of the western fur trade. The husband obtained a bed partner and a domestic worker who could keep his lodge, cook meals, tan hides, and make or mend his clothing.

That was just one phase of the Indianization of trapperdom. Men like the beaver hunters, Col. Richard Irving Dodge observed, "gladly exchanged all the comforts and advantages of civilization for the privation, hardship, danger and freedom of barbaric life." And he noted that these frontiersmen, "living among Indians, in a short time differ from them only by a shade."[47] As a matter of fact, a whiteman purchasing an Indian wife traditionally gained automatic membership in her tribe and thus safe passage for trapping in its territory.

The spectacle of Europeans renouncing civilized life and fleeing to the wilds to join the Indians had been a familiar occurrence in the English and Dutch colonies on the Atlantic seaboard. During the seventeenth century in French Canada, a significant number of young men fled their homes to join "the savages and go about naked and tricked out like Indians."[48] Descendants of such people, much Indianized Frenchmen, would one day furnish a majority of the work force employed by American fur companies.

Of the mountain men in the Far West, Washington Irving insisted: "It is a matter of ambition and vanity with them to discard everything that may bear the stamp of civilized life, and to adopt the manner, dress, gesture, and even walk of the Indian. You cannot pay a trapper a greater compliment than to persuade him you have mistaken him for an Indian brave."[49]

As a youth, Kit Carson had accepted whole-heartedly the mountain man's life style, whose configuration was shaped predominantly by Indian

a

Junction of Horse Creek (foreground, left) and the Green River, site of the mountain man rendezvous, 1835, where Kit Carson fought Joseph Chouinard and won Waa-nibe for his wife. (Photo by Henry B. Crawford)

Summer rendezvous of the mountain men. (Engraving after Peters, 1858)

b

Imaginative image
of the Carson-Chouinard
duel in 1835 on the Green
River. (Engraving after
Peters, 1858)

Reverend Samuel Parker
published the first account of
Kit Carson's duel with Joseph
Chouinard. (After Sabin, 1914)

c

Kit Carson's buckskin coat, Hawken rifle, and beaded Indian pipe bag, in the Carson house at Taos. (Marc Simmons Collection)

d

Idealized engraving of Carson's first wife, Waa-nibe. (After Cattermole, Rio Grande Historical Collections)

Kit Carson as the idealized mountain man, in buckskins, with his Hawken rifle and his favorite horse, Apache. (Engraving after Peters, 1858)

Headwaters of the Salmon River, Idaho, where Kit Carson trapped in his youth. (Photo courtesy of William Swagerty) Photographer Douglas Henderson

custom and practice. Like his companions, he fully adopted the Native mode of warfare, because survival in the wilderness required it. To a significant degree, "thinking like an Indian" became second nature to Kit, a habit of mind that later aided him when he served as an Indian agent, soldier, and treaty maker. Therefore, for him to marry an Arapaho was entirely in keeping with his self-chosen occupation and with his station in frontier society.

By the time Carson made his first entry into the arena of matrimony, the rising trade in buffalo robes had wrought profound social and economic changes in the Indian world. The impact upon the condition of Native women was primarily negative. Trading establishments like Fort Union on the Missouri River in the north, and Bent's Fort beside the Arkansas River on the edge of the southern plains could offer men of the nomadic buffalo hunting tribes an alluring array of goods, all to be paid for in tanned hides.

The labor-intensive processing of those hides fell to women, whose curing and tanning never seemed to keep up with their husband's demands for the finished product. As a result, the average number of wives per lodge increased from three to five. Since no tribe had a female population sufficient to meet this need, the net effect was an intensification of intertribal raiding for the express purpose of capturing women. As William R. Swagerty has observed, power, wealth, and prestige growing out of the flourishing robe trade flowed only to Indian men, eroding the social position of their women.[50]

Viewing Plains Indian wives from the outside, trappers and traders invariably saw them as work horses and domestic slaves of their demanding husbands who expected to be waited upon. Arikara women of the middle Missouri River were depicted at an early date as being more debased and abused by their menfolk than women of other tribes, who themselves were in a deplorable state.

Fur trader Daniel Harmon in 1820 wrote, based on his wide experience, that "all the Indians consider women as far inferior in every respect to men; and among many tribes, they treat their wives much as they do their dogs."[51] In reality there were exceptions, but on the whole the lot of Native women was not an enviable one.

Among the Arapaho, wife beating was an accepted practice, provided there was sufficient cause. As one Native informant put it, "Some of the men beat up their wives, most of them did not." However, for the crime of adultery, a woman might have the end of her nose or an earlobe cut off or her cheeks slashed by her outraged husband. Similar tribal-sanctioned punishments for unfaithful wives were fairly widespread among western Indians.[52]

Odd as it now seems, Indian women were usually accepting of their situation, undoubtedly because it was culturally approved, but also owing to the shortage of viable alternatives. Within equestrian warrior societies, no place existed for a lone unmarried female.

When the white traders and trappers came upon the scene, though, a new option quickly opened for a Native woman, particularly one born with a stubborn or independent side to her nature. Eager to marry a whiteman, she could easily tally a number of advantages to be gained thereby. She would be leaving behind her old life as an unappreciated drudge and embarking upon another one in which the foreign husband was more considerate, was apt to discipline her less harshly, if at all, and was probably more indulgent than an Indian husband would have been. Native girls counted upon being showered with richly colored cloth, beads, and metal jinglers, personal decoration close to their hearts.[53]

An Indian girl wed to a trapper found that the nomadic way of life he followed was not that different from what she had grown up with. But since most mountain men, contrary to Indian custom, kept only a single wife, the girl suddenly swept into her new and unfamiliar situation often missed the company and chatter of other wives in the lodge. As compensation, she had the undivided attention of her husband and was the sole beneficiary of his generous nature.[54]

Although no formal record is preserved of what these Indian wives thought and felt about their mates, it is clear that some were transported into their relationships on a tide of romantic passion. Author Bil Gilbert has remarked that even though the mountain men as a rule came from the hardest and least sentimental classes of their society, they were in comparison to Indian men, Lotharios in so far as romantic sensibilities were concerned. And he adds by way of memorable examples, the cases of Kit Carson and Joe Meek. "Notable ladies' men," he calls them, "who both fought duels over girls—an Arapaho and Shoshone respectively—

with whom they had fallen in love and then married."⁵⁵

From all that is known, Waa-nibe willingly yielded to Kit Carson's courtship, and theirs was a true love match. To what degree the other factors that so often inclined Indian women to wed a trapper may have entered into her thinking must be left to conjecture. The stiff "bride price" Kit paid for her, assuming Vestal's tabulation had some basis in fact, would indicate the strength of his intentions to make this Arapaho maiden his wife.⁵⁶

Stray references by others at a later date would lead us to believe that Waa-nibe was young and beautiful, probably in her mid to late teens. Her Arapaho name is often translated as Singing Grass, or occasionally as Wind Singing, but since wind moves the grass, either rendering could catch the essence of the meaning in the Native language. Singing Grass has a melodious and even an amorously feminine ring to it.⁵⁷

Edwin L. Sabin in 1914 revealed that Kit had a nickname for his pretty Arapaho, which was "Alice."⁵⁸ Not infrequently, trappers bestowed upon their Indian spouses a pet name in English. Kit, however, had no one named Alice in his genealogy, nor so far as is known any friend. The names of all his subsequent children were drawn from one or the other of those sources.

The hard fact is that the nickname Alice for Waa-nibe is entirely bogus. It derived not from the historical record, but from the fanciful yarn-spinning of an elderly Denver resident Oliver Perry Wiggins, who between 1902 and his death in 1913 gave interviews to at least ten journalists and historians, among the latter, Edwin L. Sabin. Wiggins claimed to have gone west as a runaway boy in 1838 and been adopted by Kit Carson and his [fictitious] band of forty-two trappers, with whom he remained for the next decade. Although the account of his adventures during that period was a vast web of lies, absurdities, and inconsistencies, nevertheless, for the next half century it was accepted as valid by western historians and Carson biographers, whose published works as a result bore the Wiggins taint. Not until 1964 was Oliver P. Wiggins exposed as a complete charlatan with no connection to Kit. But by that time, his rambling and deceitful narratives had badly muddied the waters of Carson's personal history.⁵⁹

In a 1902 two-part article of supposed reminiscences, Wiggins declared that he had been taken by Kit to Taos and installed in his household as an employee. In Wiggins's words: "Carson's family was an interesting one and no man ever lived who loved his home better or was more fond of wife and child. Mrs. Carson, 'Alice' we called her, was a squaw and a chief's daughter, who had fallen in love with the daring hunter. . . ."[60] When Sabin afterward asked for more details about "Alice," Wiggins confessed that he "had no clear recollection of her."[61] That was undoubtedly because he had never laid eyes upon Kit's first wife, and here confused her with the third wife Josefa. Moreover, Kit had no house at Taos in 1838, when Wiggins said that he arrived there. His assigning the name Alice to Waa-nibe has proved to be perhaps the most enduring of his fabrications, since it continues to appear in some of the Carson literature.

In his memoirs, Kit declares that at the close of the rendezvous, "on the first of September [1835], we departed on our Fall hunt. . . ."[62] If he and Waa-nibe were indeed married by this time, as Vestal described, then she must have been riding in the column among other trappers' Indian wives with one or more horses dragging the lodge poles for her new tepee.

Carson and his companions on this hunt trapped Montana's Yellowstone and Big Horn rivers, then crossed over to the Three Forks of the Missouri. As the cold season settled upon the land, they dropped south into eastern Idaho and took up winter quarters on the Big Snake River, not far above Fort Hall. That fur trading post established by Nathaniel Wyeth in 1834 had been sold by him to the British Hudson's Bay Company, which eagerly traded supplies to American mountain men in exchange for their hard won peltry.[63]

In the spring of 1836, Kit joined a small party of Hudson's Bay men, led by Thomas McKay who proposed to trap Mary's River (later called the Humboldt) that lay to the southwest in the present state of Nevada. Beaver were reported to be thick on that stream. Kit, wisely as it turned out, left Waa-nibe behind at Fort Hall.[64]

When he returned to her, he had little to show for the venture, since the beaver pickings after all had been slim. Because of the scarcity of game in the desolate country, the men ran out of food, and Kit told Waa-nibe that they were reduced to eating roots and bleeding their horses and cooking the blood.[65]

A month or so later, the Carsons struck their tepee and with others who had been encamped under the walls of Fort Hall traveled east six days to the summer rendezvous, once more on the Green at the mouth of Horse Creek. If Arapahoes were present, Waa-nibe must have enjoyed re-establishing contact with relatives and friends. She would have found more opportunities for such meetings at subsequent rendezvous, before the final summer gathering of traders and trappers in 1840.

In 1837, Carson and his fellows noticed the scarcity of their old enemies, the Blackfeet, in their normal range north of the Yellowstone. Friendly Crows informed them that the Blackfeet were being ravaged by smallpox, a catastrophe that would reduce their population by two-thirds. The disease came by way of a trader's boat up the Missouri River wiping out the Mandans and decimating other tribes.[66]

The temporary eclipse of the Blackfeet might have made the trappers' lives easier, or at least safer, since their territory was a favored hunting ground for the whitemen. But by the time of the epidemic, the beaver trade was already in sharp decline, and a way of life was dying. Kit may have had some perception of that, as from 1835 onward he watched the steep and steady drop in prices paid for beaver pelts. In the eastern states and Europe, the once fashionable men's hat made of beaver felt was giving way to top hats of imported silk. Added to that, two decades of relentless trapping had greatly reduced the beaver population on the principal rivers of the Far West.

Between early April and the first week of July 1837, Kit and Waa-nibe were again in residence at Fort Hall, as indicated by the post business ledgers that showed him purchasing supplies periodically. Harvey Carter believed that Carson spent that winter living quietly with his Indian wife, hunting for meat but doing no trapping. The most reasonable explanation for this curtailment of his activity was Waa-nibe's first pregnancy. Kit obtained some glass beads through trade, which were probably used by his wife in the beading of moccasins during her quiet hours. Arapaho women were renowned for their production of finely decorated footwear.[67]

Kit a decade later was perhaps referring to this memorable period in his relationship with Waa-nibe when he made a chance remark about her to his friend, young Midshipman Edward Fitzgerald Beale. "She was a good wife to me," he said. "I never came in from hunting that she did not have the warm water ready for my feet."[68] Lamentably, that is the only personal comment about her by Kit that has been handed down to us. From it can be gathered a faint sense of the devotion husband and wife felt toward one another.

The exact birth date of the Carson daughter is unknown. From several mentions of her age later in life, 1837 appears to be the birth year. The day could well have been within that window between April and early July when her parents were at Fort Hall. However, in mid summer the Carsons with others left for the Green River where they attended the rendezvous, for the third time in a row located at the mouth of Horse Creek.[69] It is possible that Waa-nibe bore her child there, during the twenty days the event lasted. If so, she might have had access to an Arapaho midwife and a medicine woman to assist in her delivery.

Arapaho babies were usually born in the family lodge. Waa-nibe, following tribal custom, would have knelt on the ground at the beginning of labor and grasped with outstretched arms a horizontal rod overhead. An attending woman sat in front of her to receive the baby, while another applied pressure to the abdomen from behind. A third helper cut the cord. Arapaho women who went into labor when the tribe was migrating simply turned aside to some secluded place, delivered the child alone, then hurried to catch up.[70]

The Carson baby was named Adaline. She must have had an Arapaho name as well, but if so it went unrecorded. Kit chose "Adaline" for his first child because that was the name of his favorite niece back in Missouri. She was the daughter of Kit's eldest half-brother, William, who had owned his own place next to the Carson family farm in the Booneslick country. The original Adaline, born April 3, 1810, was just a little more than three months older than Kit, and they often played together as children.[71]

Dr. Peters in the Preface of his *The Life of Kit Carson* (1858) said that his subject spoke French and Spanish fluently, "besides being a perfect master of several Indian dialects." In his use of the word master, he was probably over-stating the case a bit. Nevertheless, others too referred to Carson's ability to speak diverse Indian languages. Surely, Arapaho, of Algonquin stock, was one of those. It is unlikely that Waa-nibe spoke any English. When she and Kit met, they would have communicated in the universal Indian sign language, until such time as he learned a working Arapaho vocabulary from her.[72]

Between the close of the 1837 rendezvous and the opening of the next one, 1838, on the Wind River east of the Continental Divide, Carson ranged widely through the north country with old comrades, trapping and fending off attacks from the newly resurgent Blackfeet. Waa-nibe and little Adaline, so far as we know, remained at his side.

At the summer gathering on the Wind River, Kit seized the opportunity to discuss with other trappers the worsening state of the fur business. That would explain his decision to begin exploring other options. When the 1838 rendezvous broke up, Carson declared in his habitually abbreviated manner, "I and seven men went to Brown's Hole."[73] Although he doesn't say so, his little family was again with him on this trip.

Brown's Hole, later known as Brown's Park, situated in the far northwestern corner of Colorado, was an elongated valley, six miles wide and bisected by the Green River flowing down from Wyoming. Rock-walled on all sides, the valley could be entered only by steep and narrow trails. Its floor, however, was well-grassed and timber furnished abundant firewood. Shoshones, in whose country it lay, had long found this remote place to be a secure haven during the hard months of winter.[74]

In 1836 three enterprising men had established a trading post, Fort Davy Crockett, in Brown's Hole, naming it in honor of the celebrated figure who had died in Texas at the Alamo earlier that year. The three were Philip Thompson, Prewitt Sinclair, and William Craig. On September 1, 1838, Kit Carson and company rode into their fort, five weeks after the close of the rendezvous.[75]

"I there joined Thompson and Sinclair's party on a trading expedition to the Navajo Indians," recalled Kit. "We traded for thirty mules. We returned to Brown's Hole."[76] That is painfully little in the way of narration for a round trip of a thousand miles or so, filled no doubt with multiple adventures.

The well-travelled Thomas J. Farnham passed through the area in this period and reported seeing next to Fort Davy Crockett "the conical skin lodges of a few Snake (Shoshone) Indians."[77] It is perhaps safe to surmise that Waa-nibe had stayed behind in this camp when her husband departed for the land of the Navajo. Leaders Thompson and Sinclair planned to ride fast and hard, the pace proposed being unsuitable for Waa-nibe and a newborn infant.

According to Sabin, the purpose of the trip was not only to acquire mules, but also Navajo wool blankets and horsehair ropes. Kit did not mention those items. He does say that once back in Brown's Hole,

Thompson set out to drive the thirty mules to Fort Vásquez, a post on the South Platte River in Colorado where he bartered them for goods he could use in Indian trading.[78]

The winter of 1838–1839 Kit worked as a hunter for Fort Davy Crockett. On October 2, a twenty-three-year-old traveler E. Willard Smith ran into him and his hunting party, "composed of seven whites and two squaws" east of Brown's Hole and learned that they had been in a fight with the Sioux a few days before. There is no way of knowing whether Waa-nibe was one of the "squaws."

With the advent of spring, Carson decided to resume trapping and over the rest of the year, he roamed from the Laramie Mountains in southern Wyoming to the Yellowstone and on westward to the headwaters of Idaho's Salmon River, the latter an area he had first trapped in 1831 with famed mountaineer Tom Fitzpatrick. Sometime during this period of wandering, his wife bore their second child, another daughter. Her name, however, has not come down to us.[80]

In the expanded edition (1873) of his Carson biography, Dr. Peters wrote that "soon after the birth of this child, his wife died."[81] By "this child" the author meant Adaline, since he was unaware of the existence of the second daughter. Subsequent writers gave the cause of death as simply "a fever."[82] It seems unlikely that Waa-nibe's ailment was smallpox, since the 1837 outbreak had already run its course. So perhaps it was puerperal fever, also known as childbed fever, an infection occurring shortly after childbirth and not uncommon in those days. But the exact cause and the date of her death are probably irretrievable by historians.

As noted, one of Carson's overriding virtues was his firm sense of duty, most visible when he was called up for some military or civil service. But his devotion and responsible commitment to wife and children proved just as strong. That Kit was unwilling to speak of Waa-nibe publicly should not be taken as a sign that he was anything but deeply in love with her, or that he did not profoundly mourn her loss.

Assessing all of the evidence, including Kit's convoluted chronology for the late 1830s given in his memoirs, it appears that Waa-nibe died in the winter of 1839–1840, possibly at Brown's Hole.[83] During the summer of the latter year, Carson attended the last organized rendezvous, which was held once more on the Green River.

Present on that occasion was the Belgian Jesuit, Father Pierre Jean de Smet, known for his missionary labors among the Flatheads. Kit made the priest's acquaintance and recalled in 1858 that ". . . if good works on this earth are rewarded hereafter, I am confident that his share of glory and happiness in the next world will be great."[84]

To Father De Smet, many of the French Catholic trappers brought their half-Indian children to be baptized. Kit may have done so as well, not wanting his little girls to be without this ritual of entry into the Christian world. His affection and respect for the missionary may have helped pave the way for his own re-baptism and joining of the Catholic Church two years later in Taos.[85]

With men abandoning their traps and leaving the mountains in droves, Carson took stock of his situation. The beaver trade, if not yet entirely dead, was obviously on its last legs. Within three years, Captain John C. Frémont would declare with finality, "The race of trappers has almost disappeared."[86] Kit, however, was not quite ready to surrender a way of life that, despite its perils and hardships, he had relished for more than a decade. He decided to continue trapping a bit longer.

By Carson's own testimony, he worked the Utah country with mountain man Jack Robertson (properly Robison) in the months before the last rendezvous, and then made a fall hunt on the Grand (Colorado) River before going into winter quarters at Brown's Hole.[87]

Sometime around April 1841, he went to Fort Robidoux, located near the junction of the Uinta (called Winty by the trappers) River and White Rocks Creek, in northeastern Utah. Founded by Antoine Robidoux in the early 1830s, this trading post, like Forts Hall and Davy Crockett, catered to both the mountaineers and the Indians.[88]

Robidoux's partner, Jack Robertson, as a friend of Kit's may have volunteered to assist in caring for the Carson youngsters by having his Indian wife Marook take charge of them.[89] Some provision for the girls would have been made before Kit started on his final spring hunt into Colorado, for as Dr. Peters wrote, "His daughter[s] he watched over with the greatest solicitude."[90]

Returning to Fort Robidoux after the hunt, he disposed of his furs and sat out the summer, pondering his next step. A major change in his life was in the offing, and whatever its nature, he would have to find a way to accommodate the needs of his children.

Other hangers-on at the fort were in the same situation and joined in campfire discussions about their predicament and the future. "Beaver were getting scarce," said Kit, "and finding it was necessary to try our hand at something else, [we] concluded to start for Bent's Fort on the Arkansas."[91]

The little cavalcade that set forth in September 1841 comprised six mountaineers and their families, and included besides Kit, the irascible "Old Bill" Williams, long a legend among the trapper breed. The party moved leisurely southeastward, struck the Arkansas River not far from the headwaters, and followed it a hundred miles downstream to Bent's on the edge of the Great Plains. There a new chapter opened in the career of Kit Carson.

In the years just completed, he had profoundly enjoyed the pure freedom of life in the mountains, the constant danger that kept all his senses alert, and the inner happiness that an almost total self-reliance bestowed. Later he would look back and wonder how all of that marvelous time as a trapper had flown by so fast.

One painful memory that Kit carried with him out of the mountains was the loss of his good and faithful wife, Waa-nibe. Had she survived, the thread of his later life might have run a different course.

Some whitemen, when their adventure in the wilderness was done, thought nothing of returning their wives to the tribe and abandoning them to the charity of relatives. Or occasionally they would sell them to other trappers, at bargain prices, untroubled by moral scruples since they themselves had bought the women in the beginning.[92]

Other fur men, however, developed a lasting romantic attachment to their Indian spouses, and when they realized the trade was finished and decided to start new lives in California or Oregon, their wives and children went too. Those families often remained intact to the end.

In all likelihood, that would have been the story of Kit and Waa-nibe Carson. Since it was not to be, Kit was left with the sweet memory of the joy of family life in a buffalo hide tepee. But a chronic urge to roam still possessed him, and before he settled fully into a new domesticity, he would travel across the nation from ocean to ocean, answering the call of his country.

PART II

Making Out Road

Bent's Fort in 1841 glittered as the center of a fur trading empire, its adobe walls standing tall and solid alongside the Arkansas River. A true outpost of Manifest Destiny, its massive round towers at opposite corners of the compound looked south into Mexico, for at this date the river marked the international boundary. Bent's had rocketed upward to become not only a new focus in the Southwestern fur trade, but also a major establishment on the Mountain Route of the Santa Fe Trail, over which flowed a lucrative trade between Missouri and New Mexico.

St. Louis brothers Charles and William Bent made their first entry into the overland commerce of the region in 1829, joining a wagon caravan with their goods for the Santa Fe market. Thirty-one-year-old Charles, a natural leader with frontier experience gained in the upper Missouri fur trade, was elected captain of the merchant train. In spite of a severe Indian attack near the Cimarron River, he successfully shepherded the cavalcade to New Mexico, and back. In the process, he saw that profits could be made by investment in the developing markets of the Southwest, and so decided to fully commit his future to this new theater of activity.

In September 1830, Charles Bent formed a partnership with another Santa Fe merchant, Cerán St. Vrain, who was descended from a prominent French family of St. Louis. Initially, Bent, St. Vrain & Co. concentrated on freighting and selling goods in New Mexico's capital. But a rise in the firm's fortunes led in 1833 to the opening of a store in Taos and the beginning of construction on the fortresslike trading post situated adjacent to the Southern Plains.

William Bent, Charles's junior by nine years, was handed the job of building and then, upon completion, managing the fort. It dealt primarily in the acquisition and transport of furs to eastern buyers. That included a shrinking volume of beaver pelts, the primary domain of white trappers, and an ever expanding number of buffalo robes, a product available almost exclusively from Indians. The year before Kit Carson's arrival at Bent's Fort, the firm from its storage rooms shipped 15,000 robes to markets in the East.[1]

Even before erection of the fort, William had begun cultivating a close relationship with the Cheyennes, the most powerful tribe north of the Arkansas. Together with their allies, the Arapahoes, they moved into the Bent, St. Vrain trading orbit, bartering the bulk of their robes with the company.

About 1835, William Bent cemented his standing with the tribe by marriage to Owl Woman, daughter of the prestigious Gray Thunder, keeper of the Cheyenne's sacred Medicine Arrows.[2] Thereafter, when business did not require his presence at the fort or on the trail, he passed his domestic time living the Indian way with his wife in a tepee amid a Cheyenne encampment along the river. Soon he grew more comfortable in that setting than he was in polite white society, revisited occasionally when he had to make trips to St. Louis.[3]

On reaching Bent's in September, Kit Carson reminisced: "I was kindly received . . . by Mssrs. Bent and St. Vrain, [and] offered employment to hunt for the fort at one dollar per day. Accepted this offer and remained in their employ till [April] 1842."[4] Simple calculation, based on an 1841 arrival and 1842 departure times would seem to establish that Kit worked for the company for approximately eight months.

In fact, Carson stated only that he had left Fort Robidoux for the fort on the Arkansas in September, without giving a specific year. In editing the memoirs, Harvey Carter assessed the tangled chronology of Kit's last years as a trapper and determined to his satisfaction that he had indeed made his appearance at Bent's Fort in 1841.

At once he was challenged by the equally knowledgeable Dale L. Morgan, then at the Bancroft Library. Based on his own interpretation of the thin evidence, Morgan concluded that after all Carson had ridden down to Bent's Fort during September of 1840 rather than 1841. A gentlemanly exchange of letters passed between the two authors, each stoutly defending his position. In the end, a majority of writers and researchers deferred to Carter and accepted his conclusion.[5]

The matter is of some weight since the correct date signals the opening of a transitional period in Carson's life, during which he married for a second time an Indian woman. As will be explained below, two pieces of evidence exist that may, in reality, support the stand taken by Morgan.

As a matter of fact, the length of Carson's residency at Bent's Fort had been a subject of confusion since publication of the first edition (1858) of Dr. Peters's biography. Therein, he had inexplicably made the absurd statement that Kit served as a hunter for the fort during a period of eight years. For decades, other Carson writers blindly followed his lead, including Edwin L. Sabin in the 1914 edition of his *Kit Carson Days*.[6]

By the time Sabin published the second, and greatly enlarged, edition of his biography (1935), he had compressed Kit's supposed eight years as a Bent hunter to a mere four years, 1838 to 1842. But that still left him with the problem of explaining how Carson during that same interval managed to attend multiple rendezvous and continue trapping in the northern mountains. Sabin solved the dilemma by taking a cue from the imaginings of Oliver P. Wiggins, in whose veracity he persisted in placing his trust.

The biographer now informed his readers that Carson had conducted two large buffalo hunts a year, which supplied the population of Bent's Fort with "a reserve of meat," sufficient to last for several months. During those stretches between hunts, Sabin postulates, Carson's "contract would not [have] prevented his making excursions into the mountains."[7] Since this contrived explanation derives from Wiggins, it must be rejected out of hand.

There is no indication that Carson was anything but steadily employed at hunting by the Bents, although on occasion they sent him with trade goods to outlying Indian camps, as they did other ex-mountain men. More than a hundred persons normally worked at the fort. Beyond the company men and hired clerks, there were blacksmiths and wheelwrights, stock tenders, cooks and their assistants, common day laborers, butchers, and assorted hunters, bringing in fresh supplies of buffalo, elk, and antelope meat. Many of these persons had families that helped swell the establishment's population, although hunters with Indian wives generally lived in skin lodges outside the walls.

Kit's first priority, after landing one of the hunting jobs, was to find someone to care for his little daughters. A dogged legend claims that the task fell to Charlotte Green, the fort's chief cook. She and her husband, Dick, were family slaves brought out from Missouri by the Bent brothers. Charlotte commanded a small army of Indian kitchen helpers, and it would have been a simple task to have one of them keep a constant eye on the children. Alternately, Kit, as he had done in the past, could have placed the girls with the Indian wife of one of the fort's hunters.

In the second half of the 1830s, intertribal warfare on the Southern Plains raged with unparalleled ferocity. The once timid Cheyennes had grown in military prowess and arrogance, and together with their Arapaho allies held sway over the vast grasslands stretching between the South Platte River and the Arkansas. Raiders penetrated their territory from all sides: Utes and Shoshones on the west, Blackfeet and Crow on the north, while Pawnee and Sioux entered from the east.

Bitterest foes of the Cheyennes and Arapahoes, however, dwelled south of the Arkansas, and it was they who caused them the most damage—Comanches, Kiowas, and Kiowa Apaches (also called Plains Apaches). Against all of these peoples, and others, the Cheyennes fielded retaliatory expeditions.

In 1838 a Cheyenne war party of forty-two Bow String soldiers in a foray against the hated Kiowa was wiped out, to the last man. The tribe was so infuriated by the loss that it persuaded the Arapahoes to join them in a mass attack upon the enemy. Subsequently, a Kiowa village, also containing some Comanche visitors, was surprised and a furious battle erupted. By day's end, the Kiowa-Comanche side had suffered fifty-six men killed and an untold number of women captured. The latter were immediately butchered by the Cheyennes as revenge for the earlier annihilation of their Bow Strings.[9]

The Cheyenne victory, nevertheless, did not come cheap. Twelve of their best war leaders and warriors perished in the bloody fighting, along with elderly Gray Thunder, the arrow-keeper and father-in-law of William Bent. His wife had to take charge of the holy Medicine Arrows during the retreat north to the Arkansas.[10]

The intensity and size of the conflict left the participants traumatized. Less than two years later, the Kiowas and Comanches sent an emissary to the more tractable Arapahoes, suggesting that all tribes make peace. The Cheyennes were brought on board, and in the summer of 1840, as Lavender tells it, several thousand Indians representing five tribes assembled on both sides of the river three miles below Bent's Fort, there to exchange lavish gifts and forge a permanent peace. The site ever after was known as The Treaty Ground.

Lavender has Kit Carson present on this thunderous occasion.[11] So too does Stanley Vestal in his earlier biography. But he tosses in an added detail mentioned by no other writer. According to Vestal, it was during the pageantry of this historic gathering that Carson first laid eyes on the Cheyenne maiden,

Making Out Road, who would become his new Indian wife.[12]

The respected paleontologist and naturalist George Bird Grinnell of Yale University was the one who brought to light in 1923 the existence of Carson's second marriage. All previous authors had missed it. On earlier field trips to the West, scholarly Grinnell became fascinated with the Plains Indians and after a lifetime of association with them, particularly the Cheyenne and Pawnee, he published a series of significant studies on their culture and history.[13]

According to his own statement, Grinnell in 1917 had learned from several elderly Cheyenne informants that Kit Carson was once wed to a girl of their tribe. A very old woman called Sitting-in-the-Lodge recalled that her name was Making Out Road and that Carson had married her about 1840.[14]

If Kit reached Bent's Fort in 1840, rather than in 1841, it is still difficult to rework his schedule so that he can be placed at the grand Indian council on the Arkansas, as Stanley Vestal would have it. The problem dissolves, however, if the assembly of tribes occurred in the late summer of 1841, instead of 1840, which seems to be the case. The fuzziness of the exact dates aside, we know that in the general euphoria accompanying the peace arrangements, the Indians showered former enemies with gifts, temporarily emptying store shelves at Bent's Fort, gave elaborate feasts, and performed social dances. The festivities continued for weeks.

After he read Grinnell's 1923 statements, Vestal could have returned to his Indian sources in western Oklahoma and questioned them about Making Out Road. Possibly, they informed him that she and Carson had first crossed paths at the grand council, or Vestal, as he seems to have done on occasion, might have just made it up, to add an element of drama to the story. In any event, whatever the circumstances and date of the original meeting between the Cheyenne girl and Carson, they were shortly afterward sharing her tepee.

The name, Making Out Road, as Grinnell got it from the elderly Sitting-in-the-Lodge, has been the subject of confusion, insofar as its meaning derived from the Cheyenne language is concerned. Vestal, although knowledgeable about the culture, resorted to guessing. He suggested that the odd-sounding name evidently referred to some exploit of her ancestors and meant making out or reading signs left by enemies on a trail or road.[15] Later, historians interpreted the name to mean simply, laying out a road or path. From what her daughter (by a later marriage) said to interviewers, Making Out Road's name in Cheyenne actually conveys the sense of "laid down the law," a phrase much in keeping with her stern personality.[16]

Indeed, as far as Kit was concerned, Making Out Road would turn out to be a very different equation from his lamented Waa-nibe. In Grinnell's words, "the Cheyennes were a headstrong, obstinate people, the more so when they made up their minds about something they wanted."[17] References to Making Out Road and her mercurial disposition depict her unflatteringly as spoiled, quarrelsome, proud, and prone to fits of temper. That contrasted sharply to Arapaho women like Waa-nibe, who was known for her gentleness, accommodating nature, and domestic industry.

So what prompted Kit Carson to enter into a relationship with this assertive girl? In part it may have been her physical appearance, for frontiersmen as a whole spoke favorably of the beauty of Cheyenne women. Making Out Road, in fact, was often lauded as "the belle of the Cheyenne."

Availability rather than beauty, however, might have led Kit to her tepee door. Ordinarily in Plains Indian society, there was no place for a lone woman, unattached to a husband or the lodge of a male relative. But around mountain men and their trading posts one could usually find a small floating population of Indian females seeking refuge from intolerable conditions, or simply trying to better themselves by mating with a whiteman. From what is known about her, Making Out Road seems to have fit into that category. If Kit perceived any stain on her reputation, he easily overlooked it. Facing an uncertain future, he desperately needed to recreate a nuclear family that could provide some stability and security for his motherless youngsters.

Within the tribe at least, the "Belle of the Cheyenne" appears to have suffered no diminution of status because of her inherent independence. Perhaps that was because she had been born into the Little Bear band, the most prestigious of the ten tribal divisions of the Cheyenne nation.

The Little Bear people were recognized by the other bands as owners of the Medicine Arrows, and from their ranks always came the custodian, or Keeper of the Arrows. Because of this sacred trust, important to the entire tribe, the Little Bears were saddled with special behavioral requirements and taboos. For example, their women each morning were obliged to go to a river or stream and jump in, an act of ritual bathing and, we presume, purification. In winter they broke the ice, took a quick plunge, then raced back to their lodge wrapped in buffalo robes.[18]

Originally, each of the ten Cheyenne bands seem to have been a tightly organized unit, whose members claimed descent from a common ancestor. But by the early 1840s, such cohesion was beginning to break down. Nevertheless, at the advent of the twentieth century, the tribe still regarded fellow band members as kinsmen, so close in fact that intermarriage within the group was forbidden. Descendants of Making Out Road referred to her as a sister of Owl Woman, William Bent's wife. There is no proof that was true in the literal sense. But it could have been accurate in another way if they were looked upon as band sisters.[19]

That relationship may have caused Kit to look past Making Out Road's defects. Possibly William even brought the pair together, initially. He and Carson had first met back in 1829. They were of the same age and shared a similar temperament, being reserved in speech, swift at making decisions in a crisis, and sympathetic toward Indians, while never forgetting their unpredictable nature. Their personalities meshed easily, and once firmly established, the friendship proved life long. They died a year apart at the end of the 1860s.

In short, Making Out Road was pretty, energetic (if stubborn), a member of the Cheyenne elite Little Bear band, and she was well connected at Bent's Fort. Kit in his hurry to find a helpmate may have fixed his gaze on those positive things and ignored other signs that foreshadowed future trouble.

There is nothing to show that Kit paid a "bride price" for the Cheyenne girl. Later, however, Making Out Road's third husband after Kit, twenty-four-year-old Charles Rath, who knew Cheyenne customs well, did so. He was said to have delivered rich gifts, setting them before the lodge where she was living. They were formally accepted by a male relative, probably her eldest brother, Man Walking on a Cloud.[20] It is conceivable that Kit Carson, given his propensity for observing proper form, chose to do likewise. If so, it went unrecorded, as this second marriage very nearly did.

The forming of an alliance with an Indian woman could generally be done without serious complications. As a general rule, tribal societies spurned the use of special ceremonies to sanctify wedlock. Rather, at the beginning a couple simply took up residence together, a private arrangement that lasted as long as both parties were willing. The American trappers spoke of this as an "Indian" marriage, while the Frenchmen characterized it as matrimony "à la façon du pays," that is, "according to the local custom."[21]

Christian Americans in the East viewed such alliances as illicit, since they were entered into without benefit of clergy or proper ritual. Hence, "squaw men" were not considered to be married at all, and their children bore the stigma of illegitimacy. Carson's associate in Taos, Smith Simpson, told Sabin by letter in 1911 that from what he had heard most trappers figured that they were not lawfully married because "there was no legal authority in the mountains in them days to do the job."[22]

This was a touchy subject for Carson, but only on those rare occasions when he found himself back in cultivated society. In 1847, for instance, he stayed briefly at the Washington home of powerful Missouri Senator Thomas Hart Benton, father-in-law of his good friend John C. Frémont. Kit had just traveled across country from California with military dispatches for the government. When he appeared troubled about something, an inquiry elicited this response: "He felt it was wrong to be among such ladies [of the household] when they might not like to associate with him if they knew he had had an Indian wife."[23] He was referring to Waa-nibe, and it is clear he himself considered that to have been an actual marriage, even if the whiteman's government or church did not.

His attitude in regard to the status of his alliance with Making Out Road is less certain. On that subject, Estergreen quotes a letter written by Teresina Bent, daughter of Charles Bent, who spent part of her childhood in Kit Carson's Taos home. On one occasion, she said: "Uncle Kit was very angry when the man he had given the interview to said that he was married to a Cheyenne woman named Making Out Road. He said there was no truth in that story. . . . There are so many tales written about Uncle Kit that it is hard to know what the truth really is."[24]

On the basis of Teresina's statement, biographers Estergreen and Blackwelder both rejected the idea that Kit was ever married to Making Out Road.[25] Harvey Carter, however, explained Kit's words, as repeated by Teresina, this way: "My belief is that Carson habitually concealed these connections [Indian marriages] from the women of his family, in accordance with the standards of the time, but did not attempt to conceal them from the men. In fact, Kit's nephew-in-law Jesse Nelson (husband of niece Susan Carson) speaking to Francis W. Cragin in 1908 affirmed the second marriage to Making Out Road.[26] Then subsequently, as noted, Cheyennes provided specific details. The clincher would seem to be offered by William Bent's half Indian son George, who before his death in 1918 stated that "while living at the old fort [Carson] had married a Cheyenne girl."[27]

Having the pleasant memory of his life with Waa-nibe still fresh in his mind, Carson probably approached his new situation with unrealistic expectations. Undeniably, Making Out Road was not the gentle, demure wife who, like her dutiful predecessor, had hot water waiting for Kit when he came in tired from hunting. The sources of friction that made life in their tepee uncongenial left only faint echoes in the historical record, but taken together they spelled eventual doom for the ill-fated relationship. Carson as usual provides no clarification in his memoirs, never even mentioning Making Out Road's name.

In the first place, the role of stepmother for the half-Arapaho Carson children may not have suited the new wife. While no affirmation can be found that Kit removed one or both of his girls from their keeper at the fort and placed them in Making Out Road's lodge, it is a logical assumption that he did so, or at least tried it.

It was sometimes said that Making Out Road resented her husband's children and also his long absences from the tepee. She could have accompanied him on his extended hunting expeditions to procure game for the fort, had she wished, but it appears this beautiful young woman was unwilling to serve as a workhorse for this or any other man.

We can safely bet that it was not the hunting excursions that displeased Making Out Road, for she had grown up in a society where that activity was commonplace. Rather it must have been Kit's trips to Taos, in between hunts, that aroused her ire and perhaps jealousy.

Since Carson's first look at the town of Taos as a teenager in the latter 1820s, the place had mushroomed in population and blossomed into a vibrant and noisy trade center. In 1844 trail merchant and author Josiah Gregg would proclaim it second only to Santa Fe in importance.[28] The French Canadian and American trappers that settled there initiated the boomlet, but feeding it too was an influx of Hispanics from other parts of New Mexico, who perceived opportunities for financial improvement in a community on the upswing.[29]

Carson found it at once exciting and comfortable, with many familiar faces of men he had known in the mountains. Charles Bent and Céran St. Vrain both had homes in Taos, and were later joined by a younger Bent brother from St. Louis, George. Sometime in the mid 1830s, Charles had taken as his common-law wife the attractive and intelligent María Ignacia Jaramillo who bore him five children. George Bent also established a free-union relationship with María de la Cruz Padilla, and they had two children.[30] He was invited to join Bent, St. Vrain & Co. as a junior partner.

On his visits to Taos, Kit was progressively drawn into the Bent family circle. For a time, he also had a fling with a loose woman named Antonia Luna. She had previously been the mistress of the brawny black mountain man Jim Beckwourth. When Luna injudiciously informed Kit that Beckwourth was a better lover, he abruptly broke with her. Having been raised in a slaveholding family in Missouri, Kit probably resented being compared unfavorably to a black man.[31]

Without a doubt, it was in the home of Charles Bent that Carson first met María Ignacia's youngest sister, Josefa, a mere slip of a girl in her early teens.[32] "Her style of beauty was of the haughty, heart-breaking kind," is how Lewis H. Garrard summed up her charms a few years later.[33] Not only her physical attractiveness but a simple grace and warmth also caught Carson's eye, perhaps reminding him, as Making Out Road did not, of his beloved Waa-nibe. He made a conscious decision to bide his time until the day Josefa was of marriageable age and then let fate take its course. In the meanwhile, a pressing problem awaited his attention at Bent's Fort, and evidently he was in a quandary as to how to resolve it.

So much traffic moved between Taos and the fort, a perfect conduit for rumor, it seems unlikely that Making Out Road could have failed to hear about Carson's brief dalliance with Antonia Luna. Considerable sexual freedom was tolerated for men in New Mexico, as it was among the Cheyennes. But Kit's Indian wife, with her nonconformist views and strong sense of self, was not inclined to remain silent. When Kit returned to the fort, the subject of his straying probably fueled at least some of the quarrels reportedly marring his domestic life in this period.[34]

a

Reconstructed Bent's Fort today, on the Mountain Route of the Santa Fe Trail. Here Kit Carson entered a brief marriage with the Cheyenne girl, Making Out Road. (Photo by Marc Simmons)

Charles Bent, First Governor of New Mexico.

Charles Bent, employer, friend and in-law of Kit Carson. (After Twitchell, 1909)

b

WILLIAM BENT

William Bent, manager of Bent's Fort and close friend of Kit Carson. (After Sabin, 1914)

A Cheyenne camp on the Southern Plains. (National Archives Photo)

c

This image has sometimes been identified as Making Out Road in her later years, following marriage to Charles Rath. It seems more likely to be her half-white daughter, Cheyenne Belle. (Courtesy of Cultural Heritage Center, Dodge City, Kansas)

d

Cheyenne Belle (left), age sixteen, daughter of Making Out Road and Charles Rath; and Ada Bent (right), age fourteen, granddaughter of William Bent. (Photo courtesy of M.L. Gardner)

Soon the couple had another complication confronting them. Making Out Road was pregnant. She may have known for some time before telling Kit, but his reaction to the news, at whatever moment it came, has to be left to imagination. If he had been contemplating separation, this unexpected development might have given him pause. In the end, however, it was Making Out Road who made the decision for both of them, by ending the marriage herself.

Among the Plains Indians, wrote anthropologist Robert H. Lowie, "in the absence of religious sanctions for marriage, it could be dissolved without much ado and often was."[35] In fact, matrimonial unions were as apt to fall apart as easily as they were put together. Considering the tight boundaries placed upon women by custom, it is surprising that in most Plains tribes, a wife could take the initiative and divorce her husband, if she found it impossible to live peaceably with him. The universal procedure called for her to pile the man's personal belongings outside the lodge, thereby serving notice in public fashion that by her choice the parties were going their separate ways.[36]

The relative rarity of women initiating divorce among the Cheyennes is implied in the ethnographic literature. But the forceful personality of Making Out Road would have allowed her to take that step without hesitation. Unhappily, the frequent references to the Carson divorce, including the detail that his hot-tempered spouse tossed his saddle and other possessions outside the tepee, all trace back to the unreliable 1928 biography by Stanley Vestal.

The scene he paints of a screaming Making Out Road berating Kit while the whole camp looked on is almost certainly the author's fabrication. From one of his Indian informants, he might have actually picked up the word "divorce" and then, based on his knowledge of standard Native custom in such instances, re-created the specific details by extrapolation.[37]

Edwin L. Sabin, seven years after publication of the Vestal book, brought out his revised and greatly expanded edition of *Kit Carson Days,* and in it he introduced a paragraph about Making Out Road, who had not appeared at all in the first edition. Almost all of the information he cites comes from Grinnell's brief 1923 statement originating with the elderly informant, Sitting-in-the-Lodge. But Grinnell had said merely that "Carson lived with his Cheyenne wife for a short time only," providing no mention of how a separation occurred. Sabin added to his account a single sentence on that subject: "In about a year [of marriage] Carson, no hero to his wife, found himself and all his personal possessions including Adaline thrown out of his lodge."[38] Clearly that is a very brief and restrained distillation of Vestal's florid description of the imagined divorce scene.

Thereafter, Carson biographers and historians routinely dropped the titillating "fact" that Making Out Road had brazenly "chucked Kit, Adaline, and all their possessions from the lodge. Divorce, Indian style."[39] That Vestal in an honest moment had waffled a bit by referring to Kit's "summary divorce of—or by—the Cheyenne girl," seems to have escaped the notice of everyone.[40]

From Sitting-in-the-Lodge, George Bird Grinnell had learned the outcome of Making Out Road's pregnancy. She had given birth to a daughter that "died in infancy."[41] Sabin subsequently added this: "There had been a child which lived only a month."[42] That the life span of Kit's third girl was just one month has been generally accepted by scholars.[43]

David Roberts characterizes Carson's broken marriage as "an embarrassing mistake." Kit probably would have agreed, although he might not have phrased the matter precisely in that way. Whether the divorce occurred before or after the death of Making Out Road's baby is not clear. Its passing, however, would have severed an important tie binding Kit to his wife.

The timetable of events surrounding the marriage bears directly upon a still-dangling problem summarized earlier: the date of Carson's arrival at Bent's Fort from Fort Robidoux. As noted, Harvey Carter conjectured that Kit came to the post on the Arkansas during September 1841. Since his departure time for Missouri is well-established, as April 1842, that means he resided at Bent's Fort for something less than eight months.

That he could have squeezed into that circumscribed time frame these events seems a physical impossibility: arrival, obtaining employment, meeting and brief courtship of Making Out Road, marriage, and fathering a child who arrived nine months later and died a month after that, following which Carson left for Missouri. Reasonably considered, this schedule will not fit into Carter's eight months. But it can be accommodated effortlessly with acceptance of Dale Morgan's proposition that Carson, in fact, reached Bent's Fort during September of 1840 rather than 1841. Nevertheless, too many unknowns still surround the knotty point to permit at present a definitive resolution.

By early 1842, Carson seems to have been fully committed to pursuing the hand of Josefa Jaramillo, which suggests that the rupture with Making Out Road by then may have been complete, or nearly so. David Lavender, without citing evidence, claims that Josefa's father, "the haughty old Don Francisco Jaramillo" was cold to the attentions being paid to his daughter, his opposition mainly stemming from Kit's Protestantism. According to Lavender, "Carson's answer was to embrace the Catholic faith."[45]

Anti-Catholicism was rampant in the United States at that time, so Kit would not have converted without careful thought. His act, however, served as a measure of his new devotion to Josefa rather than as an indicator of religious commitment.

In any event, Carson submitted to baptism in Our Lady of Guadalupe Church at Taos on January 28, 1842. Performing the rite was the controversial Padre Antonio José Martínez, the same priest who would marry Kit and Josefa a year later.[46] So Carson and his future in-laws must have come to some sort of understanding, leaving the once hostile Señor Jaramillo mollified. It has sometimes been suggested, and reasonably so, that Kit promised to wait a year before seeking to marry the Jaramillos' daughter, which, if it is the case, might have helped placate Don Francisco.

The future of the two half-Indian Carson children remained to be settled. Adaline was coming of school age, but as yet there existed in New Mexico no educational facilities for girls. From his mountain man days, Kit recalled that fellow trappers, like his friends Jim Bridger and Joe Meek, had sent their youngsters out of the wilderness to be schooled either at Catholic institutions in St. Louis or in newly erected Protestant missions in Oregon. But in thinking it over, he decided Adaline would be better off with his relatives still in the Franklin, Missouri area, where he had grown up. Schools were there, as well as family for her to get to know. But it was an open question as to how she would be received.

Kit could not help but be aware of the general prejudice against squaw men and their Indian children. Since he had been gone from his Missouri home for more than a decade and a half, he possessed no current knowledge of attitudes prevailing there.

One case that is known within the extended Carson family indicates that his concern was not misplaced. Thomas Kelly Carson, a first cousin of Kit's, was one of those left behind in North Carolina by Lindsey Carson when he took his immediate family and migrated first to Kentucky and then to Missouri. When Kit Carson afterward became famous, Thomas Kelly would never acknowledge his kinship because, "being snooty," as his granddaughter said, he condemned Kit as "always a wild uncouth boy and that he married, of all things, an Indian squaw and had a little half-breed Indian girl."[47]

In his memoirs, Carson as usual is aggravatingly brief about what followed. He declared: "In April 1842, the train of wagons of Bent and St. Vrain was going to the states. I concluded to go in with them. It had been a long time since I had been among civilized people. I arrived at the states, went and saw my friends and acquaintances, then took a trip to St. Louis. . . ."[48] By compressing his narrative, Kit omits, besides any reference to Adaline, much else of significance.

Early each spring, Bent, St. Vrain & Co. sent a caravan eastward transporting the winter's hide trade to market. In 1842 it carried 283 packs of buffalo robes and 30 packs of beaver pelts according to a St. Louis newspaper that reported Charles Bent's arrival.[49]

When Kit joined the train at Bent's Fort, he had little Adaline in tow. His younger Arapaho daughter, now about three years of age, he left in Taos, presumably with Ignacia Bent, to be cared for by her servants. He would never see her again, for as a family tradition relates, the child was scalded to death in 1843 when she fell into a large kettle of boiling soap.[50] Not only her name, but everything else about her remains in the shadows.

Before the wagons set forth on the Santa Fe Trail, Charles Bent may have presented Carson a draft on P. Chouteau & Co. of St. Louis, which by this date was acting on behalf of Bent, St. Vrain & Co. in financial matters and seems to have considered the smaller firm its subsidiary.[51]

The draft was for the amount of $495.02, which he cashed the following month in St. Louis, and it represented the total sum owed him by Bent, St. Vrain & Co.[52] Since Kit, by his own admission, had been earning one dollar a day as a hunter for the fort, then the money paid to him was far more than he would have gotten for eight months of work. That means he either arrived in 1840 instead of 1841, or perhaps he received additional pay for carrying Bent trade goods to outlying Indian villages.

We cannot but wonder whether, before his departure for the East, Kit Carson had a meeting with Making Out Road. If so, it would have been their last, since no evidence has surfaced of any further contact.

In the wake of the failure of what we believe was her first marriage, Making Out Road wed two Cheyenne men in quick succession, Flat Head and Wolf Man. Both marriages proved short term and ended in divorce. By one of the men she had a daughter, Shaking Herself, who was still living on the Southern Cheyenne reservation in 1917, at age 62.[53]

We next get a glimpse of Making Out Road about 1859 when she married, Cheyenne style, Charles Rath. German-born in 1839, he had immigrated as a child to the United States where his family settled on a farm in Ohio. At age twelve, Charles ran away to the West and soon afterward joined a wagon train that took him to Bent's New Fort on the Arkansas below, what was now termed, Bent's Old Fort. Eventually, he became the commissary as well as a licensed Indian trader. His attachment to the Cheyennes grew strong, he learned their language and customs, and finally was admitted as a member of the tribe.[54]

When he decided to marry Making Out Road, who was much older than himself, Charles heaped gifts at the entrance of her lodge, and they were accepted. Their first and only child, a girl, was born near Bent's Fort during August of 1861. Rath named her Cheyenne Belle, since her mother had once been known as the belle of the Cheyennes. Belle, as the youngster was generally called, spent her early years living in the Indian camps with her uncle, Man-Walking-on-a-Cloud, or other relatives.[55]

In 1863 Charles Rath and Making Out Road were operating a trading post at the Walnut Creek Crossing on the Santa Fe Trail in central Kansas. One day Cheyenne warriors appeared, informed them that soldiers had killed one of their chiefs, and full-scale war was about to break out. After warning Charles to leave immediately or he would be killed, the intruders seized Making Out Road and returned her to the Cheyenne camp.

Charles Rath left as a prolonged war with the Cheyennes began. Under the circumstances, he considered his marriage with Making Out Road to be over. In the early 1870s, he became a buffalo hunter and hide merchant in partnership with Robert Wright, prominent Dodge City businessman. Rath suffered severe financial losses late in life and died penniless in 1902.[56]

Making Out Road and Belle remained with the Cheyennes when the tribe was confined to an Oklahoma reservation. Belle attended the Darlington School and became well educated. At seventeen she married a soldier, and when her first child was born she rode horseback to Mobeetie in the Texas Panhandle to show it to Charles Rath, who was then living there. That was the only time as an adult that Belle ever saw her father. She died in May 1939.[57]

Long after Making Out Road passed away from old age about 1890, John H. Seger, superintendent of the Darlington School gave his recollections of her. "She was a very determined woman," he said, "and was able to put Belle's husband in his place."[58]

Based upon his own rocky experiences with Making Out Road, Kit Carson would have understood those words very well.

The spring eastbound caravan of Bent, St. Vrain & Co. was captained in 1842 by Charles Bent. His brother William may have also accompanied the wagons that year, as did Lucien Maxwell, a shrewd ex-trapper destined for fame as the future owner of the baronial Maxwell Land Grant. He and Carson would develop a strong friendship and eventually become business partners. Kit found a place for little Adaline in a Dearborn, a light covered carriage often used for passengers alongside freight wagons. The five-week trip across the Southern Plains to the village of Westport, the first settlement in Missouri, was uneventful.

The Bents owned a farm just south of Westport that served as a holding ground for their livestock and as a depot for the heavy wagons. Their usual practice was to off-load peltry and other freight at nearby Westport Landing on the Missouri River and transport it by steamboat down to St. Louis. Both Westport and its landing lie within present day Kansas City.

Here, after breakup of the caravan, Kit and Adaline took lodging at the Yoacham Tavern. Daniel Yoacham had arrived in the area a dozen years before with his wife and small girls, took out a government claim, and began work on a home and hostelry built of walnut logs. The Yoachams were the first family in Westport and by 1842 had become good friends of Charles Bent.[59]

One of the daughters, Susannah, wrote down her recollections in 1906 at the age of 76. She made the following statement:

"I remember Kit Carson well indeed. He came east and stopped at my father's hotel. . . . He brought this little girl with him to be educated. . . . He bought her outfits in Westport, and had her dresses made in our home. She came to us dressed in buckskin and left dressed in as fine goods as could then be bought on the border. She was about my age, but uncivilized. She pulled up all my mother's vines and was chewing the roots when we found her at it."[60]

There at the Yoacham Tavern, Carson in providing for a make-over in little Adaline's garments began the process of assimilating her into the society he had not known since he fled Missouri sixteen years before. But after this token start, he would be dependent upon others to carry the learning forward. No doubt, he hoped the child's new clothes would help ease her acceptance by his Booneslick relations.

On that score, however, he entertained serious misgivings. So to sound out the mood of his kin, Kit arranged to leave Adaline with the Yoachams while he made a reconnaissance trip a hundred miles down the Missouri to test the waters. Upon reaching the domain of his youth, he was startled to see that pictures he carried in his mind no longer existed in reality.

Old Franklin beside the river, where he had worked as a saddler's apprentice, was gone, washed away in a flood. Its residents had moved north four miles to New Franklin on high ground and to Fayette beyond. As for the surrounding country, it no longer bore the stamp of wilderness, having long since been tamed by the spread of tidy farms and a web of fences and rural lanes. Many of the people he had known were there no longer, while those few remaining, like some of his brothers and sisters, he could scarcely recognize.

Among the missing was his mother Rebecca Carson Martin who had died the previous year. It is conceivable that Kit had received word of her passing while he was still at Bent's Fort, but if not, he got the painful news now.[61] His youngest brother, Lindsey, Jr., twenty-four years old, was tall, lanky, and educated in contrast to small and illiterate Kit. The pair eagerly restored their fraternal bonds.

All accounts agree that Kit was pleasantly surprised by the warmth of the greeting extended to him and by offers to take in five-year-old Adaline. Since he himself disclosed nothing at all about this visit in his memoirs, we are left with the confusing recollections of others concerning the history of the child's care during the ensuing nine years, while she lived in Missouri.

At first, she may have stayed with Kit's younger sister, Mary Ann Carson Rubey, but according to other reports, Adaline spent six years on a farm between Fayette and Glasgow with Mrs. Leander Amick (daughter of another Carson sister, Elizabeth), where she attended the rural Rock Springs School. In 1847, on a courier mission carrying military dispatches from California to Washington, D.C., Carson made a small detour to visit Adaline and his relatives. A similar stopover occurred again the following year when he was asked to repeat the transcontinental ride. Long afterward, Mrs. Amick's daughter wrote: "As my mother refused to accept any money for caring for his daughter, [Uncle Kit] purchased many presents for her; among them was a mahogany rocking chair which I still have."[62]

After his favorable reception, Carson returned to the Yoacham Tavern in Westport to collect his daughter and presumably deposit her with family in the Booneslick. Then he was off to St. Louis to see the sights and also cash his Bent, St. Vrain & Co. draft at the headquarters of P. Chouteau & Co.

As it happened, the pleasures and hubbub of a big city swiftly paled for him. As he put it, "[In] St. Louis, remained a few days and was tired of remaining in settlements; [so] took a steamer for the upper Missouri." And he added, "As luck would have it, Colonel Frémont, then a lieutenant, was aboard of the same boat."[63]

Lt. John Charles Frémont of the U.S. Topographical Engineers and, as noted, son-in-law of Missouri's Senator Benton, had been commissioned to lead an expedition of exploration up the Platte River to the Rocky Mountains. Reaching St. Louis in early May, he began assembling men and equipment. One of those added to the roster, as a hunter, was Lucien Maxwell who had recently come in from New Mexico in the company of Charles Bent.

Toward the end of the month, Frémont with his party boarded the steamboat Rowena, a newly built sidewheeler of 225 tons.[64] As the packet thrashed the waters on its way up the Missouri to Westport where the expedition was to begin its overland journey, Frémont stood at the rail watching the riverine landscape go by. Soon a youngish man of small height spoke to him in a soft backwoods drawl, and the two fell into conversation. As Kit remembered the incident many years later, Lt.

Frémont told of his government mission and said he was in need of a guide who knew his way around the West. "I informed him that I had been some time in the mountains and thought I could guide him to any point he wished to go."[65]

As Frémont recalled it, "I was so pleased with Carson that when he asked to go with me I was glad to take him." And the lieutenant shortly revealed that the pay was $100 a month, three times what Kit had been drawing at Bent's Fort. In referring to this initial encounter with Carson on the boat, an aged Frémont in his published memoirs (1887) said, "He was returning from putting his little daughter in a convent-school at St. Louis."[66] His statement has been accepted and repeated by many writers.

Kit's sister Mary Ann disputed it, saying: "Adaline was not sent to a convent in St. Louis as reported in Frémont's *Memoirs*."[67] Others of the Carson clan disagreed with her, insisting that the girl attended at different times both the Rock Springs country school and a St. Louis convent school. Carson's biographer Dr. Peters also weighed in on the subject of Adaline's education. "When she reached a suitable age," he wrote, "Kit sent her to St. Louis for the purpose of giving her a liberal education. Indeed, most of Kit Carson's hard earnings, gained while he was a hunter on the Arkansas were devoted to the advancement of his child."[68] If such was the case, then it seems likely that upon cashing his substantial Bent, St. Vrain draft, Carson would have used a significant portion of it to finance Adaline's entry into the Catholic convent.

Tradition has long held that the school was at the Convent of the Religious of the Sacred Heart. The early records of that institution are lost, so that Adaline Carson's attendance cannot be confirmed.[69] Yet, she probably was enrolled there or in some other Catholic school, the time period being the main question still in doubt. After all, Frémont composing his *Memoirs* forty-five years after the meeting with Kit on the Rowena might have simply made a mistake in recalling their conversation. If Adaline was taken to St. Louis later from the Booneslick, Frémont in looking back could have mistakenly thought that happened in 1842.

We simply do not know. The present writer, based on what has already been said, is inclined to believe that little Adaline was first deposited with a sister or niece of Kit's and subsequently, perhaps in 1847, he removed her to St. Louis. As in so many other instances involving Kit, his wives, or his children, it is impossible to reconcile with any confidence the conflicting information.

Kit indicated that luck had brought him together with Frémont at the very time he was at loose ends and looking for something to do. But the meeting may not have resulted from pure chance. Either Charles Bent or newly hired hunter Lucien Maxwell could have advised Kit which steamboat Frémont was taking and that he was short a guide. Whether their introduction to one another came about by accident or by Kit's design, the consequences were to be lasting because from it, in Frémont's words, "grew our enduring friendship."[70]

Kit Carson would faithfully serve the young officer on his first three expeditions: in 1842 to the Rocky Mountains; in 1843–1844 to the Great Basin, Oregon, and California; and in 1845–1846 again to California, at the time of the Mexican War. All three were filled with episodes that read now like adventures from fiction, rather than objective historical narrative.

There can be no question that the beginning of Carson's association with Frémont there on the deck of the Rowena was a turning point in his life, one that set his course on a new road leading to lasting fame. When Frémont, with the help of his talented wife Jessie, wrote up and published in 1845 the accounts of his first two expeditions, he lionized his guide Kit Carson, painting him as a daring and larger-than-life frontiersman, in the nature of a figure from the novels of James Fenimore Cooper. The book, widely distributed, was eagerly snapped up by a public hungry for information on the still-mysterious Far West. It contributed to Frémont becoming known as "The Pathfinder" and to Carson, in the words of Kent Ladd Steckmesser, seeing himself transformed "from a strictly local character into a national demigod."[71]

Unforeseen at the time by Carson was the profound impact on his future family life that ultimately emanated from his changed circumstances, first set in motion by the over-the-rail conversation with Frémont. At a moment in his life when he ought to have been thinking about settling in comfortably with his third wife-to-be, Josefa, his steps were leading him toward a career of government service, whose demands would impose painful hardships upon those closest to him.

As the Rowena ascended the mighty Missouri, it came in a few days to Boonville, located on the south side of the river opposite the site of Old

Franklin. This place in the heart of the Booneslick country was roughly half way between St. Louis on the eastern edge of the state and Westport near the western boundary. So here steamboats were accustomed to stop and take on cords of firewood needed to stoke their boilers.

Carson used the layover to make a hurried trip to nearby Fayette and in the Howard County Courthouse execute a legal document. It granted his brother Lindsey, Jr. power of attorney and authorized him to sell in Kit's behalf a small tract of land that had come to him from his mother's estate. Therein, he listed his residence as Bent's Fort on the Arkansas. As he could not write his name, Kit signed with his mark, an X, which was witnessed by his brother-in-law Robert Cooper, husband of sister Elizabeth. If Adaline was in the neighborhood, rather than back at St. Louis, he may have squeezed in a brief visit with her.[72]

The Rowena continued its journey upriver, reaching Westport Landing on June 4. After some final arrangements and a short delay caused by bad weather, Kit said, "We started for the Rocky Mountains . . . to survey the South Pass [on the Oregon Trail] and take the height of the highest peaks."[73]

Within three months, the expedition's work was done. In returning eastbound, on the last day of August it reached Fort Laramie in southeastern Wyoming, a fur trading post founded in 1834. There, as Kit stated, "I quit the employ of Frémont." He did so because the road from that point back to Missouri, being well marked, required no guide. In the next sentence, he declares, "I went to Bent's Fort in 1843." Historians have been accustomed to say that in the four months between Carson's stay at Fort Laramie and his appearance at Bent's Fort, his whereabouts and activities are unknown.[74]

If there is anything to the theory that Carson was marking time until the end of his one-year wait, so that he could marry Josefa, then this would explain the four-month gap in his personal history. Since no exciting or noteworthy incidents occurred in that brief spell, he simply skipped over it when dictating his memoirs in 1858.

Finding himself at a fur trade crossroads like Fort Laramie, Kit Carson would have encountered mountain men he had known when working the north country during the previous decade. There was news to catch up on and campfire talk to join in, much of it consisting of complaints about trapped-out streams and the continued acceleration in the fall of prices for beaver pelts. Kit may have even gone on a short hunt, for old times' sake.

Harvey Carter speculated that after a bit he slowly drifted south, visiting other trading posts until reaching Bent's Fort in January of 1843.[75] It can now be shown that Kit did not go in that direction. Rather from Fort Laramie, he shortly headed east for St. Louis to collect his guide's pay for the months that he had been employed by the expedition.

Frémont's party arrived back in St. Louis on October 17, and on October 31 individual U.S. government pay vouchers were issued to each man who had participated in the enterprise. Christopher Carson, for service as guide and hunter, received $300 plus an additional $40 for a mule sold to Frémont. He signed his mark and had it witnessed under the voucher's date of issuance, thereby placing him in St. Louis.[76]

It is a logical conjecture that before he left Missouri, he checked on daughter Adaline to see how she was adapting to the whiteman's world. Five years would pass before he saw her again.

At this point, Carson drops from the visible screen until he resurfaces at Bent's Fort in the first half of January 1843. Within a few days, he departed for Taos with serious business on his mind. He and María Josefa Jaramillo were married on February 6, 1843, by Padre Martínez.[77] She was approaching her fifteenth birthday. Kit had turned thirty-three the previous December.

PART III

Josefa

❧ ONE ❧

Willa Cather in her historical novel, *Death Comes For the Archbishop*, gives a brief description of Josefa Carson. She received visitors at her Taos home, according to Miss Cather, "with that quiet but unabashed hospitality which is a common grace in Mexican households. She was a tall woman, slender, with drooping shoulders and lustrous black eyes and hair. Though she could not read, both her face and conversation were intelligent. . . . She had a cheerful disposition, too, and a pleasant sense of humor."[1]

Although the book is a work of fiction, from what is known of Kit Carson's third wife, this literary depiction of her is fairly accurate. Only in Cather's reference to her height is there some doubt. Unlike wives one and two, Josefa emerges with some clarity from the murky precincts of the past because more documentation exists, owing to the fact that she and Kit remained wedded for two and a half decades. By all accounts, theirs was a true love match.

Popular writers of the nineteenth century, as well as Carson descendants in Missouri, tended to up-grade Josefa's background by referring to the Jaramillo family's supposed aristocratic origins and wealth. This represented a veiled attempt to protect Kit's reputation, since in the view of Easterners marriage to a native New Mexican was beneath the dignity of Anglos and barred one from full acceptance in polite society. A similar prejudice from afar had shadowed Kit in the days when he was a "squaw man" with Indian wives.[2]

Josefa's earliest known forebears, while not exactly of the elite class, were nevertheless people of solid stock. She and all of the Jaramillos in upper New Mexico (the Rio Arriba) descended from one Roque Jaramillo, who had set out in 1693 from Mexico City and headed for New Mexico with his parents, one brother, and one sister. Roque was then eleven years old. The father, José Jaramillo Negrete, was a mason by trade. His wife, Roque's mother, had been an orphan. The couple were married inside the great cathedral of Mexico City in 1672.

The family formed part of an expedition of settlers sent northward by the Spanish viceroy to help repopulate New Mexico following the Pueblo Revolt (1680) and the reconquest by Gov. Diego de Vargas (1692). Heads of households received a 300-peso stipend from the royal government to cover travel and equipment expenses. Undoubtedly, José Jaramillo saw this venture into pioneering as an economic opportunity.

Thereafter, the history of the Jaramillos remained tied to northern New Mexico, where they settled in the vicinity of the newly established town named Santa Cruz de la Cañada, some twenty-five miles above the capital of Santa Fe. Here in 1711, Roque Jaramillo gave his age as twenty-six and identified his wife as Petrona de Cárdenas, whose parents had also come from Mexico City in 1693. When she died in 1767, her will listed the couple's fourteen children, six of whom were already deceased. The Jaramillo household also included at least four Indian servants, who had been purchased or ransomed from nomadic tribes, baptized, given the Jaramillo name, and incorporated into the extended family, pursuant to local custom.[3]

Roque Jaramillo received a royal grant of land in 1746. Comprising 10,000 acres located west of the Rio Grande, it seems to have been intended originally for grazing rather than settlement. Certainly the family's principal residence remained in the Santa Cruz Valley, east of the river. At least two of Roque's grown sons with their wives and children continued to live under his roof, suggesting that together with the land grant, he held an impressive estate, at least in New Mexico terms.[4]

Roque Jaramillo's great-grandson Francisco Esteban Jaramillo was still living in the Santa Cruz jurisdiction when his first daughter, María Manuela, was born June 17, 1813. His wife, María Apolonia Vigil, would eventually bear a total of eight children, including María Josefa, future wife of Kit Carson. Church records indicate that their baptisms occurred at Potrero, a satellite of the community of Chimayó, which lay approximately eight miles up the valley from Santa Cruz, the administrative headquarters for the region.[5]

Whether Potrero was the original site of Roque Jaramillo's large dwelling a hundred years earlier, or whether Francisco Jaramillo moved there from Santa Cruz is unknown. Nor is information available regarding his activities, although it can be assumed that in the main he was engaged in farming and ranching.

For some compelling reason, he decided to pick up the entire family, soon after the fourth daughter, María Josefa, was born in 1828 and move to Taos, beyond the high mountains that filled the horizon toward the northeast. Perhaps he went in the same spirit as his distant ancestor, José Jaramillo Negrete, who had come all the way from Mexico City to New Mexico in hopes of bettering his fortunes.

It was in Taos that Francisco and Apolonia's last child was born December 15, 1830, a son named Luciano.[6] Whatever expectations Francisco may have held about Taos offering him some chance for material improvement apparently never materialized. From the bloody revolt there in 1847, his family suffered grievously. And on the first U.S. Census conducted in 1850, he was shown as owning real estate worth a mere $217, a sum just slightly above that of his son-in-law, Kit Carson. No! Taos did not prove kind to Francisco Esteban Jaramillo.[7]

Josefa Jaramillo's mother, María Apolonia Vigil, was directly descended from Francisco Montes Vigil who had brought his family of eight members from their native Zacatecas to New Mexico with the 1695 expedition of Juan Paéz Hurtado. His descendants appear as *vecinos* (citizens) of both Santa Cruz and Santa Fe.[8]

By the early nineteenth century, the Vigil clan was a numerous one in northern New Mexico. A physical characteristic, pointedly mentioned, was that the Vigils tended to be tall. It has been claimed by some writers that Josefa stood a head taller than her husband Kit, whereas, in fact, she was several inches shorter, a small and petite woman.[9] And another thing: the family line produced adept politicians.

Among them was Josefa Jaramillo's uncle, Cornelio Vigil, holder of several Taos offices, including magistrate (*alcalde*); prefect, that is, chief civil officer for the district; and probate judge. His cousin Donaciano Vigil served as provincial secretary in Santa Fe to Manuel Armijo, the last governor to preside under the Mexican flag before New Mexico fell to a conquering American army in 1846. Another relative, Juan Bautista Vigil y Alarid, in office as lieutenant governor when Armijo fled, had the unenviable task of handing over the reins of government to the invaders. But he did so with grace, serving wine and brandy at the ceremony on the Santa Fe plaza.[10]

In 1843 Cornelio Vigil had joined with fellow Taos resident Cerán St. Vrain in petitioning Gov. Armijo for a huge tract of land in southern

Colorado (then part of New Mexico) for the alleged purpose of establishing an agricultural colony. On December 9 of that year, the governor approved the Vigil and St. Vrain Grant (often called the Las Animas Grant) whose delineated boundaries encompassed four million acres. The following year, Cornelio and Cerán quietly conveyed one-sixth interest each in the grant to Charles Bent, to territorial secretary Donaciano Vigil, merchant and Bent-friend Eugene Leitensdorfer, and finally to Gov. Manuel Armijo himself. These men, together with Charles Beaubien of Taos, formed a powerful clique of commercial and political figures whose aim was to obtain control of large blocks of land in anticipation of future profits. As an heir of her uncle Cornelio, Josefa Carson with Kit would spend her last days living in a corner of the Vigil and St. Vrain grant.[11]

The first son born to Francisco and Apolonia Jaramillo was Pablo José, baptized March 7, 1819. Evidently, he died in infancy, for the next son born two years later received the name José Pablo. Something similar occurred with the daughter, born on July 26, 1826, and baptized as María Peregrine Josefa Jaramillo. She too must have succumbed, for the next child, also a daughter, was christened María Josefa Jaramillo, born March 27, 1828. Probably the grieving parents sought to honor and remember the one lost by transferring its name (omitting Peregrine) to the new arrival.[12]

All four daughters of the Jaramillos were given the first name of María, a not uncommon practice in pious Catholic families. To distinguish them, they were called by their second given name, which in the case of Kit Carson's bride was Josefa, the feminine form of José, or in English, Joseph. Thus in bearing the names of Mary and Joseph, it is supposed, she could count on the intercession of the Holy Family in times of need.[13]

The Jaramillos were in the habit of calling their youngest daughter Josefita, a diminutive that served as a term of endearment, but also differentiated her from the deceased Josefa, for whom she had been named. Major Rafael Chacón, who knew the Carson family during the Civil War, wrote: "[Colonel Carson's] wife Doña Josefa Jaramillo, was called by him by the pet name 'Chepita' and he was most kind to her."[14] Chepita, or more commonly Chipita, was a standard Spanish nickname for Josefa.[15]

In letters to her that he dictated in Spanish through others, Kit generally addressed his wife as Doña Chepita, the title denoting respect and the familiar nickname, affection.[16] But when speaking about her in

English to fellow Americans, he used "Little Jo," a literal translation of Josefita. At least that was the recollection of Marian Sloan Russell who knew Carson in the 1850s.[17]

Kit and Josefa were married by Padre Martínez in the Taos parish church of Our Lady of Guadalupe, located just west of the plaza. The date: February 6, 1843, a Monday. It is recorded in the marriage register that George Bent (younger brother of Charles) and María de la Cruz Padilla (his common-law wife) served as sponsors (*padrinos*) for the couple. One of the witnesses was José María Valdez, husband of Josefa's eldest sister, María Manuela. Subsequently, Valdez as a volunteer army officer would work closely with Kit in the Indian wars and the Civil War. In the register, the Padre speaks of "the others who were present," without naming them. That reference, however, would suggest that the Carsons stood up before Josefa's extended family as well as friends, including those of the groom.[18] In short, they appear to have enjoyed a full wedding, instead of a scaled down ceremony in front of no more than the priest and witnesses.

This was of a different order for Kit Carson from his two previous Indian marriages, both of which had been entered into according to highly informal Native custom. By submitting to Christian ritual now, he was consciously establishing the legitimacy of this union and also making a commitment to its permanency. Sensitive to personal criticism from his own society, he wished to embark upon his last excursion into matrimony following proper standards.

That may have influenced Josefa's parents to give their grudging consent to the nuptials, for it has been supposed that they had no liking for Kit. Still, they probably thought this alliance, sanctioned by a priest, to be superior to the state of their older daughter Ignacia, who since the early 1830s had lived as common-law wife with the taciturn and stiff Charles Bent. Together, that couple produced five children, all given the mother's surname, Jaramillo, at baptism and listed in public records as *natural*, meaning illegitimate. Bent's partner, Cerán St. Vrain lived with three different women, had a child by each, and provided for their financial support.[19]

In fact, a body of women in the Taos area floated in and out of relationships with American trappers and traders. But surprisingly from that situation often emerged stable and enduring unions, like that of

Charles and Ignacia Bent. As Janet Lecompte has remarked, "sexual freedom . . . was taken for granted in New Mexico," exactly the opposite of the prevailing attitude in the states east of the Mississippi. Or in the words of Rebecca McDowell Craver: "Common-law marriages were both customary and socially acceptable in Mexican frontier society."[20]

Although no shame or blame was visited upon New Mexican women bearing illegitimate children, nevertheless, upper- or middle-class parents such as Francisco and Apolonia Jaramillo, whether for economic, social, or religious reasons, preferred to see their offspring married by the Church and to Native grooms, rather than foreigners, who on occasion were known to abandon their families and depart for Missouri.

One might assume that the large differences in age between Kit and Josefa would have exacerbated any hostility the parents might have originally felt toward him. After all, Josefa was a month away from fifteen on her wedding day, while her new husband at age thirty-three was eighteen years her senior. But for the Jaramillos that evidently was not an issue.

Among southern Europeans, including Spaniards, the marriage age for a woman was often exceedingly young. Ramón Gutiérrez reports that in the late colonial period, one out of four New Mexican women were married by the time they reached fifteen. Actually, canon law set a minimum age for the contracting of a valid marriage. It was eleven for females and thirteen for males. However, marriages at those tender ages were quite rare.[21]

Large age gaps between spouses were not that exceptional in Hispanic New Mexico either, nor for that matter in the Old South to which Carson traced his own origins. And of course in his mountain man period, he knew numbers of trappers who had married Indian girls much their junior. Among them was his good friend Thomas Fitzpatrick, married at the mature age of fifty-one to a teenage Arapaho girl.[22]

Presumably, Kit actively worked to obtain parental consent to wed the Jaramillos' daughter, for although Church law permitted the couple to proceed without it, strong social pressures from the community would have led him to ask for Josefa's hand. As noted, his abiding inclination to conform to accepted procedures had prompted his re-baptism as a Catholic.[23]

Under ordinary circumstances in Hispanic New Mexico, a

constellation of rituals associated with betrothal and marriage surrounded the formal uniting of a couple for purposes of founding a new family. Beyond the sacrament of the marriage ceremony conducted by Padre Martínez, we have no further information revealing which of the accustomed practices, if any, might have been observed at the time Kit and Josefa wed.

It has long been voiced that Carson bought an adobe residence of four rooms, built originally in 1825, and presented it to Josefa as a wedding gift. Over time, he gradually expanded it to twelve rooms as the family grew. Owing to the money he had earned guiding the first Frémont expedition, it would have been within Kit's financial means to make such a purchase.[24]

Because of the lack of any deeds, thus far discovered, it is impossible to corroborate this claim, although it now forms part of the interpretation provided by the Kit Carson Museum, located in Kit and Josefa's home. In reality, another tradition persists among some of the old Taos families, to the effect that the building first belonged to Josefa's parents, who presented it to the new couple, most likely as part of her dowry.[25]

With roots extending back to the Middle Ages, the dowry by tradition was composed of goods, money, or property the bride's family presented to the groom, representing her contribution to the economy of the marriage. In New Mexico, real estate was rarely included in dowries since here the new husband's family was expected to meet that need.[26] But since Kit had no family on hand, it is entirely possible that the Jaramillos did provide the couple with their home.

Upon his marriage in early 1843, Carson's life began a realignment in new directions. Now with a wife, a permanent home, and the prospect of more children, he had to face stern realities. Foremost, was the challenge of finding a way to make a living when the work skills he had developed over the previous dozen years, in wilderness craft, were of little value in a community like Taos.

And then there was the necessity of learning to settle in, which required the curbing of his instinctive love for roving, an impulse Kit had been able to indulge freely while living as a trapper. Waa-nibe and their two little girls had followed him blindly across vast distances, or waited patiently at trading posts while he skittered off on some lengthy and hazardous enterprise, like his Navajo trade venture out of Fort Davy Crockett.

Finally, Kit Carson had to deal with assimilating into still another society, since his acquisition of a Spanish-speaking wife and in-laws put him on a new cultural footing. Raised in the Missouri back country among Anglo Protestants, he had spent his young manhood with the Indianized fraternity of trappers. Now, as an outgrowth of his marital status, Kit began the process of becoming Hispanicized, domestically at least.

If Josefa expected to have her man around the house, at least for any extended interval, she was doomed to disappointment. A scant two months after the wedding, Kit again took a job as hunter for the Bent, St. Vrain wagon train, hauling the winter's accumulation of buffalo robes to Missouri. In central Kansas, it encountered the spring westbound caravan. Encamped at Walnut Creek, the merchants were fearful of continuing on to New Mexico because of reports that a large force from the Republic of Texas led by Jacob Snively was raiding Santa Fe Trail traffic.

At once they hired Kit Carson for the sum of $300 to return to New Mexico with a petition for Gov. Manuel Armijo, requesting that he send out a military escort to protect them. Accepting the assignment, Kit rode to Taos where he persuaded the alcalde to dispatch a courier to Santa Fe with the petition. While awaiting the reply, he was able to spend welcome time with Josefa.

The response arrived, and Carson started eastward again. At Bent's Fort, however, William Bent imparted the news that U.S. Dragoons had captured and disarmed the Snively marauders so that the Santa Fe–bound merchants no longer feared attack. That word released Kit Carson from his obligation to them. At the same time, he was surprised to hear that his former employer John C. Frémont was encamped seventy-five miles up the Arkansas, just beginning his second, more ambitious exploration of the West.[27]

"I wished to see him," Kit recalled. "My object was not to seek employment. I only thought that I would ride to his camp, have a talk, and then return. But when Frémont saw me again and requested me to join him, I could not refuse, and again entered his employ as guide and hunter."[28]

In this recital can be discerned a pattern that would recur throughout the remainder of Kit Carson's married life. Owing to his growing reputation as a reliable and competent frontiersman, he would be repeatedly offered opportunities that, as in this case, he felt he "could not refuse." His loyalty toward Frémont now was one reason. But another and stronger consideration for him was that this second expedition, like the first, was a government enterprise, meaning that his fierce sense of patriotism would not permit him to decline a call to serve his country.

The number of such official summonses would grow in the furrowing of the years, imposing a progressively heavy burden on Carson and straining attempts to fulfill his role as husband and father. The competing demands for his attention, he would never entirely reconcile.

Frémont needed extra mules and upon hiring Carson sent him back to Bent's Fort to purchase ten or so. We must assume that once there, Kit arranged to get a message to Josefa, advising her of his changed circumstances but conveying only a vague notion of when he might return. In fact, the second Frémont expedition, after crossing the desolate Great Basin, visiting the Oregon country as far north as Fort Vancouver, wintering at Sutter's Fort in northern California, and at last picking up the Old Spanish Trail eastward, did not again see Bent's Fort for almost a year. Of Kit's many hair-raising adventures, his wife knew nothing until his arrival home in mid July of 1844.[29]

For the first decade of her marriage, Josefa Jaramillo Carson found herself obliged to deal with the prolonged absences of her beloved Kit, a task made all the more difficult because of her tender age and lack of worldly experience. Hispanic women of New Mexico found their sense of identity in belonging to *la familia,* an extended family in which their role as housekeeper, bearer of children, and caregiver was highly valued in the community.

Nevertheless, authority was tightly concentrated in the hands of the male head-of-household, so that his wife and other female members were accustomed to having his paternalistic rule, be it benevolent or harsh, guide them in everyday matters both large and small.

Like the Indians that the trappers had known, a Hispanic father turned over complete responsibility for his daughter to the husband upon her marriage. In the normal course of things, Josefa would have passed from under the patriarchal wing of her father to that of an equally patriarchal Hispanic husband. On marrying Kit, however, she found herself attached to a man whose authoritarian tendencies were mild by comparison, even though he too had been raised in a society on the Missouri border where male dominance prevailed.

Josefa Carson, thus in a formative period of her youth, did not have a steadying masculine hand to provide guidance and share the running of a home. And domestic burdens weighed even more heavily on her shoulders because Kit with his periodic travels could only be an occasional husband. So although wed, in the beginning at least, she had no nuclear family of her own.

Throughout the forties, whenever Kit was away Josefa would move in with relatives. That was easily done since various branches of the Jaramillo-Vigil family possessed houses spacious enough to accommodate not only children and servants, but a young woman who could glide easily into the daily routines. More often than not, however, Josefa went to stay with her sister Ignacia in the adobe house of Charles Bent, just north of the Taos plaza.

María Ignacia Jaramillo was Josefa's senior by thirteen years, the difference in ages allowing her to assume the role of elder adviser and confidante. Kit Carson affectionately referred to her as "The Old Lady" and in various small ways depended upon her generous nature and support.[30]

Both women demonstrated a streak of independence by their willingness to enter into cross-cultural marriages, a shared experience that probably brought them closer together. It is a plausible surmise that Ignacia supported her younger sister's wish to marry Kit Carson when their father initially opposed it.

Although Josefa and Ignacia both entered alliances with foreigners, a significant distinction existed since one marriage was Church sanctioned while the other was not. That situation highlighted a fundamental difference in attitude held by their two husbands. Carson had navigated with ease and confidence in the Indian-like world of the mountain men, and he had been in New Mexico long enough to master Spanish and to absorb local custom sufficiently to be classed as "Mexicanized." Only upon infrequent returns to his birth culture in the East did he experience social discomfort that was painful and obvious.

Charles Bent by contrast made no attempt at personal assimilation, beyond establishment of his Hispanic household in Taos. Quite the contrary. Overbearing and wooden, he once stated in a letter that Mexicans were "stupid, obstinate, ignorant, and vain."[31] His younger brother William had married into the Cheyenne tribe and become accepted as one of them. Such a thing would have been unthinkable for Charles.

During his dozen or more years living with Ignacia, he never tried, so far as is known, to legitimize their union. A profound unwillingness to convert to Catholicism may have been one reason. For the rest, we can only guess. Perhaps being of the prominent St. Louis Bent clan, he feared a loss of status should he marry "down." So far as can be told, not once did he take Ignacia with him back to Missouri on his yearly business trips, as other Americans with Hispanic or Indian wives sometimes did.

The couple had at least five children, two of whom appear to have died in infancy. The three surviving offspring were Alfredo (usually called Elfego by the family), born in 1837; Estafina (various spellings), 1839; and Teresina, 1841. As already noted, the Church considered all of them as natural (illegitimate) children.[32]

During some years, Charles Bent was away from Taos almost as much as Kit—on his annual trip to the States, tending to business at the fort, or looking after the Santa Fe store. In his place, Ignacia presided over the running of the house, which sheltered her three young children, a couple of servants, Josefa on occasion, and her older daughter Rumalda Luna, the product of her first marriage in 1829 to Don Rafael Sena de Luna, Jr.[33]

Kit returned home in July to find Josefa a year older and, no doubt, more womanly looking than when he left. She was filled with girlish delight to have him back in her constricted universe once more. But at the same time, she was bound to have known that his residency would be short term.

In fact the Carson memoirs are silent about his activities for the next eight months. However, within that period a lanky six-foot Santa Fe trader James Josiah Webb ran into Kit on the Rio Culebra sixty miles above Taos, in the fall of 1844. He was traveling with friends Lucien Maxwell and Tim Goodale, each man leading a pack horse. They were returning to Taos from a visit to the rag-tag settlement of mountain men known as El Pueblo on the Arkansas River.

Unfortunately, in his recollections set down in 1888, Webb failed to indicate the purpose of their trip. Nevertheless, the mention shows that

Kit remained on the move, perhaps examining new occupational possibilities.[34]

The following March, 1845, Carson tells us that, "Dick Owens and I concluded that, as we had rambled enough, . . . it would be advisable for us to go and settle on some good stream and make us a farm."[35] Richard L. Owens had become friends with Kit when both were trapping in the northern Rockies. About the time the latter had left the mountains for Bent's Fort, Owens settled at El Pueblo and then several years later followed Carson to Taos.[36]

Kit's belated recognition that having rambled enough, he needed to settle down, comes as a significant admission. So too his decision to turn to agriculture, something with which he was passingly familiar, having grown up on the family farm. Whereas his earlier marriages to Indian wives, who had been raised in nomadic cultures, interposed no obstacle to pursuing his penchant for wandering, Kit's entry into Hispanic culture was an entirely different matter. He needed to find productive work, which meant becoming sedentary, and farming seemed to provide the solution.

Irrigable crop land was in short supply in the Taos Valley, as was pasturage since that area was badly overgrazed. Hence, he and Owens crossed over the Sangre de Cristo Mountains, 45 miles, to the eastern foot of the range facing the plains, found a plot to their liking on the little Cimarron River and went to work. Dr. Peters claims that they purchased the site, and Harvey Carter says that the seller was Lucien Maxwell, Carson's close associate.[37] That sounds reasonable since the area was inside the vast Beaubien-Miranda land grant and Maxwell, as son-in-law of Carlos Beaubien, had an interest in introducing settlers, one of the terms for receiving a government grant.

Of his and Owens's efforts to develop the property, Kit said that we "built ourselves little huts, put in considerable grain, and commenced getting out timber to enlarge our improvements."[38] They had brought over workers from Taos, which permitted this progress during the forepart of the summer. It is not difficult to imagine that Kit periodically broke away from the job to make a quick excursion over the mountains to see Josefa and bring her up-to-date on the farm project. He might even have taken her back to the Cimarron for short stays, notwithstanding that the danger from hostile Indians was acute.

a

Believed to be an image of María Josefa Carson, in her early to middle years. (Rio Grande Historical Collections, Las Cruces)

Marriage register for Christopher Carson and Josefa Jaramillo, Taos, New Mexico, February 6, 1843. Signed by Padre Antonio José Martínez. (Courtesy Archives of Archdiocese of Santa Fe)

b

Donaciano Vigil, uncle of
Josefa Jaramillo Carson,
served as interim governor
of New Mexico following the
assassination of Governor
Charles Bent. (Museum of
New Mexico photo, negative
number 11405)

Kit Carson's old home at Taos, New Mexico, as it looked in 1880. (Photo courtesy of
Lee Burke)

c

John Charles Frémont
whose narratives of
western exploration first
brought Kit Carson to the
attention of the public.
(Marc Simmons
Collection)

Taos Indian Pueblo, assaulted by United States troops following the insurrection of
1847. Note remains of wall at right. (Bureau of American Ethnology photo)

d

María Ignacia Jaramillo Bent (Mrs. Charles Bent) toward the end of her life. (Courtesy Kit Carson Historic Museums, Taos, New Mexico)

Teresina Bent. At the age of five she went to live with Kit and Josefa Carson, after the assassination of her father Charles Bent. (TBS Collection #4178, NMSRCA)

Teresina Bent's husband Aloys Scheurich who was at Kit Carson's deathbed. (Museum of New Mexico photo, negative number 71471)

On August 1, 1845, John C. Frémont at the head of his third government expedition reached Bent's Fort from the East. At the conclusion of the previous venture, Kit Carson, as he was being discharged, had promised Frémont, now a brevet captain, that should his guide services ever be required again, he would willingly join him.

Ostensibly, this new expedition, like the first two, was for purposes of western exploration, survey, and mapping. Earlier in the year, however, the United States had annexed Texas, in spite of serious protests from Mexico, which still claimed the lost province. Americans were also at formidable odds with Great Britain over their joint occupancy of the disputed Oregon country.

Frémont's official instructions contained only limited survey directions, to locate the headwaters of the Arkansas and Red rivers. But he may have been given secret orders to visit both Oregon and Mexican California to gather intelligence and with his sixty armed men establish a temporary American presence. In reality, that was exactly what he did.

Josefa Carson may not have known about her husband's prior commitment to Frémont, but it would have made no difference. Although Carson experienced much anxiety upon receiving an express calling him to Bent's Fort and the expedition, it never occurred to him to violate his word and refuse, or so the sympathetic Dr. Peters declares.

He had already invested substantially in a house and barn under construction, and in livestock, tools, and wagons. After consultation with Owens, who also agreed to join Frémont, they swiftly sold the farm for half of what it was currently worth. The purchaser quite likely was the canny Lucien Maxwell, who then decided to throw in with Frémont himself. Peters wrote that "Kit Carson once more bade his family and friends an affectionate farewell."[39] At that moment, he had no idea how many thousands of miles he would travel horseback before he would again share a bed with his wife.

The sudden and unexpected departure of her Kit must have been a blow to Josefa. They had enjoyed a husband-and-wife existence for scarcely eight months before he and Dick Owens had trundled off to the Cimarron to begin the creation of new homes and farms. When the main buildings were up, she had expected to go and contribute her share in the venture. Now with Kit gone and the property sold, her vision of what might have been vanished like a dream.

Josefa again went to live in the Bent house with her sister Ignacia and Charles. Kit may well have arranged the matter before his departure, perhaps even depositing some of the money from the farm sale with the Bents to cover her expenses. He surely felt she was safer there than in her own home, an important consideration given recurring civil unrest in the Taos area. Citizens from that corner of New Mexico had a lengthy history of disobedience to the Santa Fe governors and to local established authority.

Charles Bent and Cerán St. Vrain on June 12, 1846, again took up the road for Missouri, but without their usual freight wagons. This year the trip east had a different air about it, for the pair of merchants traveled with a sense of urgency. Rumors of pending war with Mexico were rife at both ends of the Santa Fe Trail. To all that heard them, it appeared certain that New Mexico and probably California would be enveloped by the storm.

In western Kansas, Bent and St. Vrain chanced upon a messenger from Washington who informed them that war had indeed been declared the previous month. Hearing that, the two pointed their horses toward Fort Leavenworth. There, Charles conferred with Col. Stephen Watts Kearny, then readying his 1,700-man Army of the West for the invasion of New Mexico. Bent outlined conditions in the province and gave an opinion upon the amount of resistance the American force might encounter. Kearny was grateful and suggested that Bent complete his business in Missouri and hasten back to New Mexico where his services would be needed.[40]

Toward the end of June, news that war had broken out reached Charles Bent's home in Taos. Ignacia with three small children and her fourteen-year-old daughter Rumalda was immediately apprehensive about the family's safety. Rumalda had recently married Tom Boggs, age twenty-three, a kinsman and current employee of the Bents, and also a son of Missouri's ex-governor Lilburn Boggs. Young Tom and George Bent decided it best to gather up the women and children, including Josefa Carson, and remove them to the security of Bent's Fort.[41]

Advance units of the Army of the West began reaching the fort in the final days of July. They halted to await arrival of the full column before crossing the river into Mexican territory. In the meantime, William Bent put on a fandango to honor and entertain Col. Kearny and his officers. Mrs. Luz Trujillo Metcalf, who was there, reported that the following ladies attended the dance: Mrs. Tom Boggs, Mrs. Kit Carson, Mrs. Charles Bent, Mrs. George Bent (María de la Cruz Padilla), and some Indian women.[42]

The Army began moving out of Bent's Fort on August 2. By the 18th of the month, it had marched unopposed into the Santa Fe plaza, seizing the city and running up the U.S. flag over the historic Palace of the Governors. Charles Bent, in his earlier interview with Kearny at Fort Leavenworth, had actually predicted that the province might be claimed with little or no fighting. When tidings of the successful taking of New Mexico made their way to Bent's Fort, Tom Boggs conducted his wife Rumalda, her mother Ignacia, and aunt Josefa back to Taos. George Bent and his wife remained behind and thus were spared becoming victims of the tragedy that followed.[43]

While Josefa, with her sister, was experiencing the inevitable dislocations and stresses associated with war, Carson, Owens, Maxwell, and the rest of Frémont's company underwent a series of dangerous trials in California. The small American population there banded together and beneath a banner emblazoned with the figure of a bear, proclaimed the Bear Flag Revolt, whose aim was the separation of California from the Republic of Mexico. Frémont with his men joined in the ensuing hostilities, and when the prize seemed to be won, he began to organize a civil government with himself as its provisional head.

Kit Carson after participating in this dramatic episode was assigned by Frémont to carry military dispatches to Washington. With an escort of fifteen men, including Maxwell, he left Los Angeles on September 5, 1846, and struck out on the Gila Trail that threaded its way across the deserts of the Southwest. Reaching the Rio Grande below Socorro, New Mexico, on October 8, he unexpectedly intercepted Gen. Kearny (recently promoted) leading 300 U.S. Dragoons. With this stripped-down force, Kearny had descended the river from Santa Fe intending to pick up the southern trail and march to the conquest of California.

From Carson, however, he learned, perhaps with some disappointment, that the job had already been done. In a subsequent letter to the adjutant-general of the Army in Washington, Kearny reported that Carson had told him "the American flag was flying from every important position in the territory," and the war in California ended with "peace and harmony established among the people."[44] In view of that,

Kearny decided to send two hundred of his men back to Santa Fe to rejoin the occupation troops remaining there, while he continued to California with only one hundred Dragoons.

Kit for his part was astonished to run into soldiers in central New Mexico because until this moment he had no inkling that the United States was in possession of the province. Throughout his 26-day ride from California, he had been yearning for the sight of Josefa, having planned his route east so as to pass through Taos. Now, finding out that New Mexico was on a war footing, he was suddenly beset by concern for her safety.

Gen. Kearny was elated to have one of the most respected guides in the West suddenly within his grasp. During the Bear Flag disturbances, John C. Frémont (now a lieutenant-colonel) had bestowed a temporary appointment of lieutenant on Carson. Kearny, learning that, insisted that he turn around and guide the Dragoons back to California, since Kit had just come over the Gila Trail and the condition of pasturage and the scant waterholes was fresh in his mind.

Carson was stunned. He told Kearny that to Col. Frémont he had pledged on his honor to deliver the dispatches to Washington with first news of the California conquest, and then immediately return with instructions from the War Department and the president. As Kit related the exchange to Senator Benton in Washington the following year, "General Kearny would not hear of any such thing as my going on."[45] In fact, Kearny ordered surrender of the military dispatches so that another messenger might carry them east, while he took advantage of Kit's guide skills.

Carson's strenuous objections derived partly from his intense disappointment over not reaching home just a few days short of his goal, and that occurring after his year of dedicated government service. But he also felt that his honor would be compromised and loyalty questioned on account of his inability to keep his word to Frémont. Moreover, a strong possibility exists that he carried in his head secret verbal intelligence for Senator Benton and President James K. Polk regarding controversial matters in California.[46]

In his anger, Carson made preparations to desert in the middle of the night, but luckily his friend Lucien Maxwell cooled him down and dissuaded him from that impulsive folly.[47] In any event, Kit put aside thoughts of his dear Josefa and led Gen. Kearny on to California.

For that, his fellow soldiers praised him. Pvt. John T. Hughes, the unit historian, wrote that "Carson turned his face westward again . . . when he had set his hopes on seeing his family. It requires a brave man to give up his private feelings thus for the public good." And, Capt. Philip St. George Cooke wondered whether Gen. Kearny fully appreciated that he was asking a man who had ridden 800 miles across a desert and was near the residence of his family to stop and retrace his ride over the same distance. "That was no common sacrifice to duty," the captain said admiringly of Kit Carson.[48]

Gen. Kearny made his exit from New Mexico, leaving behind a rump civil government that he had created soon after reaching Santa Fe. New officers under the American regime included Charles Bent, governor; Donaciano Vigil (Bent's in-law), lieutenant-governor and secretary; Frank Blair of Missouri, attorney general; and Charles's close friend from Taos, Carlos Beaubien, one of three judges on the superior court. Real power resided in the military commander of the occupation troops, Col. Sterling Price, who had arrived soon after the Kearny conquest with reinforcements. As Bent was aware, the country seethed with discontent, especially in the Taos district where Ignacia and the children remained.

Presiding from a small office in the old, primitive Palace of the Governors, Charles made some rudimentary stabs at administration, including the preparation on November 10 of a short but comprehensive report on the condition of Indian tribes within the jurisdiction of New Mexico, which he sent to the commissioner of Indian Affairs in Washington.[49]

As early as October, Gov. Bent began to receive reports of a widespread conspiracy meant to overthrow American rule and restore Mexican sovereignty. As Christmas approached, details of the plot were revealed and arrests made of leading citizens in the capital who were implicated. By December 26, Bent concluded that the danger had passed and disaster averted. It proved to be a fatal miscalculation.

On January 14, the governor prepared to leave Santa Fe for a visit to his home and family. Donaciano Vigil and others urged him to take a military escort, but he dismissed their pleas as unnecessary. The small party that accompanied him to Taos through cold and snow included Ignacia's twenty-six-year-old brother, Pablo Jaramillo, and Carlos Beaubien's son Narciso, fourteen, who had recently returned from school in St. Louis. Reaching home Charles found the town's atmosphere combustible, yet still he held to the conviction that his own calming influence could succeed in maintaining order.

Before dawn on January 16, a frigid Friday morning, a crowd of Indians from the pueblo two miles out of town stormed into the jail and demanded release of a pair of tribal members being held on petty charges. Leader and spokesman was a Pueblo firebrand, Tomasito Romero, who nursed a bitter hatred for Americans, based on his accumulation of real and imagined grievances.

Hearing of a disturbance at the jail, Sheriff Stephen Louis Lee came running. Suddenly finding himself helpless in the face of the Indians, and town residents who had joined them, he yielded to threats, brought out the prisoners, and began to unshackle them. Cornelio Vigil, ranking civil officer of the district, arrived and began to sternly scold the noisy mob. It instantly turned on him and hacked him to pieces. Lee attempted to flee but was killed. The aroused throng, some of them drunk on Taos Lightning, then followed Tomasito to the house of Charles Bent.

An Indian servant was already at work in the kitchen, but the Bent family was still asleep or just rising. Hearing a tumult in the street, Charles went to the front door. There were no other men in the residence at that time, Kit being away in California and Rumalda's husband, Tom Boggs, having gone to Fort Leavenworth as a courier bearing Army dispatches. Huddled anxiously behind Charles were the three women, Ignacia, Rumalda, and Josefa, together with the children, Alfredo, Estafina, and little Teresina.

Charles opened the door and tried to reason with the frenzied mob. For his pains, he was shot several times with arrows and staggered back into the room. Ignacia, who had also been wounded by an arrow, slammed and bolted the door. Josefa led Rumalda into an adjoining room that shared a common wall with the house next door. Using an iron spoon and a poker, they frantically began opening a hole in the adobe bricks. When it was large enough for a person's body, they pushed the sobbing children through, and then the three women followed. Charles, with blood streaming down his face and staining his chest crimson, came last.

The assailants by now had broken down the front door and also cut a hole in the roof. Tomasito charged into the apartment where the family had taken refuge, and he found Rumalda cradling the bleeding Charles in her arms. According to her account, related fifty years after this day of horror, Tomasito lifted Bent's body by the suspenders and slammed it on the hard floor. Then, in her words, "he proceeded to scalp [Charles] with a bowstring while he was yet alive, cutting as cleanly with the tight cord, as it could have been done with a knife."[50]

The governor shortly died, sparing him further agony. His clothes were at once stripped from the lifeless corpse. It appeared that Ignacia and the Bent children would be slain next. One story that cannot be confirmed relates that Josefa and Rumalda dropped to their knees and pleaded with the mob to spare them. At that point, a town resident, Buenaventura Lobato, entered and seeing what the Indians were doing cried out: "I did not tell you to kill him, but only to take him prisoner."[51] For Charles, Lobato's intervention came too late, but it probably saved his wife and children. In any case, the attackers departed to seek out other victims, leaving the Bent family in a state of shock.

The defiant insurrectionists poured through the streets of Taos. They caught Ignacia and Josefa's brother Pablo Jaramillo and his friend Narciso Beaubien hiding in a stable and lanced them to death. Young James W. Leal, a volunteer who had come with Kearny and had been made district attorney, was grabbed, tortured hideously, scalped alive, and left to suffer in the street. Anyone who had a connection with Charles Bent was hunted down. Rumalda's grandfather, José Rafael Sena de Luna, Sr., saw much of his personal property destroyed.[52] The Carson house, according to a newspaper report, was pillaged, the mob robbing it of everything.[53] An assault upon local government offices resulted in the loss of valuable public records, including all those of the Probate Court.[54]

At the height of the tragedy, Bent's scalp pinned to a board with brass tacks was paraded through the streets as a war trophy.[55] Some of the people targeted for attack managed to save themselves by fleeing to the large fortified house of Padre Martínez. He received and sheltered every one of them. Then he armed his Indian servants and instructed them to defend the building at all costs.[56]

As Teresina remembered the aftermath, her badly bruised family, still in their night clothes, remained in the house through the day and into the following night. At 3:00 A.M. brave friends slipped in with food and blankets. Two days later, Ignacia and the children escaped to the home of

Juan Catalina Valdez. A friendly old Mexican, in the words of Teresina, took Josefa and Rumalda to his house, where he disguised them as squaws and set them to grinding corn on the metates.[57]

On February 3, 1847, U.S. troops from Santa Fe, many of them frost-bitten, marched into the Taos plaza. With them was a company of volunteers headed by Cerán St. Vrain, which had been quickly raised in the capital on news of Bent's assassination. They were nicknamed the "Avengers" and included many prominent names, both Hispano and Anglo.[58]

When the soldiers appeared, those citizens of Taos active in the insurrection fled to the pueblo and joined their Indian allies in fortifying the old mission church. Against it the Army launched an all-out attack, supported by artillery. Stiff resistance led to heavy casualties, but by day's end, the church and pueblo fell. The next morning, women and children from the ruined pueblo, holding crosses, walked out on their knees suing for peace. It was granted.

During the height of the conflict, Cerán St. Vrain at the head of his Avengers encountered enemy ringleader Pablo Chávez, wearing Charles Bent's blood-stained coat and shirt. St. Vrain promptly shot him.[59] In all, 150 of the pueblo's defenders died in the stand-up fighting.

During the series of trials that followed, Ignacia, Josefa, and Rumalda testified as eyewitnesses to the murder of Gov. Charles Bent. The American youth Lewis H. Garrard, who was in attendance, stated that, "The dress and manner of the three ladies bespoke a greater degree of refinement than usual." And he noted that when Mrs. Bent gave her testimony, "the eyes of the culprits were fixed sternly upon her and on pointing out the Indian who killed the Governor, he [Tomasito] was aware her evidence sealed his death warrant."[60] In all, fourteen men were condemned to the gallows, the sentence being carried out in a series of public hangings.

In 1881, thirty-five years after the slaying of her husband, as Ignacia Bent related the brutal circumstances to interviewer Lt. John G. Bourke, her eyes filled with tears and her voice quavered with emotion.[61] Josefa, no doubt, was equally affected by the assassination and by the stressful legal trials that, for the women at least, were almost as traumatic. Through all her sufferings, she was without the support and guiding hand of her adoring but conspicuously absent husband. Three months in fact would pass before Kit Carson learned of the Taos revolt and the depth of the horrors to which Josefa, his in-laws, and his close friends had been exposed. The impact upon him proved lasting, for in the wake of the tragedy he inherited new responsibilities that he could not ignore.

❧ TWO ❧

Pedro Sánchez, a contemporary of Padre Antonio José Martínez, wrote a short biography of the priest in which he suggested that had not Kit Carson, Carlos Beaubien, and other Americans been absent from Taos at the time of the 1847 insurrection, they too doubtless would have perished.[1] Kit not only thought otherwise, but earnestly believed that had he been present he could have prevented the tragic deaths of his friends. Historian Ralph E. Twitchell concurred, writing in 1912 that "if Carson and [Tom] Boggs had been at Taos, [it is believed] Bent would not have been murdered, as Carson had great influence with the Mexicans and Indians."[2]

It will be remembered that Charles Bent, also, had remained satisfied upon setting out from Santa Fe that he could deal with any public disturbance in Taos. He himself misjudged the depth of the mob's fury, and it appears that even after the fact, Kit did so as well. With all of his experience at confronting crises, acquired in his trapper days, Carson nevertheless would very probably have been killed had not destiny placed him in California at the hour of the tumult.

One other idea that he harbored to the end of his life was that Padre Martínez, a fierce political foe of Charles Bent, had been the mastermind behind the revolt and thus the blood of those slain was on his hands.[3] Inasmuch as Martínez was a Mexican super-patriot and had close ties to conspirators in both the capital and Taos, on the surface that is not an unreasonable assumption. But from the possible fact that the Padre may have supported resistance to the American army, it does not necessarily follow that he aroused the lowest orders of society to take to the streets on a rampage of bloodletting. The weight of evidence attests that Martínez was horrified by the violence and as indicated, at some risk to himself turned his large home into a refuge for both Anglos and Hispanos. And there also, Col. Price upon his arrival to quell the revolt, found lodging, quite likely at the direct invitation of the priest.[4]

Kit Carson, despite evidence to the contrary, never wavered in blaming Father Martínez for the tragic events that caused himself and Josefa so much grief. It would also be surprising if he did not experience some flicker of guilt upon realizing that in his wife's moment of supreme need, he was not available for her.[5]

After his meeting with Gen. Kearny's dragoons on the Rio Grande and his enforced return to California with them as guide, Kit was astonished to learn that the Mexicans of that province, far from being defeated as he originally informed the general, had in fact regrouped and resumed hostilities. He fought in two battles before an American peace was established by the Treaty of Cahuenga on January 11, 1847 (five days before the Taos revolt). Carson, having rejoined Lt. Col. Frémont's battalion, was sent by him once more "as a bearer of dispatches for the War Dept." in Washington.[6]

With a new escort, Kit retraced the Gila Trail to New Mexico. At the point on the Rio Grande where Kearny had interrupted his previous courier mission, he turned north toward Taos, eager to see Josefa. He must have moved very fast, not stopping for idle conversation, because he got all the way to Santa Fe before learning of the recent upheaval that claimed Gov. Bent's life.

On April 9, 1847, just forty-three days out of California, an anxious Carson finally rode into Taos. Twenty months before, he had disposed of his Rayado property and dashed off to join Frémont's third expedition. Of all that had transpired since then, particularly the sad and chilling events that began on January 16 last, Josefa poured out her story. Kit listened somberly, tallying the loss in lives and in his own personal property. His house was a shambles, looted of furnishings and perhaps at least partially burned. Charles Bent and other American friends were dead, as well as members of the extended Jaramillo-Vigil family. The situation could hardly have been worse, and Carson came away from it embittered.[7]

He stretched his layover time to ten days, consoling his wife and perhaps discussing with Tom Boggs, George Bent, and Cerán St. Vrain the future of Charles's bereaved family. But his pause in Taos proved all too brief. Kit remained in government service, and duty called him to finish his transcontinental courier assignment. Josefa watched regretfully as he once again mounted his horse and rode away, to return she knew not when.

Barely nineteen years old when Kit departed, Josefa Carson again found herself to be a wife without a husband. There is no way to measure the toll taken by recent shattering events upon her mental and physical state, but given her youth and limited experience, it must have been substantial. On the other hand, from descriptions of her by others shortly afterward, the dolorous episode seems to have produced an early maturity, a new resilience, and a deepened sense of self-possession. In his short home-stay, Kit must have noticed something of these changes, but if so, he made no mention of it in his reminiscences.

Tom Boggs, as the husband of Ignacia's daughter Rumalda, had become the man-of-the-house in Charles Bent's battered residence. Josefa was staying there when Kit found her, and upon leaving for Washington, he was no doubt comfortable that she remained with her sister.

Carson's lightning mission continued by horseback to St. Louis where he transferred to a steamboat, and finally to a railway car that bore him the last miles to the nation's capital. While there, he enjoyed the hospitality of Senator Benton's elegant house. On June 7, 1847, the senator's daughter Jessie (Frémont's wife) introduced him to President Polk, and after a brief conversation, Carson was quietly invited back for a private meeting with the president that same evening. Polk wrote in his diary, "I saw Kit Carson again after night, and had a full conversation with him concerning the state of affairs in California."[8]

Two days later, the president, as a reward for his patriotism and service to the country, appointed Kit to be a second lieutenant in the Regiment of Mounted Riflemen.[9] When he left Washington on June 15, carrying new dispatches for military commanders in New Mexico and California, Lt. Cristopher Carson was "swathed in his new uniform and stiff round crowned dragoon cap, tightly buttoned long-skirted coat, and heavy wool trousers."[10]

At St. Louis he took a steamboat up the Missouri River to his home ground, now organized as Howard County. A nephew, George H. Carson of Fayette, afterward testified that Kit had visited all of his relatives. The one he most fervently wished to see was twelve-year-old Adaline, now very much acculturated and as far as book-learning went, far ahead of her father. Dressed in proper "civilized" clothes, she showed her Indian heritage only in the strong lines of her face and in her coal black hair.[11]

While visiting there, Kit is reported to have told his kin that as soon as Adaline was a bit older, he planned to return for her and move to California with his wife, Josefa. If true, his intention to relocate might reflect his disenchantment with Taos in the wake of the troubles that had so recently enveloped it.

Carson hurried on to Fort Leavenworth where he joined fifty raw volunteers on their way to service in New Mexico. Evidently in Howard County, he had sent an express to Josefa in Taos, telling of his military appointment and asking her to meet him in Santa Fe where he would halt to organize the last leg of his journey to California.[12] Both Josefa and Ignacia, in fact, descended the seventy-five miles to the capital and met Kit on the plaza. We can be certain that they were suitably impressed by his Army uniform, dusty and trail worn as it must have been.

Carson now engaged sixteen civilians to accompany him to California as protectors of the mail. Knowing from recent experience that on the southern Gila Trail water and forage were scarce, he elected to take the Old Spanish Trail, extending in a broad parabola from northern New Mexico, across western Colorado and central Utah, before dropping southwestward through the Mojave Desert to Los Angeles. The plan allowed him extra precious days with Josefa, since his party could escort her and Ignacia back to Taos, before picking up their trail to the Pacific.

Carson reached Los Angeles in October and continued on to Monterey with the express pouches where he delivered them to the new military governor, Col. Richard B. Mason. Stepping off his horse after the long ride, the first person he met was young red-headed Lt. William Tecumseh Sherman, serving as Mason's adjutant. It marked the beginning of a life-long friendship.

Lt. Carson remained in California on active military duty through the winter. In early May 1848, he received orders again to carry official dispatches to Washington. His 27-man escort included youthful Lt. George Brewerton, who subsequently published a stirring account of their perilous eastbound ride over the Old Spanish Trail. Reaching Taos, Brewerton wrote: "I was hospitably entertained by Carson and his amiable wife, a Spanish lady and a relative, I believe, of some former governor of New Mexico."[13] The governor to which he referred was Donaciano Vigil.

A brief rest restored the haggard mail party, which continued on, reaching Santa Fe on June 19, 1848.[14] Carson reported to the military commander at Fort Marcy, Col. Edward W. B. Newby, who informed him of receiving news from Washington that the U.S. Senate had rejected his lieutenant's commission submitted by the president.[15]

His rejection, apparently, was based upon political reasons that had little to do with Kit himself. His partisans, Sen. Benton and Lt. Col. Frémont, were embroiled in controversy over the latter's conduct in California, where Gen. Kearny had accused him of disobedience and mutiny. As a result, in 1848 Frémont was court-martialed and resigned from the Army. His and Benton's arch enemies in the Senate must have taken delight in denying their friend Kit Carson, his presidential commission.

On learning at Santa Fe the fate of his appointment, Kit says that friends advised him to turn his dispatches over to Col. Newby instead of carrying them on through to Washington. But ever true to his character and firm sense of patriotism, he declared afterward that, "I determined to do my duty. . . . [It] mattered not to me . . . [that] the Senate of the United States did not deem it proper to confirm on me an appointment of an office I had never sought."[16]

When he heard from Col. Newby that Comanches were preying upon Santa Fe Trail travelers, Kit decided on the next leg of his journey east, to swing north to the Platte River, thereby avoiding Comanche country. That course took him back to Taos for another brief visit with Josefa, and while there he reorganized his escort, adding young Jesse Hodges Nelson and the grizzled ex-trapper Louis Simmons. Kit and his men departed Taos on June 25, 1848, heading northeast toward Sangre de Cristo Pass.[17]

Before they left, survivors of a party from Colorado, who had been attacked by Apaches in the Raton Mountains, stumbled into Taos. Among them was Kit's companion of former years, Lucien Maxwell, one of those wounded in the affray. Maxwell had been bringing a herd of horses and mules back to Taos, along with buckskins traded from the Utes. Later Carson would tell a reporter for the *Missouri Statesman* (August 4, 1848) that Mr. Maxwell had lost everything, including the livestock.[18]

Arriving at Fort Leavenworth, Kit, perhaps with some members of his party, took passage on a steamboat for St. Louis. On the way, he quite likely stopped in Howard County to see his Adaline, and if Louis Simmons and Jesse Nelson were still accompanying him, they might have made their first acquaintance with their future wives. Three years later, Simmons would marry Adaline, and Nelson, Kit's niece Susan.

After giving an interview to the *Missouri Statesman* in St. Louis, concerning details of his trip from California, Carson made his way by public transportation to Washington and delivered the mail pouches to the government a second time. By October of 1848, he was back home in Taos, and for the first time in a long while, free to live his own life.

His several courier missions, by best estimates, had led him to travel some 16,000 miles. As Blackwelder notes, "In the six years of their marriage, Kit and Josefa had lived together less than six months."[19] Now that he was to be home for the winter, or most of it, the couple had plenty of opportunity to discuss plans for their future.

A month after Kit arrived back from Washington, John Charles Frémont, now a civilian, appeared once more at Bent's Fort. He was beginning a fourth expedition, this time privately financed, whose purpose was to find a suitable central route for a proposed transcontinental railroad along the 38th parallel. He was planning to make a winter crossing of the southern Colorado mountains to prove the feasibility of year around travel in that area.

It has been generally assumed that Frémont, as in times past, sought out Kit Carson to serve as his guide in this latest exploration, and that Carson declined partly because he thought it foolhardy to be in the high country during snow season, but also perhaps because he was unwilling to leave Josefa so soon. In any event, Frémont settled for the irascible mountain man, Old Bill Williams, who led the expedition into a catastrophe.

Crossing La Garita Mountains, the 33-man expedition was trapped by heavy snow, and before the ordeal ended, ten members had perished from cold and starvation. With several of his weakened followers, Frémont rode slowly south to Taos seeking help. When he staggered exhausted and hollow-eyed into Carlos Beaubien's store on the plaza, Carson, Owens, and Maxwell, who were there, at first failed to recognize him.

A relief party promptly started back to the beleaguered men still in the mountains, while Carson took his friend and former employer home to Josefa. Frémont convalesced three weeks under their roof. In a long letter to his wife Jessie, he told what had befallen him and expressed gratitude for the good and generous care he was receiving from the Carsons. That very morning a cup of chocolate had been brought to him in bed, and he wrote her how much he had relished that small luxury.[20]

Elsewhere in his letter, Frémont said: "Carson is very anxious to go [to California] with me now, and afterwards remove his family thither, but he cannot decide to break off from Maxwell and family connections."[21] Earlier, it will be recalled, Kit had suggested to the Missouri Carsons that when he came back for Adaline, he would be taking her on to California. Apparently he was still chafing to relocate on the West Coast, so maybe it was Josefa holding back, not wishing to sever those all important familial ties. Coincidentally though, Kit was moving into a new business relationship with Lucien Maxwell, and that too may have altered his thinking about going to California.

As Frémont recruited his strength and mental equilibrium, with encouragement of both Kit and Josefa, he made plans to leave for California by descending the Rio Grande to pick up the snow-free Gila Trail. When his small party left Taos, it included Tom Boggs and Lindsey Carson, Jr., both of whom were eager to scout the relocation possibilities in the Far West. Lindsey had accompanied his older brother back to Taos on Kit's return from his last courier mission east, and since then had been living with the Carsons.[22]

Long afterward, Jessie Frémont wrote to Kit and referred gratefully to the time her husband had recuperated "in your home where your wife cared so kindly for [him] when he came all starving and worn out to your care."[23] Frémont himself retained fond memories of Josefa. His biographer Charles W. Upham wrote in 1856 of Carson's wife that she was "a New Mexican lady of great worth and respectability," words that no doubt reflected Frémont's exact sentiments.[24]

Except for a brief reunion at Washington, D.C. in early 1868, Kit Carson and John C. Frémont would hereafter go their separate ways. They would remain long-distance friends, nevertheless. In 1857, for instance, Frémont addressed a letter to Kit from his residence in New York City where he was beginning to write his memoirs. He had started an account of the third expedition, which covered California's Bear Flag Revolt, and he needed to discuss the details with Carson to refresh his own memory.

In the letter, he inquired whether Kit entertained any plans of traveling east that year, and if so, "could you not arrange your affairs so as to come on here for a short visit."[25] But Carson, by then enmeshed in the business of the Taos Indian Agency, was making no trips outside the region.

With the shadow of any further obligation lifted from his horizon, Kit could, in a sense, return to the life interrupted in 1845 when he had sold out his promising new farm on the Little Cimarron beyond the mountains and hurried away to join the third expedition. Josefa could now look forward to being with her husband on some regular basis, an even more welcome prospect when in the late summer of 1849 she became pregnant with their first child.

For some while, Kit had been contemplating the family's future expansion and considering how he would financially provide for it. According to his own statement, in April of 1849, "Mr. Maxwell and I concluded to make a settlement on the Rayado. We had been leading a roving life long enough and now was the time, if ever, to make a home for ourselves and children." And he adds that both of them were getting old, and realized that they could not continue to make their livelihood in the same way they had in the past.[26]

There was actually more to Kit's simple statement than meets the eye. In fact, Lucien Maxwell early the previous year had joined with James H. Quinn to secure a nine-month contract to supply beef to the Army. That may have been the catalyst that led to founding of the firm of Maxwell & Quinn, which soon operated a store on the south side of the Taos plaza.[27]

Quinn, a Marylander and a lawyer, had come to New Mexico as a member of Kearny's army in 1846. Early the following year at age twenty-four, he was listed among the company of "Avengers" who joined in putting down the Taos revolt.[28] He and Maxwell suffered a severe financial loss when Jicarilla Apaches got off with the firm's eighty horses and mules and six hundred tanned buckskins at the Manco Burro Pass fight in the Raton Mountains. One source claims that Kit Carson made a personal loan to Maxwell of $1,000 to bail him and Quinn out of their difficulties.[29]

If true, that could explain why shortly thereafter Carson is referred to as a partner of Maxwell's. The exact nature of their business arrangement, perhaps sealed by a handshake rather than through a legal document, is unknown.[30]

Biographer Harvey Carter did not believe that Kit possessed any great amount of "aggressive, ambitious drive" to accumulate wealth, certainly

a

Portrait of Kit Carson, possibly
taken in Washington, D.C., 1847.
From a daguerreotype.
(After R. Gabriel)

Padre Antonio José Martînez,
controversial priest of Taos,
who married Kit and Josefa
Carson in 1843. (Museum of
New Mexico photo, negative
number 71308)

b

Jessie Benton Frémont who knew and wrote about Kit Carson. (After J.C. Fremont's Memoirs, 1887)

Lucien B. Maxwell (in his later years), participated with Carson in the Frémont expeditions and became his business partner in the early 1850s. (Photo courtesy of M.L. Gardner)

Remains of Kit Carson's home at Rayado, New Mexico, as they appeared in the early twentieth century. (Photo courtesy of Audrey Alpers)

C

Very imaginative nineteenth century depiction of Kit Carson's Arapaho daughter, Adaline, as a young adult. (Marc Simmons Collection)

Tom Boggs, nephew-in-law of Kit Carson, who participated in the ranching venture at Rayado. (Courtesy of John Carson)

Lt. George Douglas Brewerton in 1848 accompanied Kit Carson on a military courier mission over the Old Spanish Trail from California to New Mexico and published a stirring account of the trip. (After Brewerton, 1856)

d

Bronze plaque near the grave site of Adaline (or Adeline) Carson, showing Mono Lake in the background (Photo courtesy of Charles E. Randall)

Text of plaque, containing several errors. (Photo courtesy of Charles E. Randall)

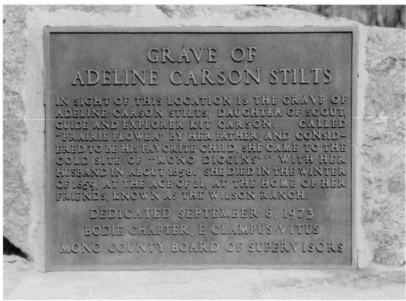

GRAVE OF
ADELINE CARSON STILTS

IN SIGHT OF THIS LOCATION IS THE GRAVE OF ADELINE CARSON STILTS, DAUGHTER OF SCOUT, GUIDE AND EXPLORER KIT CARSON. CALLED "PRAIRIE FLOWER" BY HER FATHER, AND CONSIDERED TO BE HIS FAVORITE CHILD, SHE CAME TO THE GOLD SITE OF "MONO DIGGINS" WITH HER HUSBAND IN ABOUT 1858. SHE DIED IN THE WINTER OF 1859, AT THE AGE OF 21, AT THE HOME OF HER FRIENDS, KNOWN AS THE WILSON RANCH.

DEDICATED SEPTEMBER 8, 1973
BODIE CHAPTER, E CLAMPUS VITUS
MONO COUNTY BOARD OF SUPERVISORS

not to the degree that Maxwell did. If we accept that, then it is logical to assume that Carson remained a junior partner, perhaps even doing Maxwell's bidding.[31]

Kit's statement that he and Maxwell made a settlement on Rayado Creek (forty miles east of Taos), at the foot of the mountains during April of 1849 appears to be a bit off target. It can be shown that Maxwell with a small party of workmen, including former trapper Tim Goodale, had started such an undertaking as early as February 1848, raising a number of preliminary structures. That was prior to the Manco Burro Pass incident.[32]

The Rayado Valley, located a few short miles below Kit Carson and Dick Owens's 1845 farm on the Little Cimarron, opened outward onto the eastern plains, and with its heavy mantle of grass was a paradise for stock raisers. "The cattle on the Rayado are beyond comparison," wrote Capt. Henry B. Judd, commander of a small garrison stationed at Las Vegas on the Santa Fe Trail.[33]

The area was just inside the southern boundary of the massive Beaubien-Miranda Land Grant. Carlos Beaubien had struggled for some time to induce settlers to take up land on a system of shares, paying as rent 50 percent of the grain harvest or livestock increase. Maxwell acted as collection agent for his father-in-law.[34] The effort to make the grant pay had been badly hindered, however, by the depredations of Utes, Jicarilla Apaches, Comanches, and other hostile tribes.

In a report of June 1, 1849, Capt. Judd spoke of the exposed state of the settlement established on the Rayado by Messrs. Carson, Maxwell, and Quinn. He stated that "the two former have been twice driven from that place with the loss of all their stock, in [previous] efforts to obtain a foothold there."[35] Of those failed attempts, Carson says not a word. Speaking of what was evidently the third and successful try in April 1849, he remarks simply: "[We] commenced building and making improvements, and were in a way of becoming prosperous."[36]

Soon after his work began, Capt. Judd established a temporary grazing camp on Rayado Creek, whose soldier guard served to protect not only government livestock but the new settlers as well. To his superior in Santa Fe, he indicated that having a permanent garrison at that place would help shield interior communities from Indian raids.[37]

Charles E. Pancoast, a gold seeker from Pennsylvania on his way to

California, passed through Rayado on July 26, 1849, and left us the earliest description of the first buildings. "The Ranch House ... was a two-story log affair, surrounded by Adobe walls for purposes of fortification. Inside the walls were several Adobe Houses, and outside a number more, as well as a large Corral, ... Stables, Slaughter Houses, etc." Traveler Pancoast saw nothing stylish or bucolic in this rough western scene.[38]

The following October 24, a small party riding in advance of a larger caravan, was attacked by Apaches at Point of Rocks on the Santa Fe Trail east of Rayado. One of the fatalities was James M. White, whose wife and infant daughter were carried away. Troops from Taos, sent in pursuit, paused at Rayado long enough to enlist Kit Carson as guide. The Indians were overtaken beyond the Canadian River and dispersed. The still-warm body of Mrs. White, with an arrow through her heart, was recovered, but the baby was never found.[39]

Uncharacteristically, Carson devoted considerable space to the episode in his memoirs. The tragedy became a public sensation and led military officials to permanently garrison the "Post at Rayado." On May 24, 1850, some forty-three men of the First Dragoons arrived and took up station there.[40]

The presence of the troops provided Maxwell and his business partners new economic opportunities. Through Army contracts, they were able to sell forage, meat from the slaughter houses, livestock, and supplies freighted over the mountains from Taos. A building contractor, John Holland, had been finishing a large mansion for Maxwell, and even before completion it was rented to serve as officers' quarters, until troop buildings could be constructed.[41]

Kit Carson began a more modest house of his own, a flat-roofed adobe structure about six hundred yards below Maxwell's. On the side, he was ranching on shares, raising cattle, horses, and mules, and marking them with his own Cross J brand, and also a CC branded on the left hip. He probably expanded the residence as funds and the availability of laborers allowed.[42]

From the beginning of this entire venture on Rayado Creek, Kit had been planning to develop a seasonal home here, so that his wife could spend part of the year with him, in some comfort and safety. Teresina Bent in later years said that in November of 1850, when only nine years old, she had gone with her Aunt Josefa to the Rayado.[43]

On May 2, 1850, Josefa Carson had given birth to a son in Taos, and four days later the child was baptized, according to parish records, under the name Carlos Adolfo Carson.[44] The first name Carlos (Charles), all sources agree, was chosen in memory of Charles Bent. Nowhere in the Carson or Bent genealogies, however, has there been discovered a precedent for use of the middle name Adolfo. Inasmuch as the Carsons subsequently named two of their daughters after Bent's daughters, Estafina and Teresina, it seems possible that little Carlos's true middle name was Alfredo (after Charles Bent's son) and the church's priest made an error on the certificate.

Three days after Charles's birth, Kit started for Fort Laramie, five hundred miles to the north on the Oregon Trail. He and Tim Goodale were driving forty to fifty horses and mules, intending to trade or sell them to emigrants and 49ers headed west. His departure must have been an inconvenience at best for Josefa, who as a first-time mother struggled to cope with frail little Charles.[45] She may have moved in with her parents, whose household already included their youngest son Luciano and grandson, Nicanor. Or, as in times past, she could have gone to stay with her widowed sister, Ignacia.

Kit returned two months later from his successful trading trip. He stopped in Taos for several days to be with Josefa and the baby, then hurried over the mountains to check on conditions at Rayado. As he reported, the Indians had run off every head of stock in the valley during his absence. They descended in such large numbers that the newly arrived Dragoons had been unable to prevent the theft.[46] That evidently gave Carson pause about bringing his wife to this dangerous place, which might explain Teresina Bent's statement that she and Josefa had not come to Rayado until November. By then Indians would have gone into winter camp, when they did little raiding.

In March 1851, Carson says that he left "for St. Louis with twelve wagons of Mr. Maxwell for the purpose of bringing out goods for him."[47] Among those in the caravan was Jesse Nelson who had gone with Kit on the second leg of his 1848 courier mission to Washington. We suppose that along the way he had met niece Susan Carson in Missouri and was now going back to marry her.

In St. Louis, Kit made the required purchases for Maxwell and shipped the freight by steamboat down the Missouri River to Kansas City, where he had left the dozen wagons. Returning across the state, he stopped in Boonville, Missouri, a river town that occupied a high bluff opposite the site of Old Franklin, where as a boy long ago he had run away from the saddle shop to begin his career in the West.

At Boonville, he apparently attended the wedding of Jesse Nelson (24) and Susan Carson (20). Afterward, he crossed the river to Howard County and collected his sixteen-year-old daughter Adaline, at last fulfilling his promise to take her with him back to New Mexico.

The small party hurried on to Kansas City, where Kit saw to the loading of the wagons. Then the train launched itself upon the great prairies. The cousins Susan and Adaline traveled in a covered carriage. In western Kansas, the travelers found themselves seriously menaced by hostile Cheyennes. The two women were terrified, but Kit through his skill at dealing with Indians was able to extricate them all from the perilous situation.[48]

In New Mexico, the Nelsons would divide their time for the next several years between Kit Carson's house on the Rayado and Santa Fe. For the rest of his life, Kit remained very close to the couple. Jesse, who died in 1923 at age 98, became a chief resource for scholars and writers seeking information on his illustrious uncle-in-law.[49]

On his return to Josefa in Taos, Carson learned of the passing of his first son, Charles, the previous May 21, 1851. Even given the fact that frontiersmen, such as himself, were accustomed to bearing grief with restraint, still it must have been a telling blow.[50]

After the loss of their child, Josefa spent longer stretches of time at Rayado, even though security there had deteriorated. In the second half of July, Col. Edwin V. Sumner founded Fort Union on the Santa Fe Trail, about 35 miles south of Rayado. As a result, the Post of Rayado was closed and its troops transferred there.[51] Maxwell and Carson still had their contracts with the Army, only delivery now to Fort Union was a bit less convenient.

Jesse Nelson told Cragin that when the troops left Rayado, Carson bought from the Army the hospital building, which then became his residence and remained so as long as he was in the area.[52] Military Inspector Col. George A. McCall, however, reported earlier that the post had no hospital, although Assistant Surgeon David L. Magruder did serve there for several months before being transferred to Taos.[53] Maybe Dr. Magruder had occupied the building that Carson purchased and had seen patients in his own quarters, prompting civilians like Nelson to speak of it as "a hospital." The question of the Carson house's original identity seems beyond resolution today.

It was in the period after the Army abandoned Rayado when two incidents occurred that serve to illustrate the uncertainties of life on the New Mexico frontier. The first happened upon an occasion when Kit was at his house alone with Josefa and Teresina. A combined party of Comanche, Cheyenne, and Arapaho Indians (as many as 300 according to one account) descended upon the settlement and surrounded the Carson home.

As the earliest published version of this story tells it, Kit informed his wife and niece that he had only two shots for his pistol. Should the assailants break down the door, he intended to kill them both. As improbable as that sounds, it must be recalled that on the woodland frontier in the East, where Carson grew up, a standard rule called for men to slay their families when Indians breached the cabin door or overran the walls of palisaded forts. The aim was to spare loved-ones the horrors of captivity, including possible death by torture.

Although making a hostile demonstration, the Indians withdrew after two days and two nights, seemingly doing no serious damage. Teresina related that as soon as they were gone, Kit quickly gathered up the scattered settlers of the neighborhood and led them all to safety at Taos.[54]

The second incident took place at a time that both Carson and Maxwell were gone from Rayado. Tom Boggs, however, was staying in the Carson house, and when a band of Cheyennes, bristling with weapons, rode up one morning and demanded food, he took charge. Several women were then in the home, and he told them to prepare a large meal for the Indians, while he quietly sent a runner to Fort Union, summoning aid.

Recalling her fright, Teresina fifty years later said: "I was twelve years old and the chief of the war party saw me and wanted to buy me to make me his wife. He kept offering [more] horses. . . . My, I was so frightened! And while I carried platters of food from the kitchen, the tears were running down my cheeks. That made the chief laugh. He was bound to buy me."

When his offers of horses for Teresina were spurned, the chief with his warriors withdrew to a spot in front of the house. He said they would wait there until sundown, and if Teresina was not delivered they would take her by force.

Tom Boggs made preparations for a defense. But providentially, just as the sun dropped toward the horizon, troops from the fort dashed up, accompanied by Kit himself who had been there on business. "The Indians saw them and went away," concluded Teresina. "Then I cried some more, I was so glad."[55]

Carson places himself at Rayado during the fall and winter of 1852.[56] In line with his habitual reticence regarding personal matters, he fails to allude in his memoirs to the growth of the family during that period. On October 1, 1852, Josefa gave birth at Taos to their second son, Julián, called in English William, or Billy. Being so close to Taos, Kit had ample opportunity to arrive in time for the blesséd event, although no known record confirms that.[57]

Another significant landmark within the immediate Carson family was seventeen-year-old Adaline's marriage to Louis (Louy) W. Simmons, forty-five, a trapper who had worked for the Bents and more recently served in the escort for Kit's 1848 courier mission. S. P. Dillman, who knew Simmons in the 1870s, was told by him that he had asked Kit for his daughter's hand, and Kit gave his consent.[58] No document has come to light showing that the couple married according to the requirements of the Church, and it may be that they were wed, very simply, "Indian style."

In February 1853 Carson and Maxwell launched a new venture that would consume most of the year and in the end bring them a huge financial reward. California in the wake of the gold rush was booming and commodities of all kinds fetched staggering prices. New Mexican sheep, driven overland, found a ready market.

Kit in February 1853 rode down to the Rio Abajo, the lower section of the New Mexico Territory where the great sheep barons reigned, and with the financial backing of Santa Fe merchant Henry Mercure and Taos merchant John Bernavette, he purchased a herd of 6,500 animals, predominantly sheep but intermixed with a large number of goats. These he drove back to Rayado.[59] Maxwell acquired another herd of sheep, said to be about the same size as Kit's, probably with whole or partial backing of his father-in-law, Beaubien.

They concluded to make their long drive to California by a roundabout route, going north to Fort Laramie in Wyoming, then west to South Pass, and thence by the California Trail through the Great Basin and over the

Sierras to Sacramento. The extra miles were offset by better water and forage on that course. For convenience in handling the sheep, the partners elected to travel a week apart.

Carson departed first, about the beginning of March. Joining him were his backers Mercure and Bernavette; nephew-in-law Tom Boggs; a cousin from Glasgow, Missouri, George Jackson; Adaline and her new husband, Louy, who were planning to relocate in California; and assorted herders with their sheep dogs.[60] Their trip, though taxing, was fairly uneventful, Kit paying animals as toll to Indians met along the way to forestall thefts or hostilities.

The *Sacramento Daily Union* reported arrival of "the world-renowned mountaineer, Kit Carson" on September 3. It added: "We regret to hear that the adventurous pioneer is at present suffering somewhat from ill-health."[61] That would appear to be the first published notice that Carson was afflicted with an unidentified health problem, one that would recur over the years ahead.

Kit and his associates sold their herd, now about 5,000 animals, in Sacramento to a livestock speculator Samuel Norris for $5.50 per head. Thus, the sum received was $27,500.[62] When the expenses are subtracted, including approximately one dollar per head originally paid for the animals in New Mexico, it will be seen why an elated Carson chortled that they had "done very well."[63] No doubt, he relished the idea of returning to Taos and informing Josefa of their windfall.

From Sacramento, he went on to San Francisco, having arranged to reunite with Maxwell, then still on the trail, so that they could return to New Mexico together by the lower Gila route. San Francisco, since Kit last saw it in 1847, had exploded in population, now 40,000. Well-wishers pestered him everywhere he went, as he was a celebrated public figure. Therefore, he and Tom Boggs, with Adaline and Louy, left the city and rode north to the Napa Valley to visit Tom's younger brother William, who had come to California from Missouri in 1846. In his recollections of the reunion, William Boggs afterward wrote that Kit and Tom "had associated together for so many years they were more like brothers."[64]

From there, the party continued forward to the Russian River where Kit's youngest brother, Lindsey, had been living since his arrival in California with Frémont in 1849. Other Carson brothers, Moses and

Robert (father of Susan, Jesse Nelson's wife), were also in the vicinity and joined in a small family get-together.

Later, when Kit left to meet Maxwell in Los Angeles, he unknowingly parted with daughter Adaline for the final time. One story, which cannot be confirmed, has him settling the couple on their own farm, paid for by some of the profits from his sheep drive. Lindsey wrote on August 1, 1854 to Kit in New Mexico: "I have not heard anything of Lewis (*sic*) Simmons and Adaline for some time, the last I heard from them they were well."[65] Thereafter, what Kit Carson may have learned about the subsequent fate of his daughter, his only link to Waa-nibe, remains a mystery.

Frontiersman James Hobbs, who claimed to have been a companion of Carson's, wrote in 1872 that young Adaline, "was a noble looking woman, of mixed complexion; black eyes and long black hair, and could excel most men in the use of the rifle."[66] Another source pictured her as "handsome and in form and features resembling her [Arapaho] mother."[67] Observers tended to notice that she was well-educated, in sharp contrast to her father.

Hobbs seems to have popularized the fiction that Adaline's Indian name [translated from Arapaho] was "Prairie Flower." No evidence has ever appeared to support his assertion, and it was probably his own fanciful invention.[68] Nevertheless, the name continues to surface in the Carson literature, in each case ultimately deriving from Hobbs. In fact, he almost certainly borrowed it from a romantic novel by J. P. R. James, *Lena Leota, or The Prairie Flower*, published in 1853.

Adaline's marriage to Louy Simmons did not last. The exact cause and date of their separation are unknown. However, Jesse Nelson in a cryptic remark to Francis Cragin, said: "She didn't do right and he [Simmons] had to leave her."[69]

In 1859 occurred a minor gold rush to Mono Diggings, located a few miles from Mono Lake in east central California. Adaline showed up there with a new husband, George Stilts, said by Hobbs to have been a reckless man and a fiddle player in a Santa Fe, New Mexico, dance hall about 1840.[70] Reports suggest they arrived in the area with the R. M. Wilson family, who established a 160-acre farm by the lake.

When Adaline died, soon after 1861, she was buried on the Wilson place, not far from the water's western edge. Visiting Mono Lake in the summer of 1869, James Hobbs was shown Adaline's grave, marked only by a wooden head board. He wrote: "I employed a man to build a fence around it, as a mark of respect to, and in memory of her father, with whom I had been pleasantly acquainted."[71] So Adaline Carson passed from the scene, cause of death unknown, scarcely having reached the age of twenty-five. There is no indication that her short life held much in the way of happiness.

Toward the end of October, Carson and Maxwell reconnected in Los Angeles and set out at the head of a small company for New Mexico. After a quiet trip, they reached Santa Fe on Christmas Day, 1853. William W. H. Davis, the U.S. Attorney serving there, witnessed the arrival and made note that their journey from the Pacific had taken sixty days.[72]

At Santa Fe, Kit saw the Utah delegate to Congress, Jacob Bernhisel, who had just traveled west from Washington and now informed him that he, Carson, had been named United States Indian Agent at Taos for the Moache band of Utes. That news must have come as a surprise to Kit, since so far as we know he had not sought the appointment.[73]

Upon arriving home in Taos a few days later, he thus had another piece of good news, beyond the profitable outcome of the sheep drive, to convey to the forbearing Josefa. The office of Indian agent provided him a regular salary into the foreseeable future and also would keep him fairly close to home, the headquarters for the agency having been previously established in Taos.[74]

At age forty-four, Carson was now at the peak of his physical and mental powers, the full measure of which he would need in the carrying out of his official responsibilities and in the accepting of challenges imposed by a growing family. On being greeted by the smiling faces of Josefa and little William, Kit Carson must have regarded his world as rosy, indeed.

THREE

Josefa Jaramillo Carson liked to sew and excelled as a talented seamstress. According to a daughter-in-law, Kit provided a bolt of imported material for her wedding dress, and afterward adopted the custom of presenting his wife a gift of cloth each time she gave birth to a new baby.

Soon after he returned to Taos, flush with profits from the sheep drive, he bought her a new-fangled treadle sewing machine, the first ever seen by anybody in the community. That would have been the one patented in 1851 by Boston inventor Isaac M. Singer.[1]

Josefa's acquisition of the wonderous sewing machine stands as something of a landmark, denoting the end of the first decade of her marriage, which was filled with repeated separations, heartache, and tragedy, and perhaps, for her, symbolizing a more promising future with husband and children at her side.

In point of fact, Kit's twenty-five-year-old wife was entering the sunniest period of her life, which would extend from his homecoming in late 1853 to his resignation from the Indian Bureau in the second half of 1861. In that interval, Carson's marriage solidified and matured, while Josefa grew ever more resourceful in the management of the expanding family domicile, a role Kit willingly surrendered to her. Actually, New Mexican women of all but the poorest class had long run the household while their menfolk roamed the country, hunting, trading, or performing militia service.

In early 1854, Carson made arrangements to transfer his main residence from Rayado back to Taos. Although agency duties now promised to engage the bulk of his time, he continued breeding horses and mules at the Rayado ranch for sale to the government and to Santa Fe traders. Jesse Nelson with his wife Susan then managed Kit's ongoing livestock operation on shares.[2]

When Carson took over the Ute, or as it was usually termed, the Utah Agency at Taos he was forty-four years old and considered by many to be something of an expert in dealing first hand with Indians. His predecessor E.A. Graves had left him an indifferent adobe building on the south side of the Taos plaza, serving as official quarters to which Indians regularly came when they had business with their agent, or wished to make complaints. Before long, Kit seems to have moved the office to his home, two blocks eastward, whether on his own initiative or upon orders of the Indian superintendent in Santa Fe is unknown.[3]

As a condition of government employment, Carson was required to be bonded in the amount of $5,000, with two co-signers acting as sureties.[4] One co-signer was aging Carlos Beaubien, leader in the Taos clique of

American businessmen and entrepreneurs. The other was a Portuguese, born in the Azores, Peter Joseph (originally Pedro José de Teves, or Tevis) who had come to New Orleans in 1830 at age sixteen.

Upon moving to St. Louis, Peter Joseph took a mulatta slave, Mary Ann, as a common-law wife, by whom he had a son, Antonio. After spending several years in the fur trade, he settled at Taos during the early 1840s and opened a store on the northeast corner of the plaza. Absent during the 1847 revolt, he enlisted in St. Vrain's company of Avengers and subsequently served on the jury that condemned insurrectionist leaders to death. Peter Joseph became a close friend of the Carsons, and when Kit was away on Indian service business, he was among those who kept a protective eye on the family.[5]

On January 9, 1854, Kit Carson visited Santa Fe to take an oath, post his bond, and receive instructions from Gov. David D. Meriwether, who was also ex-officio Superintendent of Indian Affairs for the Territory. He was a stern and inflexible by-the-book bureaucrat, believing that Indians should not be coddled and that expenses on their behalf ought to be curtailed. James Collins, who succeeded him as superintendent in 1857, when that office was separated from the governorship, declared that "Meriwether never had anything good to say of any of his agents and was cordially disliked by them."[6] Carson during his first years on the job would face his own conflicts with the imperious governor.

On becoming Indian Agent in January, Kit began receiving a salary of $1,550 per annum, paid in quarterly installments of $387.50. In addition, he was allocated $500 for an interpreter, plus a discretionary fund to purchase annuities and foodstuffs needed to feed Indian delegations when they visited the agency. That amounted, in Carson's case, to some $3,600 yearly, a sum sufficient to explain the relatively high bond required of him.[7]

A serious handicap faced by Kit in the management of the agency was his inability to read or write, or as an Army officer who knew him put it, "Carson never wrote a line of manuscript in his life."[8] This personal deficiency particularly irritated Gov. Meriwether, and at one point he complained to the commissioner of Indian Affairs that Carson, owing to his illiteracy, "fixes his name to such papers as are written by a very unscrupulous clerk."[9]

Sometime in the mid to late 1840s, Christopher had learned to sign his name, a simple "C. Carson." Ordinarily, in that day and place lack of literacy was seldom a major impediment to gainful employment. Kit's Portuguese friend, merchant Peter Joseph, for instance, had to sign documents with an X and rely on an assistant to write out all business records and correspondence.[10]

But for one holding the office of Indian Agent, with its requirement of monthly reports, quarterly accounting statements, and assorted correspondence, illiteracy loomed as more than just an inconvenience. Initially, Carson simply ignored the paperwork, an easy matter since he was fully engaged in dealing directly with his troublesome charges. Stern reprimands from an unforgiving Meriwether, however, forced him to confront the problem.

No provision existed for the hiring of an agency clerk, but an interpreter was allowed, so Carson appears to have engaged several in succession, not to interpret, since the Indians communicated in Spanish and Kit spoke that language well, but to handle clerical duties.[11] His friend Smith Simpson stated that when Carson traveled to Santa Fe at the end of the month, he sometimes was able to persuade John Ward, a functionary serving in the superintendency office, to take down his reports from dictation, and the affable Ward even headed them, "Utah Agency, Taos," as if they had been prepared there.[12]

Historian Sabin believed that Carson, in a pinch, also depended upon friends and associates in Taos to act as scribes for both his business and personal writing needs. And, supposing that Josefa was literate, at least in Spanish, he suggested she too assisted her husband with that chore. It is clear, however, that when Kit was away and sent dictated letters to Josefa, she had to summon others and have them read aloud.[13] Gen. William T. Sherman thought, mistakenly, that Kit could write nothing, his wife always signing his name to his official reports.[14]

For the acquisition of food, clothing, livestock, and gifts presented to the Utes, and on occasion to Jicarilla Apaches and Pueblos, Carson depended upon merchants of Taos and Santa Fe, most of whom were close friends. They included Lucien Maxwell, James Quinn (until his untimely death on New Year' Eve, 1856), Peter Joseph, and the three Beuthner brothers (Solomon, Samson, and Joseph), all of Taos, and in addition, the firm of Spiegleberg Brothers at Santa Fe. Kit was in a position to steer large purchase orders their way, but nothing has ever surfaced to hint that any transactions were handled improperly. He often carried sizeable quantities of cash on their behalf during his monthly trips between Taos and Santa Fe, indicative of the confidence in which he was held.[15]

Biographer Harvey Carter contends that Kit Carson was not a shrewd and sharp trader like Lucien Maxwell, nor was he an aggressive and acquisitive businessman after the manner of the Bents. Although Carter's case may be over-stated, it also contains a grain of truth. Owing to his natural simplicity and paucity of education, Kit throughout his later years struggled to earn money and to manage it wisely. He was motivated by ever-enlarging family responsibilities. But regrettably, he seems to have failed in his central aim, which was to bequeath his children an estate sufficient to care for them until their majority.[16]

The most puzzling question concerning his personal finances has to do with the disposition of the significant block of capital realized from the California sheep sale of 1853. Tom Boggs's younger brother John declared that when Carson and Maxwell got back to Taos, "they had so much money, they didn't know what to do with it."[17] Maxwell, it appears, invested part of his share in expansion of his farming and ranching operation on the Rayado, and in transformation of the residence there into "a mansion of lofty ceilings."[18]

Carson might well have spent something on his own dwelling in Taos, particularly if it still bore scars dating from the 1847 revolt. But as that structure was always described as modest, it is doubtful that any rehabilitation could have soaked up a sizeable amount of Kit's assets.

A curious sidelight on his business affairs is handed down by George Douglas Brewerton who in 1848 had accompanied Carson on his last courier mission from Los Angeles. In December 1853, while stopping over in Westport, Missouri, Brewerton received news of his former comrade delivered by a frontiersman just arrived from Taos.

According to the man, who claimed to have seen Carson earlier in the year, the celebrated trapper of the Rocky Mountains had settled down for good, "laying aside the rifle and Bowie-knife to take up the yardstick and scales." In other words, "Kit Carson keeps a store, or as they say out West, is engaged in selling goods in the city . . . of Taos." And concluding, Brewerton divulged that "Carson has entered into partnership with Mr.

Maxwell. The style of the firm is Carson & Maxwell." And he added that Kit continued in his job as Indian Agent.[19]

This reference is very strange. The earlier partnership that included James Quinn had long since dissolved and faded into history. Progressively, Lucien Maxwell had been transferring his occupational interests east of the mountains to the lands of his father-in-law Beaubien, which shortly would pass into his own hands, becoming known as the Maxwell Land Grant. Nevertheless, Lucien, true to his habit of staying involved in diverse enterprises, did not relinquish his long-standing toehold in the Taos mercantile trade.

If there was any substance to Brewerton's report of a new partnership, we have to wonder why Carson took top billing in the firm's title. As the one with acumen and a drive for money-making, Lucien ordinarily would have occupied the role of senior partner. But in this instance, he may have deferred to Kit, believing that the famous Carson name, out front, might attract more customers. Or possibly Kit earned his primary spot in the letterhead by putting up most of his California cash to fund the store where he reputedly "took up the yardstick and scale."

In reality, it is difficult to imagine Carson finding time or even having the inclination to be an over-the-counter tradesman. His multiple duties as Indian Agent, constantly accompanying troops into the field when his charges made war, or attempting to solve their many everyday problems when at peace, would seem to preclude his assuming the role of even a part-time shopkeeper. Only Brewerton mentions in print Carson & Maxwell, and no records of the business, if it ever existed, have come to light. Notwithstanding, the possibility remains that Kit somehow lost a hefty portion of his sheep drive earnings in the ill-fated venture. If not there, then in loans to high-flying Maxwell, or through his well-known generosity to friends, Kit may have dissipated his nestegg. By the second half of the 1850s, Carson, even with his backup Indian agency salary was coming under financial strain.[20]

On June 23, 1855, Kit Carson's first daughter with Josefa was born. Named Teresina, presumably after Teresina Bent, she would say in a 1907 interview that others had told her how strongly she resembled her mother.[21] With a new infant in the house, Kit's monetary concerns took on added meaning.

Taos merchant Jesse Turley, not long afterward, approached him with a seductive proposal. He urged Kit to dictate an autobiographical narrative of his stirring adventures, so that Turley could prepare the manuscript for publication and market the book. Glowingly, he spoke of the profits that both men were sure to realize. Beyond that, Carson may have been attracted to the idea because it furnished him an opportunity to correct many outlandish or untrue stories published about him by literary drudges in the East who exploited his name unmercifully.[22]

Through 1856, during his leisure hours, Kit Carson related his personal history, to be recorded by dictation. The identity of the scribe was originally thought to have been Jesse B. Turley. However, Carter built a case in 1968 showing that the most likely candidate was actually Kit's interpreter-clerk in the Indian agency, John Mostin.[23]

The final product was a rather thin manuscript, straight-forward and unembellished, but terse and dry, compressing entire episodes of exciting adventures into a colorless recital of a few words. Poor Turley despaired of whipping the text into something that might sell easily to the public, and he finally turned the endeavor over to Dr. De Witt Clinton Peters, a young military surgeon then stationed in the Taos area.

Through padding and artful decoration, the enthusiastic surgeon puffed up Kit's narrative and by the end of 1858 got it published in New York, illustrated with engravings. That same year, he wrote to Turley saying that by a recent letter from Carson, "I judge he disponds [*sic*] of ever seeing much come out of the undertaking."[24] Months later, Dr. Peters sent a letter to Kit, declaring candidly that he should not expect to receive much from sales of his book, even though the national press had given it lavish praise.[25]

Carson was probably already resigned to the financial failure of the Peters biography. In 1866, he remarked to Army physician George Gwyther that he was mortified by the book since Dr. Peters had taken the commonest actions described in his memoirs and transformed them into heroics. That galled the ever-modest Kit.[26]

A notice that appeared on the front page of the *Santa Fe Weekly Gazette*, May 22, 1858, may or may not serve as a clue to Kit's fiscal condition at the time. The paper in listing its agents in the northern counties, who were procuring subscriptions and advertisements, included the name of

Christopher Carson, Taos. That sounds as if he was moonlighting to bring in a few extra dollars, although it is unclear whether the *Gazette* was paying its designated agents, or merely seeking their help as a courtesy.

How Kit and Josefa managed domestic life in their home, like so much else, is left substantially to our imagination. Here and there in the available record, we are granted occasional glimpses of small incidents that convey something of the tone and character of their family circle. Not surprising, given Kit's known fondness for his two previous Indian daughters, the children born at Taos moved to the center of his affections.

After Julián or William (1852) and Teresina (1855) came Cristóbal, usually called Kit, Jr. (June 13, 1858), a second Charles (August 2, 1861), Rebecca, named for Kit's mother (April 13, 1864), Estefana or Estella in English (December 23, 1866), and finally Josefita or Little Josefa (April 13, 1868).[27] At the birth of the last child, Kit was fifty-eight years old, and Josefa forty. Their offspring had come so late, the parents would miss the special joy of seeing them reach adulthood.

From the statements of Kit, Jr. and others, it is acknowledged that Josefa was a motherly type who relished being a stay-at-home housewife, tending to her maternal duties in the manner of Hispanic women. However, she sometimes accompanied her husband, probably at Kit's urging, on his monthly trips to Santa Fe, if the recollections of Marian Sloan Russell, who claimed to have seen her there, are accurate. "I remember how [Kit's] eyes grew tender when he looked at her," said Marian. "I am sure that he loved her very much."[28]

Major John Stevenson met Carson briefly in 1868, just after the birth of Josefita, and observed that "his home and family were his chief delight [and] he literally worshipped his infant daughter."[29] That Kit passionately loved all his children cannot be doubted. They brightened the Taos household, according to journalist Albert Richardson who was there in 1859.[30]

In late 1861, when Kit had become commander of the First Regiment of New Mexico Volunteers and was stationed at Albuquerque, he sent for Josefa and the children to join him there in time for Christmas. One of his junior officers, Capt. Rafael Chacón, recorded the following in his own memoirs: "He was very loving toward his family. I remember that he used to lie down on an Indian blanket in front of his quarters, with pockets full of candy and lumps of sugar. His children then would jump on top of him, and take the sugar and candy from his pockets and eat it. This made Colonel Carson very happy, and he derived great pleasure from these little episodes."[31]

Kit Carson had an easy way with all young people, not just his own. Marian Russell saw a natural shyness in him, "which he wore before his face like a veil," and she surmised that only with children was he able to lay that shyness aside.[32] Jessie Benton Frémont, on the occasion of Kit's first visit to the Benton home in Washington, D.C., saw with amazement how devoted he became to her seven-year-old daughter Lilly, speaking to the child seriously and comforting her on his knee when she sobbed over a sad story. "Sensitive to every generous and refined impulse, he was charming to children," judged Jessie.[33]

Kit proved a doting father, not only to his own brood, but also, as Blackwelder phrases it, "taking unto his care . . . several nieces and nephews and any waifs who were lucky enough to cross his path."[34] In fact, the first child to find a home in the Carson household was Josefa's niece, Teresina Bent.

Upon Charles Bent's death in early 1847, his younger brother George, who had his own family in Taos, seems to have assumed care and support of the grieving Ignacia and the three Bent children. George started east on May 16 of that year with the late Charles's son Alfredo, intending to place him in a St. Louis school. The pair reached Bent's Fort on May 26 and continued on to Missouri in the company of a small party that included Cerán St. Vrain. George Bent did not return to Bent's Fort until September 20. He died there at age 34 on October 23, apparently from malaria.[35]

Subsequently, Cerán St. Vrain and Kit Carson became the guardians respectively of Estafina and Teresina Bent.[36] Teresina moved in with the Carsons and was with them at Rayado during the Indian scare already recounted. Many years later, she would describe her Aunt Josefa in the following terms: "Rather dark [complexion], very dark hair, large bright eyes, very well built, graceful in every way, quite handsome, very good wife and the best of mothers."[37]

Clearly, Josefa and Teresina developed a special relationship during the late 1840s, before Kit was back from his last courier mission and before the birth of the first Charles and then William. When Josefa became a mother, she would have found eight-year-old Teresina a useful helper, a role the girl filled until she left for boarding school in Santa Fe early in 1853.

Sometime after that date, young Nicanor Jaramillo, son of Josefa's lamented brother Pablo, came to live with her and Kit. Francisco Jaramillo and his wife Apolonia, Nicanor's grandparents, had cared for the boy in the years immediately following his father's murder in 1847, and he was still with them, at age eight, as indicated by the 1850 census.

Charles Carson in the early twentieth century told Edwin Sabin that "my father and mother educated Nicanor Jaramillo." That was an expense and familial obligation Kit willingly assumed. In March 1859, Nicanor wrote a letter in Spanish to Kit from Mora, where the youth was staying temporarily with his aunt Manuela and her husband, José María Valdez. Addressed to, "My much esteemed uncle with all my regard, and love," the letter asked that the boy's Spanish grammar and Third Reader be sent to him.[38]

During the campaign in the final Navajo war when Kit was in the field, his Taos friend Joseph Beuthner wrote to him, January 6, 1864, with local news. He reported that three weeks earlier, Nicanor had returned to the Carson residence where "he is . . . a very good boy and a great assistance to your family."[39] By then Nicanor was twenty-three years old.

The composition of the household extended beyond Kit and Josefa's children and niece Teresina Bent and nephew Nicanor Jaramillo. As was the custom in Hispanic New Mexico, it included assorted non-relatives in the persons of ransomed Indians who were incorporated into the family. Here as in Spain, co-residence was considered more important in defining a family than blood relationship.[40]

Charles Carson reported that his parents reared three Indians from childhood. All were Navajos. Juan Carson was baptized at Taos, December 23, 1860, being thirteen or fourteen years old according to the officiating priest, Father Gabriel Ussel. On the same day, he baptized also a five-year-old Navajo child, given the name Juan Bautista Carson. The eldest Carson children, William and Teresina stood as godparents (*padrinos*). Both Indian boys, the padre indicated, had been adopted by Kit and Josefa, "according to the custom of the country."[42]

Nothing is known as to how the first Juan came to the Carson home, but Kit, Jr. in 1928 related the story of the second Juan. One day Josefa looked out and saw Utes on horseback standing in the dirt street.

a

Dr. De Witt C. Peters, friend and biographer of Kit Carson. (After Peters, 1858)

b

Kit and Josefa's eldest son, William (Billy) Carson, as a young man. (After Sabin, 1914)

Teresina (left) and Stella (right) Carson, eldest daughters of Kit and Josefa. (Courtesy of Taos Historic Museums, Taos, New Mexico)

c

Juan Carson, Navajo, as a small child was ransomed from the Utes by Josefa Carson and was raised in the Carson household. (Colorado Historical Society photo)

d

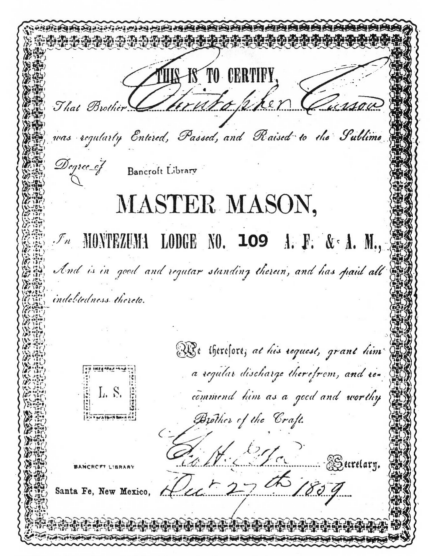

Kit Carson's certificate raising him to the degree of Master Mason.
(Original in the Bancroft Library. Used by permission.)

Obviously, they wanted to speak to their agent. So Josefa went out to tell them that Kit was away.

Then she spotted a three-year-old boy on a horse with one of the men. Upon inquiry, she was told that the party had just come from a raid on the Navajos, and the child was a captive. As Kit, Jr. related it, "The Ute chief told mother that the boy was a bother to them and they intended to kill him. She knew an appeal for his life would be useless, so she asked what they would sell him for."[43]

The price named was a horse. Now, Kit Carson was often described as a fancier of fine horseflesh, thus he must have had several animals in the corral behind the house, Josefa led one forward and exchanged it for the child. When her husband arrived home, he discovered that he was short one horse and that he had a new mouth to feed at his table. From what Kit, Jr. said, we can assume his father accepted the arrangement with good grace. And he also said that Juan "lived to young manhood, married a [New] Mexican girl, but not long afterward died."[44]

In November of 1858, a dozen Utes rode into Taos, where Kit learned that they had attacked a cluster of five Navajo hogans, and after a fight seized, in his words, "one squaw and forty horses."[45] On December 8, he wrote to Supt. Collins at Santa Fe, saying that the Indians were trying to sell the woman, and rather than see her go into the hands of New Mexicans, he purchased her for the price of two horses and other articles, the total amounting to some $300.

"The squaw shall remain in my possession subject to your orders," he advised Collins. "I am ready to deliver her to the Navajos by their paying me the sum I gave for her, or they may have her without paying the sum, as you direct."[46] The "squaw" was actually a fourteen-year-old girl. Her status, in fact, was never resolved, and she remained under the Carson roof for the next six years, at which time she was baptized in the Taos church with the name María Dolores, and her age was listed as twenty. She went with Kit and Josefa when they moved to Colorado in the second half of 1867.[47]

The majority of New Mexican households that had pretensions of some wealth were apt to have Indian servants, baptized and bearing the family name. The custom traced far back into the colonial period, and when Kit Carson first reached New Mexico in 1826, he found the traffic in human beings well-established. Writers in English invariably referred to them as slaves, but under Spain's king, enslavement had been illegal. Hence, New Mexicans referred to captives euphemistically as *criados* (servants), which they actually were.[48]

Those held had certain legal rights that aided in controlling abuses. Upon marrying, they were entitled to their freedom, and as new Christians they enjoyed protective sanctions imposed by the Church, whose purpose was to gain them fair treatment. Carson, having grown up in the slave state of Missouri, and having spent his youth among mountain men, for whom Indian women were regarded as lawful commerce, found little difficulty in adjusting to New Mexican society where Hispanic settlers raided Indian tribes for captives and the Indians themselves engaged in a similar practice, carrying off scores of Hispanic boys to use as livestock herders. We encounter no evidence that Kit indulged in moralizing over this issue. He merely accepted conditions as he found them.[49]

During his term as government agent, however, Carson had occasion to deal officially with captives, both Indian and white. In January 1859, for example, he wrote Supt. Collins that he had taken charge of a young Apache woman who had fled to him for protection. She had been seriously mistreated by her Hispanic mistress, and Kit outlined his plan to find her a better home.[50]

Later that same year, he went to Mora, east of the mountains, on agency business and there discovered a twelve-year-old blonde, blue-eyed German boy, William Hoerster, who had been stolen by Kiowas from his father's ranch in Mason County, northwest of San Antonio. A Mora resident, trading with Indians on the Texas plains bought him for a mule and assorted trinkets, together worth about $100. When Kit learned the boy's circumstances, he took him in charge after agreeing to see that the New Mexican was reimbursed for the sum paid.[51]

There were other similar cases, which usually led to youthful captives spending time with the Carsons while arrangements were being worked out for their future. The Hoerster boy, for instance, boarded several months until negotiations with the government of Texas resulted in Carson sending him to Santa Fe where he could catch a stagecoach for home. Kit and Josefa's fondness for children no doubt eased the inconvenience of having such youngsters intrude on their family for prolonged stays.

The couple was also linked, through the Spanish system of *compadrazgo* (godparenthood), to numerous Taos families. Upon baptism, confirmation, and marriage, young persons were usually sponsored by a godfather and godmother who assumed specific obligations for their welfare. The practice built strong kinship networks in the community resulting in reciprocal patterns of mutual aid.[52]

Men of standing were sought after by parents in search of a godfather for their offspring. Understandably, Kit was much in demand for that role. Author Paul Horgan interviewed Fr. José S. Garciá, age 99, who indicated he was the godson of Kit Carson. Garciá sated that Kit "gave his parents a twenty dollar gold piece as a gift for the newly baptized child, which was prudently hidden behind a brick in the Garciá family fireplace at Taos."[53] Moreover, all of the Carson children had sponsors, leading son Charles to declare that there were so many godfathers and godmothers in line of his family connections that Kit had a hard time to name them all.[54]

One would think perhaps that with his vast extended family on hand, and with occasional stays by his Missouri relatives, among them brothers Lindsey, Jr., Hamilton, and Moses Carson, and niece Susan with her husband Jesse Nelson, that Kit Carson would be satisfied by the size of the crowd he customarily sheltered or entertained. Far from it. His sociability and hospitality, in part no doubt borrowed form his wife's culture, became legendary. And this in spite of his personal reserve and shyness, which he displayed on occasion and were frequently noted by others.

Albert Richardson, being an invited guest in the Carson lodgings for several days in 1859, described Carson as "leading a quiet domestic life," but pointed out at the same time that "his residence in ... Taos is a popular place of resort for travelers passing through the country, and one often meets there a motley array of Americans, Mexicans, and Indians." Army surgeon Gwyther, remembering when Kit was commander of Fort Garland, Colorado, in 1867, confirmed Richardson's observation. "At Garland," he wrote, "Carson kept open house, exercising the most unbounded hospitality to all visitors and passers-by, who were often sufficiently numerous, and these ... included the Ute Indians."[55]

In early July of 1865, Kit and Josefa received as overnight guests in Taos, members of the Doolittle Congressional Committee, sent to the Southwest to examine the condition of Indian affairs. One of the party was Connecticut Senator Lafayette Foster, who as the senate's president pro tem was then next in line to the presidency, since Vice President Andrew Johnson had assumed the highest office upon the assassination of Lincoln. While in New Mexico, Foster was customarily addressed by dignitaries and the media as Mr. Vice President.

The Carsons charmed the distinguished Washington visitors, and after the evening meal, Kit allowed Vice President Foster to draw him out, and he related an incident or two from his adventurous career. He also gave the commissioners formal testimony concerning the state of the Indians, adding his recommendations on policy.[56]

Kit's willingness to host a stream of visitors must have imposed a burden upon his wife, even though the work load could be distributed among family members, dependents, and servants. In fact, the Hispanic upper class, from which the Jaramillos came, was accustomed to seeing their large houses regularly filled with people, all of whom consumed prodigious quantities of food. Josefa, we guess, took the company in stride and probably found in catering to her many guests nothing unusual or particularly vexsome.[57] Indeed on occasion, she seems to have enjoyed herself enormously, as an incident that occurred soon after Kit became Indian Agent illustrates.

A party of travelers from the States had arrived in Taos and set up tents on the edge of town, intending to stay a few days before continuing their journey. Carson wandered over to the camp and soon found that four of the men were from Missouri and were acquainted with persons he knew there. After several hours of lively conversation, he invited the quartet, which included R. J. Alexander and a Capt. Doak, to take noon dinner at his house on the following day.

Alexander described the welcome event. "The [Carson] residence was built of 'dobies,' whitewashed a pure, snowy white. It was about 50 feet long, four small windows (8x10 glass), and a low porch running the length of the building. It was the only house in Taos that had glazed windows."

He spoke of Josefa Carson as "a fair young Spanish lady, height about five feet four inches, weight somewhere around 110 pounds, black hair and eyes, very pleasant countenance and good features."

The guests dined at several round tables in a large room, the meal consisting primarily of wild game. It was cooked and served, as the narrator remembered it, by Mexican servants.

"Capt. Doak," said Alexander, "spoke Spanish fluently and sat with Mrs. Carson who was [delighted to] take a lesson from him in English. She laughed pleasantly at the mistakes she made in pronunciation and comprehension."

After dinner, the men smoked and drank a light, sweet wine while Josefa Carson entertained by singing Spanish songs and accompanying herself on the guitar. Mr. Alexander attests that she had a most enjoyable afternoon, as did those in attendance. His brief sketch provides evidence of the prevailing atmosphere in the Carson home, and of the sociable nature of its host and hostess.[58]

The reference here to Josefa's English lesson serves as further proof that she knew little or nothing of the language, although in later years she might have acquired some slight proficiency. The two surviving letters that Kit sent to her during his Civil War service in 1862 were dictated by him in Spanish.[59] He was fluent, and that was the language of his household.

It is reasonable to assume that the Carson children spoke little or no English in their earliest years. The first person in the house to learn it, actually, was Teresina Bent who with her sister Estafina were boarding members of the inaugural class of Our Lady of Light Academy, a school for girls operated by the Sisters of Loretto in Santa Fe, which opened early in 1853. Students were taught Spanish, English, and French. On business in Santa Fe the following year, Carson encountered little Marian Sloan [Russell] in a Loretto uniform on her way home from school. After some polite questions, he remarked, "Them nuns do a heap sight of good in this god-forsaken country." Marian may not have recalled his exact words, but in all likelihood she caught his authentic sentiments. Having missed out on a formal education himself, Kit was a firm believer in its merits and much desirous of seeing his children grow up literate.[60]

On February 25, 1858, six-year-old Billy (William) Carson, attending the Lux Academy in Taos, received a quarterly report card certifying as to his conduct. Little is known about this short-lived school, other than that a mysterious John T. Lux was principal and probably the only teacher. Certainly, Billy received no more than a minimal start on the path to education.

In 1862, while stationed at Fort Union, Kit sent his wife a letter in which he stated: "I much recommend that you place little Julián in school and tell him for me to apply himself as much as possible so that he may learn . . . and I shall have the greatest pleasure in doing for him."[62] It is not known what school Carson had in mind.

A year and a half later, Joseph Beuthner, one of Kit's Taos friends who wrote him letters on Josefa's behalf while Carson was absent on military duty, told him this: "Little Teresina [Carson] goes to the Convent [of San José] daily, opposite your house, where old James Quinn (deceased) used to live, and she learns very quick. Only girls are admitted to this convent; it is free of charge . . . and a very strict and good institution. Shortly, a Convent for boys will be established in the house of Theodore Wheaton and Billy, Charles, [and] Kit will go there."[63]

If the second "convent" opened and the Carson youths attended, it has not been recorded. In the summer of 1865, Billy just short of fourteen still could not read letters that arrived at the Carson house for him.[64] After Kit's death, his friend Gen. William T. Sherman attempted to provide Billy Carson with some higher education at an eastern college. But he was so deficient in fundamentals, the general had to concede that he possessed "no appetite for learning."[65]

In passing, it can be mentioned that Teresina Bent in her latter teens married the schoolmaster John T. Lux. However, in 1860 he deserted her and disappeared from Taos. Subsequently, in 1865 she wed Aloys Scheurich, an immigrant from Bavaria who had joined the Army at St. Louis in 1853 and was eventually posted to Cantonment Burgwin, ten miles outside of Taos. Being discharged in 1858, Scheurich engaged in freighting over the Santa Fe Trail and merchandising in Taos, acquiring a large house near the center of town. He and Teresina both remained great favorites of the Carsons.[66]

Although Kit enjoyed the comforts of home and fireside gatherings with his family, he had been a man on the move and had lived at the center of stirring events too long to surrender easily to idleness and domesticity. As Indian Agent, his duties took him into the field with enough regularity to keep boredom at bay. And he further stilled his hunger for adventure by making hunting trips of some duration to the Colorado mountains.

The monthly rides to Santa Fe, moreover, allowed him not only to file his official reports and accounts with the Indian superintendent, but in addition to indulge his taste for socializing. That was mainly accomplished through Kit's entry into the world of Freemasonry.

During the first half of the century, anti-Masonic sentiment had been rampant along the East Coast, but on the frontier the craft flourished. In the New Mexico of the fifties, many of the most influential Americans, including political figures, merchants, lawyers, and high-ranking Army officers were Masons.[67]

The quasi-religious posture of Freemasonry and its notions of chivalry, vaguely tracing back to the medieval Order of St. John and the Knights Templar, strongly appealed to Kit Carson as did the comradeship with men of intellect and social status.[68] The Grand Lodge of Missouri in 1851 had issued a charter for establishment of a Lodge in Santa Fe to be named Montezuma. There Kit was initiated in First Degree on April 22, 1854; Second Degree, June 17, 1854; and Third Degree of Master Mason, December 26, 1854.[69]

At the end of that year, Carson evidently participated in his first public celebration held by Santa Fe's Montezuma Lodge. The local press reported that on December 24, the Christmas holidays brought to the capital Col. Thomas T. Fauntleroy, two of his officers and several citizens from Fort Union, one hundred miles to the east. They were accompanied by the post's Dragoon band. The story added that on the same day, Judge Perry Brocchus, Attorney General Theodore Wheaton, and Agent Kit Carson "arrived from Taos to spend their Christmas in the city of the Holy Faith."[70]

All these men, except members of Fort Union's First Dragoon band, were Masons, and they had come to Santa Fe as much to attend their own fraternal gathering as they had to observe the religious holiday. The *Weekly Gazette* informed residents of the capital that: "The Masonic order of Santa Fe united in celebration on the 27th [December], in honor of St. John the Evangelist, the father of the fraternity. They turned out at eleven, clothed in their proper regalia, and preceded by the Dragoon band, marched through the principal streets of the city to the courthouse, where the exercises were held . . . . A large concourse of people filled the building."[71]

Apparently, Col. Fauntleroy, as commandant at Fort Union, had brought the military band with him to march and play in the Masonic procession. And local officials made the district courthouse available so that the public could witness the fraternal exercises. Such was the prestige and acceptance of Freemasonry in New Mexico of the fifties.

Although no mention of the fact has appeared, it is safe to assume that Kit Carson was one of those who, dressed in proper regalia, strode in line with his Masonic brothers to the courthouse to the accompaniment of military music. And, he was back the following year, riding down from Taos in weather 32° below zero, to participate once more in the Montezuma Lodge's celebration of St. John's Day. On that occasion, he was accompanied by his future biographer, Assistant Surgeon De Witt Clinton Peters, who despite the intense cold declared, "We had a very jolly time."[72]

We know that Carson was often able to arrange his schedule of business trips to Santa Fe to coincide with Masonic lodge meetings, which over the years became increasingly important to him. He also probably spent the majority of his Christmases in the capital to take advantage of the St. John's activities, at least until 1860 when the Bent Lodge (named in memory of Mason Charles Bent) was authorized and established in Taos.[73]

How can Kit Carson's repeated absences from his Taos home during the Christmas season be explained? And what were the reactions of Josefa and the children? There are no ready answers to those questions. The rich constellation of holiday activities offered by the Hispanic culture of the Taos Valley would have certainly kept the Carson family occupied while its breadwinner was away. But that scarcely compensated for his not being at home during such meaningful occasions.[74]

Kit's aforementioned natural restlessness and his wish "to fraternize with the boys," in this case with his Masonic brethren at Santa Fe, were traits that traced back to his free-wheeling trapper days. They can provide a partial explanation of his behavior. But more is needed. It can perhaps be found in the words of writer Edwin L. Sabin. In the first years of the twentieth century, he interviewed numbers of Carson's old-time associates in Taos and from them learned that Kit "willingly absented himself from home by reason of the meddling, as he thought it, of the parish priesthood in his domestic affairs. He found it hard to submit to the customs of the Catholic Church."[75]

Sabin interpreted this as evidence of Kit's rejection of Catholicism, when in fact it appears to have been an expression of his lingering resentment toward Padre Martínez and his several clerical supporters in the Taos Valley. When Father Joseph Machebeuf, Bishop John B. Lamy's vicar, traveled to Taos on 1857 to read an edict excommunicating Padre Martínez for insubordination, Carson was one of those who marshalled armed volunteers to provide him protection.

At that time, Carson stated forcefully: "We shall not let them do as they did in 1847, when they murdered and pillaged.... I hate disturbances among the people, but I can fight a little yet, and I know of no better cause to fight for than my family, my Church, and my friend the Señor Vicario."[76]

Notwithstanding such an unequivocal declaration, it would be surprising if some of the animosity Kit felt for Padre Martínez did not spill over to color his view of New Mexico's Catholic Church. Capt. Nelson Thomasson, who knew him, proclaimed that Carson was a great believer and lover of pure religion, but would have nothing to do with theology. When men at the campfire sought to direct conversation toward theological argumentation, Kit invariably turned his back upon them.[77]

All signs point to Josefa possessing the necessary grit to weather the stresses of her marriage to Kit, including his voluntary excursions to Santa Fe during Christmas week. Nothing exists to suggest that she became a scolding wife or resented his short-term abandonments of the family. Indeed, after ten years of wedlock, she appears to have developed an inner toughness and a constitutional resilience quite uncharacteristic of the feminine dependency prevailing in the society from which her husband came.[78]

Josefa's ability to act quickly and decisively on her own is nowhere better exemplified than in the ransoming, or purchase, from the Utes of the Navajo toddler, Juan. One suspects that by that time, the latter 1850s, she and Kit were so in tune that she had no hesitation in swapping his horse for the boy.

New Mexican women, in contrast to American women, kept their own property and any wages earned, had distinct legal rights, and retained their maiden names after marriage. Kit's wife was usually referred to as Mrs. Carson by Americans, but local Hispanics persisted in calling her Josefa Jaramillo. In addition, women of her status were customarily honored with the respectful title of *Doña*.[79]

Records show that Josefa owned real estate, three lots in the Taos area, perhaps inherited. In addition, she was possessor of twelve jacks and jennys, probably for use by her boys or the servants in hauling firewood.[80]

The Carsons kept a running account with family friend and merchant Peter Joseph, allowing Josefa to draw upon his stock for household necessities. A few pages from a Memorandum Book, beginning in 1860, show her purchases leaning heavily toward children's clothes, among them a pair of boy's boots and a boy's coat, specifically designated "for Billy." For herself, we see linen handkerchiefs, a pair of lady's kid boots, and a hoop skirt. She also regularly bought cloth, such as calico and French dress goods by the yard, suggesting that she filled her slack time by making the sewing machine hum.[81]

From such fragments as heretofore described comes the faint outline of Josefa Jaramillo's life as wife and mother during Kit's years as Indian Agent. As new duties progressively devolved upon her shoulders, she slowly gained mastery over her own limited world, the one that held the Carson children at its center. In the second half of 1861, however, Josefa's domestic tranquility would suffer interruption as the curtain lifted upon a national trauma, destined to affect even the remotest precincts of the American frontier.

Ⳑ FOUR Ⳑ

Kit Carson never gave up his love of hunting, and the wild game that appeared on the family table to delight visitors was largely furnished by his own Hawken rifle. "Carson was reputed one of the best hunters in the West," commented a writer in 1881. And the celebrated Francis Parkman in his classic account of western adventure, *The Oregon Trail*, declared: "Kit Carson I believe stands pre-eminent in running buffalo."[1] It is ironic, therefore, that a serious mishap on a hunting trip left him so severely impaired that in time it would lead to his premature death.

When his duties as Indian agent allowed, Kit would organize a fall hunt to obtain meat for the long winter ahead. His companions on such excursions might include friends from Taos and Rayado, as well as Utes, with whom he had become exceptionally close. Besides having a practical function, the trips gave him the welcome opportunity to return to the wilderness and during a brief span resurrect the former life he had known as a free trapper and hunter for the Bents.

In October of 1860, Kit guided his party from Taos northwest to the San Juan Mountains of southwestern Colorado, an area rich in game. While there, he suffered his accident. Based on what he told Jessie Benton Frémont seven years later, she described the event this way: "A refractory young mule had contrived to so wind his lariat about himself and Carson too that as the mule fell over a steep hill-side, Carson was dragged over—the rope tightening about his body and the left side getting badly hurt and jammed among rocks."[2]

Assistant Army Surgeon Henry R. Tilton, who attended Carson in his last days, also heard the story from him. According to the doctor's recollection, incorporated in a letter of January 7, 1874, "[Kit's fall] happened while he was descending a mountain. The declivity was so steep that he led his horse by the lariat, intending, if the horse fell to throw it from him."

"The horse did fall, and although he let go the lariat, it caught him and carried him a number of feet and severely bruised him."[3]

William F. M. Arny, who knew Kit and succeeded him as Ute agent in 1861, added this detail. ". . . Carson and his mule fell from the mountain into 40 feet of snow and came near losing his life."[4]

Whether the animal causing the accident was a mule or a horse cannot now be determined, although most secondary sources today say the latter.[5] The imprecise descriptions of what happened certainly sound like a horse, since that animal is prone to panic and generally regarded as less sure-footed than the mule. Kit, however, although very much the horseman, might have indeed been leading a saddle mule in that rough country. And there are undeniably instances from history of mules tumbling off precipitous trails, dragging riders or handlers with them.

When Kit reached Taos, a startled Josefa was able to view his bruises and abrasions, which would heal with time. But the internal injuries were something else, and no doubt raised her immediate concern. At the time, Josefa could not foresee that her husband's unfortunate fall was to have a lasting impact, not only upon his physical condition, but on the fate of his family as well.

In reality, Kit had been suffering from one or more health problems for years. Toward the end of his life, he alluded to persistent pain in his legs owing to enlarged veins, the cause of which he traced to a foot race he was forced to run in his youth, escaping from Blackfeet Indians. That particular incident he failed to included in his memoirs.[6]

The scarcity of paperwork issuing from the Utah Agency in Taos during the winter of 1860–1861 suggests that Agent Carson may have spent the bulk of his time recuperating. Following standard Hispanic practice, Josefa would have fed him nourishing quantities of chicken soup and *atole,* that is boiled gruel of blue corn meal. If so, they contributed to Kit's feeling much better by spring, although occasional twinges of pain in his chest served notice that something was still wrong.

As remote as New Mexico was from the centers of power in the East, the territory could not avoid the rising tide of political discord that engulfed the nation in late 1860 and the first half of 1861. Republican Abraham Lincoln's ascendancy to the presidency and the strident debate that led to secession of the South and formation of the Confederacy, raised anxiety among Americans living in the far Southwest where news of these events reached them belatedly.

From the beginning, Kit Carson was fully aware of the volatile issues that produced the rupture in the Union. Owing to his Southern birth and background, he must have felt at least some pull toward the infant Confederacy. So far as is known, all of his Missouri kin turned in that direction, as did his youngest brother Lindsey, Jr. in California. When that state stayed loyal to the federal government, Lindsey moved with his family to Texas. A Confederate soldier who met Kit following the battle of Valverde reminisced long afterward that Carson's "heart was really with us, but his judgement as to his duty took him to the Union side."[7]

Historian David Roberts, while acknowledging that Carson's own fierce loyalty to the nation forced him to cast his lot with the North, also suggests that his years with Frémont may have instilled abolitionist and Republican views in him. That scarcely seems likely since Kit is not known to have shown any interest in the abolitionist movement. As to his possible sympathy to the Republican Party and Mr. Lincoln, that is contradicted by contemporary statements that clearly place him with the political opposition. As early as 1857, a Missouri newspaper profiling "the far-famed

Kit Carson," identified him as "a strong states-rights Democrat."[8]

In any case, when a May 4th call went out from the War Department for volunteers to defend the Territory, Kit Carson resigned as Indian agent and responded. What discussion within the family his decision might have elicited is not recorded. Presumably, his health had improved enough over the winter that he felt up to the strenuous campaigning which lay ahead. Actually, the mere prospect of action could have lifted his spirits and animated the blood so that he set forth convinced of his capacity to meet all challenges. Josefa, as we know, was consumed with worry.

On June 6, Taos merchant Solomon Beuthner wrote to Kit from New York City, on his way to visit relatives in Germany:

> My dear friend,
> With great pleasure I have seen in the Herald that you are appointed by the President as [Lt.] Col. of one of the Mounted Regiments called out by order of the Government to serve in N.M. . . .

Precisely when Carson received formal notice of his appointment is not known. However, on June 21, he was in Santa Fe where he appeared before territorial Chief Justice Kirby Benedict to accept the commission and swear allegiance to the United States, promising to defend it against all enemies.[9]

During the spring, high-ranking officers with Southern origins, on duty in New Mexico, had been resigning and departing for the Confederacy. Some attempted to persuade enlisted men beneath them to join in their defection. Kit, it appears, was also approached and perhaps even offered bribes, as rumor hinted. But he stood firm for an insoluble Union, and with his lieutenant colonel's commission in his pocket, he reported for duty at Fort Union, where he was formally mustered into active service.[10]

Carson's old friend, Cerán St. Vrain, appointed regimental commander with the rank of colonel, had already brought in a company of volunteers that he had recruited at Mora on the eastern flank of the Sangre de Cristo Mountains. Captain of the new unit was José María Valdez, husband of Josefa's elder sister Manuela. In the ensuing conflict, he would rise to the rank of lieutenant colonel and afterward win election to the territorial legislature.[11]

In the following weeks, Kit was kept busy seeking out Utes to serve as scouts and in August leading four companies of volunteers eastward to the Cimarron River to meet and protect in-coming military supply trains. We can be sure that if any small window of opportunity opened, he made a quick trip to Taos, not that distant, to check out matters at home.[12]

On September 17, 1861, Col. St. Vrain suddenly quit the Army, declaring in his letter of resignation that owing to "a multiplicity of private business," he was unable to perform efficiently in the service. The real reason, stripped of his vague phrasing, had to do with his physical condition. Nearing 60, overweight, and apoplectic, he was not up to the herculean demands on mind and body the job required.[13]

With the vacancy, Kit Carson on September 20 assumed command of the regiment, and the following October 4, Gov. Henry Connelly at Santa Fe promoted him to colonel, and the well-educated José Francisco Chaves to lieutenant colonel.[14] With no military background, other than his brief aborted appointment as a lieutenant in 1847, Carson took on daunting responsibilities. But no hesitancy can be detected on his part.

Through the summer just closed, Confederate forces had made significant gains in southern New Mexico. In July 1861, Lt. Col. John R. Baylor with 300 Texans had advanced up the Rio Grande from El Paso to seize the Mesilla Valley and neighboring Fort Fillmore. On August 1 he created the Confederate Territory of Arizona, extending west to California, and designated the town of Mesilla as its capital.

Col. Edward R. S. Canby, head of the Military Department of New Mexico, began concentrating available Federal troops at Fort Craig on the river below Socorro. In mid October, Col. Carson received orders to move most of his First Regiment to the town and post of Albuquerque, approximately 100 miles north of Fort Craig. That strategic location would allow him to shift his forces quickly down to Fort Craig should an emergency arise.

Carson took command of Albuquerque on October 19, where he would remain headquartered until the end of January.[15] During that period, he was principally occupied with recruitment, to bring the regiment to full strength, and with seeing to the training of his men who were by and large simple Hispanic farmers or wage laborers.

He also had orders to put patrols in the field, one of which under

Capt. Rafael Chacón was sent west to warn the Navajos to keep clear of the settlements. Other patrols ranged east-southeast on the lookout for Texan scouting parties.[16]

On the whole, the atmosphere in Albuquerque seemed so quiet, with no immediate threat of danger, that a number of officers sent for their families. In early December, Kit brought Josefa and their children, William, Teresina, Christopher (Kit, Jr.), and baby Charles down from Taos to share his quarters. Charles, named for the first Charles who had died, was born the previous August 2 while Kit was on duty at Fort Union.

The joy of this reunion was shared by all the Carsons, as Kit and Josefa struggled to restore a bit of normalcy to their lives. Capt. Chacón, as already noted, took pleasure in observing Col. Carson's rollicky brood tumbling around their father in play. Josefa too must have worn a smile, for not only did she have her husband at her side, but owing to her status as wife of the regimental commander, she should have been much in demand for whatever social activities Albuquerque afforded.

About the time his family arrived, Carson received two odd recruits sent him by Col. Canby. From Colorado, the pair had shown up in Santa Fe seeking to enlist so they could defend the Union. As Canby explained to Kit by letter, the men lacked all qualifications for soldiering, except one. They were excellent musicians. He suggested they be put to use in Albuquerque organizing a military band for the First and Second Volunteer Regiments.

Kit was not only agreeable, but delighted. Martial music could enspirit the troops, and entertain civilians, including his own children. At once he submitted a requisition for twelve brass instruments, and the musicians made drums, allowing them to begin giving instruction to band applicants.

Hardly was the noble effort under way before Col. Carson received a new set of regulations from the War Department in Washington. As his clerk read aloud General Order No. 91, he was dismayed to learn that separate military bands for Volunteer Regiments were abolished forthwith. It was no doubt an economizing measure. Now, stuck with two musicians and brass instruments, Kit appealed to Col. Canby at Santa Fe. "Will you please advise me what I had better do with them?"[17]

Christmas came and went, then 1862 opened, and still the Carsons basked in the warmth of family togetherness. But the pleasant interlude, as everyone knew, could not last. January was well along when word filtered in that a Confederate force of three regiments and 2,500 men had left El Paso and was moving north, intent upon conquering upper New Mexico. In its way stood Fort Craig on the west bank of the Rio Grande where Col. Canby had gone to prepare defenses.

The post and depot at Albuquerque was thrown into a swirl of activity, as preparations went forward in anticipation of marching orders. On January 23, elements of the First Regiment and other troops began the descent to Fort Craig. Kit's parting with his wife and youngsters had to have been emotional in the extreme. There was no certainty they would ever see one another again.[18] Josefa was delayed a week before she could get safe passage home, but on January 31, she and the children finally left for Taos where they expected to wait out the war.[19]

Carson and his reinforcements reached Fort Craig on February 1 and pitched their tents just outside the garrison walls. The invading rebel army, commanded by Gen. Henry H. Sibley, arrived on February 16. The Volunteers engaged in light skirmishing with the enemy, and there on the 21st joined in the major battle of Valverde. On that date, Canby had ordered his troops to march several miles upriver to contest possession of the Valverde Ford, which led to the confrontation with Sibley's Texans.[20]

Kit's green regiment found itself near the center of the attenuated Union line and fought gallantly. Capt. William W. Mills reported that in the thick of battle, Col. Carson walked up and down encouraging his men with the words, "*Firme, muchachos. Firme!*" (Steady boys. Stand firm.)[21] According to another officer, Capt. Edward W. Wynkoop, Carson "knew how to lead men into battle and keep them there."[22]

Unfortunately for the Union side, one of their artillery batteries was overrun, whereupon Col. Canby prematurely ordered a general retreat to the fort. Lt. Col. J. Francisco Chaves of the First Regiment stated many years later that he and Carson were dumbfounded by the withdrawal order, believing they were winning on all sides.[23]

Leaving the federal soldiers bottled up in Fort Craig, licking their wounds, the victorious Confederate army continued its advance up the Rio Grande. Like toppling dominos, Socorro, Albuquerque, and Santa Fe fell into its hands. Finally on April 1, Col. Canby with the main body of troops started north, intending to outflank the enemy.

a

ALBUQUERQUE AND THE SANDIA MOUNTAINS.

Albuquerque as Kit and Josefa Carson knew it during the Civil War. (Nineteenth century engraving, Marc Simmons Collection)

Colonel Edward R.S. Canby, commander of Union forces in New Mexico during the Civil War. (Museum of New Mexico Photo, negative number 54169)

b

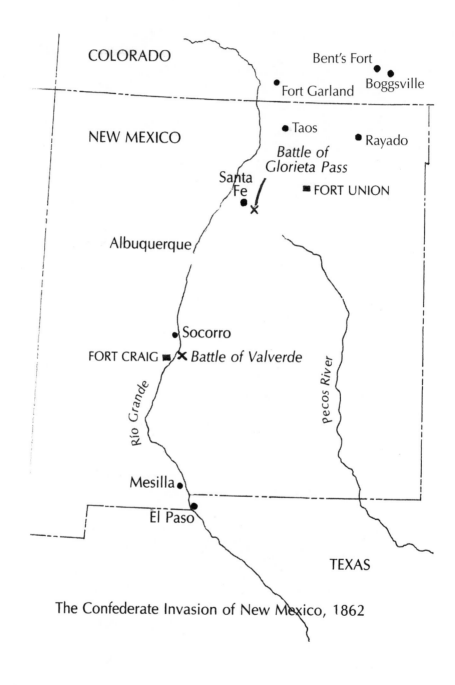

The Confederate Invasion of New Mexico, 1862

A gathering of Masons in Santa Fe, 1865. Kit Carson seated, center. Next to him on the right is General James H. Carleton, his superior military officer. (Museum of New Mexico photo, negative number 9826)

Juan Santistevan, Taos merchant and friend of the Carson family in the 1860s. (Nineteenth century engraving, Marc Simmons Collection)

d

FORT GARLAND.

A distant view of Ft. Garland, Colorado, Kit Carson's last duty post. (After Thayer, 1888)

Plaque at entrance to Ft. Garland National Historical Site. (Photo by Marc Simmons)

e

Parade ground at Ft. Garland today. (Photo by Marc Simmons)

f

General Carson as he appeared
during his Fort Garland period,
using a cane and wearing a
mustache. (After Inman, 1897)

Carson's Oath of Office
taken upon his appointment
as Brevet Brigadier General
of Volunteers, January 4, 1866.
(NMSRCA)

Near Socorro, a courier reached him bringing the first news of the Battle of Glorieta east of Santa Fe on March 28. There, Gen. Sibley's brigade was stopped and obliged to begin a slow retreat down the river by a combined force of Federals and Colorado Volunteers from Fort Union.

Upon Canby's departure from Fort Craig, Kit Carson had been left in command with ten companies of volunteers. A smaller Confederate troop in the Mesilla Valley posed a threat, as later did the main rebel army in the course of its flight southward. In a report of April 3, Carson said that he would defend Fort Craig "to the last extremity," even if it meant arming convalescents in the post hospital and putting them on the walls.[24]

Matters did not come to that since the fleeing Confederates, unwilling to face the redoubtable Kit Carson, chose to bypass the garrison. Col. Canby arrived back at Fort Craig on April 22 and resumed command. Relieved of that duty, Carson was soon ordered to Albuquerque to begin recruiting a new volunteer unit, the First New Mexico Cavalry. The more than three months he had spent on duty in the south was the longest period he had been separated from Josefa since his sheep drive to California in 1853.

From Fort Craig on April 26, he had sent a letter to Josefa in Taos, informing her of the Confederate repulse and of his coming through the episode unscathed. The letter, received May 6, was read aloud to the Carson family by close friend, merchant Juan Santistevan, who had been looking after them and handling Kit's personal business affairs in his absence.

In reply to Kit the following day, Santistevan wrote: "The receipt of your letter has been a source of great relief to Mrs. Carson, and indeed to all your friends . . . as we were very anxious to know how you had come out in the late struggle." And he added that Josefa was eagerly "awaiting the 20th day of May." Evidently that was the date Kit had indicated in his letter (now lost) that she should start south with the four children to rejoin him in Albuquerque. Santistevan's correspondence closed with this message: "Mrs. Carson and the children send their best love and prayers to you."[25]

By the end of the month, the Carsons were reunited and had settled into quarters at Albuquerque again, where they were destined to spend the rest of the summer in comparative quiet. Kit remained busy, organizing the new cavalry regiment and handling mundane matters of military administration, in which he was coached by a sergeant of the regular army. That included training and discipline.[26]

Toward the tag end of August, he received Special Orders to move south with Companies A and G of the First Cavalry and take up a temporary station at the post of Los Lunas, sixteen miles down the Rio Grande. That position was deemed more useful in intercepting Navajos and Mescalero Apaches bent upon raiding Albuquerque and its environs. With whitemen distracted and fighting among themselves, those Indians and others on the margins of the Territory had progressively expanded their raiding.

The entire family accompanied their breadwinner to Los Lunas, but the stay there proved short. On September 21, Kit wrote to Canby (recently promoted to general) in the capital, acknowledging receipt of orders that said his regiment would be participating with others in a full scale Navajo campaign. In view of that Carson asked permission to travel to Santa Fe, in his words "to have a full and explicit conference with the General Commanding as regards my duty . . ." And he added: "I would like to send my family to Taos where they will be at home, and I would like to accompany them as far as Santa Fe, as I do not consider the road safe for women and children . . . . I would thank the General if he would give me permission to proceed with them that far."[28]

The ink was scarcely dry on this letter when Carson learned that Gen. Canby had been transferred to the war theater in the East, to be replaced by Gen. James H. Carleton as departmental commander. Kit, while Indian agent, had worked with Carleton on occasion, and come to respect him, even though others thought the officer stern, unbending, and zealous. Now, the General decided to put Canby's plan for a Navajo campaign on hold for the moment, and instead go after the Mescalero Apaches.

To that task, he assigned Col. Carson, whom he described as having a reputation for performing anything that may be required of him ". . . with skill and high courage, for which he is justly celebrated." And he directed that Carson's regiment should muster at Fort Union, then strike south to reoccupy Fort Stanton, abandoned to the Confederates in August 1861, and which lay in the heart of Mescalero country.[29]

In light of the new circumstances, it is not clear just how Kit arranged to get his family back to Taos. His son Kit, Jr., remembering more than a half century later, declared:

My mother had a considerable amount of money and some jewels. Father was not with the party when we started, although he joined us before reaching Taos. My mother still fearing the possibilities of meeting some of Sibley's stragglers . . . concealed her valuables in the garments of a faithful Navajo servant girl. [Dolores Carson?]

The trip of three days was made without incident, and . . . my father caught up with us, but at once returned to Fort Union to join his regiment.[30]

Kit Carson's brief war waged against the bellicose Mescalero Apaches in the winter of 1862–1863, marked the beginning of the second phase of his rather improbable military career. In the first phase, as the untrained commander of a volunteer regiment, he had fought against his own kind in a single Civil War battle at Valverde. But with expulsion of the Confederates six weeks later and prospects of a further invasion from Texas seemingly dim, the reason for Kit's original enlistment—to preserve the Territory for the Union—appeared to be accomplished.

Indeed, upon arriving back in Albuquerque from Fort Craig, he sent a letter, May 4, 1862, to Capt. William Nicodemus, department adjutant, asking as a friend and fellow Mason whether his discharge from service was imminent. Kit had learned that some of the regiments were being disbanded, and if the one he had recruited was on the list, he preferred to resign than await discharge. When Canby was shown the letter, he replied in a brief note that Kit's regiment was to be kept, and he very much "wished Col. Carson not to resign." In fact, Kit had made a point of saying that if his services were still required he was quite willing to remain on duty.[31]

Canby and his successor Carleton both recognized that Kit Carson, despite his illiteracy and lack of military training, was the very man to serve as field commander for a final push against hostile Indians. His long experience among the tribes, his knowledge of Spanish and the New Mexican culture, which eased his acceptance by the Hispanic volunteers, and his common sense approach to frontier warfare admirably fitted him for the task of bringing a long-sought peace to the Southwestern frontier.

So when Kit rode south in late September to face the Mescaleros, he was embarking upon the second and longest phase of his military career, one that would extend over the next four years. It was just as well that neither he nor Josefa had the slightest inkling of the toll his soldiering would take upon their lives and marriage. However, that period, for all its rough sledding, would produce some of the foremost achievements in Carson's entire life.

The Mescaleros, numbering but a few hundred people, were soon brought to bay. Kit saw to the beginning of their removal to a new reservation at Bosque Redondo on the middle Pecos River in eastern New Mexico. There, Gen. Carleton had established Fort Sumner to prevent the Apaches and eventually the Navajos from returning to a life of raiding.[32]

On February 3, 1863, Kit from Fort Stanton dispatched a letter to Gen. Carleton in Santa Fe, submitting his surprise resignation. Pointing out that a new Confederate invasion remained unlikely, he promised "to serve my country" and return to active duty should New Mexico be menaced again. "At present I feel that my health as well as happiness directs me to my home and family, and trust that the General will accept my resignation."[33]

Carleton was by no means prepared to release the one man upon whom hinged his future plans for subjugating other Indians still at war in the territory. He summoned Carson to Santa Fe, expressed his displeasure, and refused to grant him his wish, offering him instead a couple of months leave at home. Kit went along, reluctantly. This proved to be just the first in a string of unsuccessful resignations he would tender to Gen. Carleton, before finally leaving military service in 1867.[34]

The prolonged break at home, conceded by Carleton, permitted Kit to enjoy the company of his wife and William, Teresina, Kit, Jr., and baby Charles, now twenty months old, but also to rest and restore his fragile health. The next assignment looming on the horizon—the long-expected Navajo campaign—hovered like a tar-black cloud over the household during his stay. At last the dreaded call-up came and at the end of April, Kit hugged his loved ones and set forth to confront the most arduous and challenging of his military undertakings.

On May 2, 1863, the *Santa Fe Gazette* reported that Col. Carson had passed through town en route to Fort Wingate in western New Mexico where he would assume command of the Navajo Expedition. For the Carson family members left behind in Taos, a new semester of apprehension now began.

During the seventeen years Americans had occupied New Mexico, they negotiated no less than six treaties with the Navajos, all of which had been promptly broken. The tribe's war with the Hispanic residents of the Rio Grande Valley had dragged on intermittently for more than two hundred years, the raids leading to an expansion of Navajo population and a steady growth in their prosperity. The Indians' success had bred a way of life, so well-entrenched, that some government officials despaired of seeing it redirected along peaceful and productive lines.

It was Gen. Canby in his last months as commander of the Department of New Mexico who conceived the strategy that eventually worked—that of sending an overwhelming force into the heart of the Navajo lair, soundly defeating the Indians, and then removing them from their homeland to a distant reservation where they could be transformed, through education, into tranquil farmers. With Canby's departure, Gen. Carleton was left to execute the plan, while adding to it a few touches of his own.

First from Fort Wingate and then from Fort Canby just across the boundary in eastern Arizona, Carson had his troops fan out in all directions to pursue the scattered Navajos. By destroying their hogans and fields and capturing their livestock, thousands of Indians were reduced to starvation. They streamed into Fort Canby through the bitter winter to surrender and be transferred to the Bosque Redondo Reservation on the Pecos. The "scorched earth" strategy, while brutal, did serve to accomplish Carson's aim of subduing the Navajo with minimal casualties, the action resulting for the most part in limited skirmishes and no large-scale battles.

By fall, Kit was tiring, the strenuous marches reminding him of the serious infirmities that were now part of his permanent physical condition. He began petitioning headquarters for an extended leave of absence.

On November 1, he again addressed Gen. Carleton, requesting specifically a leave of two months beginning December 15, 1863. By that date, as he explained, the weather would be so severe that the wide sweeps he had been conducting throughout the Navajo homeland would become impractical. By returning to the field in mid February, when the weather had moderated, he could pick up where he left off.

Carleton was having none of it. Curtly, he told Col. Carson to remain with his regiment and continue to press the Navajo roundup, snow and sub-zero temperatures notwithstanding. He did, however, offer some hope. As soon as Carson had managed to clean out the forbidding Navajo stronghold of Canyon de Chelly, northwest of Fort Canby, he could leave the expedition in charge of its quartermaster Capt. Asa B. Carey, the only officer of the regular army with the volunteers, and come to Santa Fe for consultations. Kit earnestly hoped, once there, to persuade the general to allow him home leave, as he put it in his original request, to handle "some private business of importance."[35]

That may have been a discreet reference to Josefa who was expecting their sixth child in the spring, or more likely it was a disguised plea for time to recuperate from his latest responsibilities and labors. Approaching his fifty-fourth birthday, a gloomy Kit was experiencing the full effects of a hard life spent on the frontier. Nevertheless, by the last week in January 1864, he had directed his troops in a lightning swoop through Canyon de Chelly, and a few days later set out for the capital with several of his officers.

Gen. Carleton at Santa Fe must have been shocked when he observed his field commander's worn and sickly appearance. At the conclusion of the conference dealing with progress in the Navajo campaign, he placed Carson on detached service in Santa Fe, or so it showed on the record. In reality, the general allowed him to go home to Taos, as offering the best prospects for improvement of his health.[36]

The welcome reprieve meant that Kit was on hand for several weeks to give Josefa comfort in the last stages of her pregnancy. By mid March, he was ordered back to Fort Canby, and so, unhappily, missed the arrival of daughter Rebecca on April 13. Capt. Carey reported that when the colonel reached the fort on the evening of March 19, he appeared "unwell and very much fatigued."[37]

Blessedly for him, Kit was able to report to Gen. Carleton less than a month later that "the Navajo War, so far as active operations are concerned, is ended." That being the case, he stated, "My services here are no longer required, and I ask it as a favor that . . . [you send] me to some post where I can have my family with me, or that I may tender my resignation. My children are small and they need my presence to look after their education . . . and [they] have the next claims on my time and attention."[38]

Despite the urgent appeal, Carleton failed again to accept Col. Carson's request to resign, nor did he respect his desire to be stationed at a location suitable for his family. He did summon him to Santa Fe to participate in court martial proceedings against a junior officer, then on May 30, he assigned him to Fort Sumner and the Bosque Redondo Reservation as supervisor of the captive Navajos, some 8,000 of them. Kit was disturbed at the condition he found among the ill-fed Indians, and frustrated that his efforts to improve matters brought him into conflict with the post commander, Capt. Henry B. Bristol. After a few months, he once more submitted his resignation.[39]

At that point, Carleton was still not inclined to grant Kit Carson his wishes. The general, in fact, had another mission for his field commander, which like earlier ones would take him away from family and home.

The Plains Indians, especially the allied Kiowas and Comanches, had also taken advantage of the military disarray caused by the Civil War. Their favorite target became the richly laden freight caravans traveling from the East over the Santa Fe Trail. As this was the only artery of supply and communication for New Mexico, Carleton committed himself to its protection. From department headquarters at Santa Fe came an order of October 22, 1864, authorizing a quick campaign against the two tribes.

Earlier Gen. Carleton had notified Kit as to what was pending, and instructed him to recruit Utes as scouts and warriors for the punitive force. "Your knowledge of the haunts of the Indians of the plains and the great confidence the Ute Indians have in you as a friend and leader, point to yourself as the most fitting person to organize, direct and bring this enterprise to a successful conclusion," he wrote convincingly.[40]

After a short time in Taos, Col. Carson led an expedition of 325 troops and 75 Ute warriors, accompanied by two twelve-pounder mountain howitzers, down the Canadian River and into the Texas Panhandle where Kiowas and Comanches were known to make their winter camps. There, on November 25, 1864, at a place called Adobe Walls Carson's men encountered the two tribes and their allies, the Kiowa Apaches, initiating an engagement that Robert M. Utley has characterized as "some of the most savage fighting known to the Indian frontier."[41]

Kit always claimed that without the two pieces of artillery, his little army would have been overcome. As it was, he beat a strategic retreat, saving his regiment, while serving notice on the hostile tribes that no place in their High Plains domain remained a safe sanctuary.

Subsequently, an elated Carleton relayed to Kit his congratulations. "My thanks for the handsome manner in which you met so formidable an enemy and defeated him. This brilliant affair adds another green leaf to the laurels you have so nobly won in the service of your country."[42] Of course, the Indians were "defeated" only in the sense that they failed in their counter attack to destroy the soldiers.

Adobe Walls was the last battle of any kind that Kit Carson was destined to fight, though it by no means marked the end of his military career. Like men everywhere, he had initially enlisted at the outbreak of the Civil War, in the belief that answering a call to the colors was his civic duty. When Gen. Carleton afterward needed Carson for a very different purpose—to fight Indians—he was careful to couch his solicitation in patriotic terms, understanding well that his illiterate, backwoods colonel could not bring himself to resist his country's summons.

As observed, the two abiding problems that prolonged military service imposed upon Kit were those attendant upon his absences from home and his deteriorating health. The former he conscientiously attempted to mitigate by writing regularly through dictation to Josefa while he was in the field. This private correspondence was apparently large, although most of it, regrettably, has not survived.

In one letter to his *Adorada Esposa* ("Beloved Wife"), dated October 10, 1862, he told her: "Do not worry about me because with God's help we shall see each other [again]. . . . I charge you above all not to get weary of caring for my children, and to give each one a little kiss in my name. . . . I remain begging God that I return in good health to be with you until death. . . ." And he closed with this touching declaration: "Your husband who loves you and wishes to see you more than to write to you."[43]

On occasion, in the midst of campaigning, Kit proved unable to send off his regular letters to home. That was the case during the intense weeks of the Navajo expedition. On December 23, 1863, he managed to include with outgoing army dispatches from Fort Canby a note for Josefa, addressed in care of Joseph Beuthner. It arrived on January 5.

Beuthner hurried to the Carson house and read Kit's words to Josefa and the children. In his reply to Kit, written the next day, he remarked: "I am often visiting your family, and if I cannot take them your letters every week, as they desire to receive them, I try to console them that you are well and get along fine, as they feel always very anxious about you."[44] His words convey the magnitude of the apprehension experienced by the home-bound Carsons when Kit was abroad in the path of danger.

Kit's precarious health, the second abiding problem, remained a matter of serious concern for the duration of his army years. As early as 1859, journalist Albert D. Richardson while in Taos took note that his host Kit Carson had recently decided, "thenceforward to avoid horseback riding and travel only in carriages." Since Carson was often mentioned as an expert horseman, his use of a carriage would indicate that some physical disability had forced upon him a more comfortable means of transportation. Inasmuch as Richardson saw him prior to the accident in the San Juan Mountains, the problem with circulation in his legs, referred to earlier, may have been the cause of his distress at that time.[45]

In fact, even after his autumn 1860 accident, Kit enjoyed intermittent periods of improvement during which he could mount a horse and ride long distances. But increasingly in later years, he traveled in an army ambulance when on government business, and when on private matters, in his own carriage.[46]

As he was not one to complain, we have to assume that Carson's repeated references to the poor state of his health in military correspondence reflect the weakness and pain that routinely assailed him. The rigorous Navajo campaign, prosecuted through the bitterest of winters, left him utterly exhausted. A month after his release from that duty, Capt. Herbert M. Enos of the army's Quartermaster Corps, reported that Col. Carson "is very unwell and has gone to the Hot Springs." He was referring to Ojo Caliente northwest of Santa Fe, whose waters to this day are renowned for their healing properties.[47]

In the months following the Adobe Walls episode, Carson was kept busy with a variety of government assignments. At home in May 1865, he received word that Gen. Carleton had decided to establish a temporary post on the Cimarron route of the Santa Fe Trail, to protect overland traffic from raids by Plains Indians. Handed the task, Kit marched east from Fort Union with some of his New Mexico Volunteers and spent the forepart of the summer in constructing Camp Nichols inside the western end of the Oklahoma Panhandle.[48]

Before the job reached completion, he received a summons to appear before the traveling congressional Doolittle Commission investigating Indian affairs. His housing of the Washington dignitaries when they passed through Taos in July has already been narrated.

Senator Doolittle, from information gathered, concluded that the time had come to hold a meeting with the southern Plains tribes in hopes of curbing their attacks upon travelers and settlements. Having become favorably impressed with Kit Carson's knowledge of Indians, he recommended his appointment as a special commissioner to participate in a grand council the following October at a site in south central Kansas.[49]

On the subsequent trip east, Kit rode in an officer's ambulance, escorted by six soldiers and army wagons with teamsters and a cook. At the council grounds on the Little Arkansas River, above today's Wichita, Kansas, he helped in forming treaties with the Cheyennes, Arapahoes, Kiowas, Comanches and others.[50]

In a memoir, early-day hunter and trader on the plains, James R. Mead, speaks of his attendance at the Little Arkansas gathering. He mentions sitting in a tent where Kit Carson and Charley Rath were engaged in conversation. Rath was probably there to serve as an interpreter for the Cheyennes. Mead gives no clue as to the subject of the pair's talk, but since both had once been married to Making Out Road, surely her name came up. It would have been surprising had they not shared their respective opinions of the headstrong Cheyenne woman.[51]

At the conclusion of the treaty-making, Kit was ordered to St. Louis to confer with generals John Pope and William T. Sherman about the status of Indian affairs in the West. He had first met Sherman in California upon returning there from Washington with military dispatches in 1848. They now renewed their friendship.

With the official business finished by month's end, Carson received orders sending him back to his regiment in New Mexico. On the way, he paid a brief visit to his kin in the Booneslick country, as it turned out, the last time he would see them.[52]

After a token stay with his regiment, Kit hurried home to Taos, arriving there on November 29, 1865. Josefa and other members of the household were surprised and delighted to see improvement of his physical condition, or, as Kit expressed it, he was "in somewhat better health than when [he] left there."[53] The trip out and back on the Santa Fe Trail, riding comfortably in an ambulance, had proved to be therapeutic.

Husband and wife had much catching up to do: Kit describing his government travels, and Josefa imparting news of the Taos community, along with a summary of the children's latest achievements and problems, and a review of the couple's current economic situation.

At the beginning of his service as colonel, Carson had drawn pay of $95 a month, which was somewhat less than he had enjoyed as an Indian agent. Although his officer's pay was later increased to $110, the amount scarcely covered his personal expenses and those needed to keep a family in food and clothing during war-time inflation.[54] No evidence exists that Josefa ever complained, but that she made deep sacrifices so that Kit might pursue his course of duty cannot be doubted.

Carson was scarcely back from St. Louis before he received an order from Santa Fe, dated December 8, 1865, assigning him to take command of Fort Union.[55] After tending to some Taos business and packing up, he started across the Sangre de Cristo Mountains a few days before Christmas. He arrived at the fort on December 24th, his 56th birthday.

Since his first appearance here after enlistment in 1861, Col. Carson had gone on to command forts Craig, Stanton, Wingate, Canby, the posts of Albuquerque and Los Lunas, and Camp Nichols. Now he assumed charge of Fort Union, the largest in New Mexico. All of this had been accomplished as an enlisted volunteer, rather than as a trained soldier of the regular army. Kit Carson's ability to lead men overrode his numerous other military deficiencies.

In the early part of 1865, Gen. Carleton had persuaded Carson "not to leave the service while I remain here." By receiving such a commitment, the general hoped to keep under his wing the one man who could be counted upon to win success in the field. As he put it directly to Kit, "A great deal of my good fortune in Indian matters . . . is due to you."[56]

The placing of Carson at Fort Union, at that moment a quiet post, was meant to be temporary. Carleton was on the lookout for a new hot spot to which he could dispatch his seasoned firefighter. Although Kit remained at the fort's helm for four months, mainly engaged in administrative duties, he did not bring his family over the mountains to live with him. He knew his earlier request to Carleton to find him a semi-permanent command where Josefa and the children would be comfortable had not been forgotten. For the moment, he bided his time.[57]

While at Fort Union, Kit was in for an unexpected but altogether pleasant surprise. Back on March 13, 1865, by order of President Lincoln, Carson was breveted brigadier general, U.S. Volunteers, specifically for gallantry at the battle of Valverde and for other distinguished services in New Mexico. The brevet, a rather empty but much-coveted honor, entitled an officer the courtesy of using a title higher than his permanent rank. Kit, for instance, while still receiving a colonel's pay and wearing a colonel's insignia on his shoulder straps, was hereafter to be addressed as general.[58]

Owing to bureaucratic delays and slow mail, Gen. Carson did not receive notice of his new rating until early November. On January 2, 1866, he dictated a letter to the Secretary of War acknowledging that his brevet although "unsolicited by me, I accept with grateful pleasure." And he went on to say generously that he interpreted it as recognition of "the exertions of the New Mexico Volunteers."[59]

Was Josefa pleased? Perhaps she accepted the belated news from Washington as a welcome sign that the painful years of sacrifice by Kit and herself had not gone unnoticed by the nation. She may even have attempted to explain that to her progeny, in terms a child could understand.

On January 6, the *Santa Fe Gazette* published a notice that Col. Kit Carson of Taos had been breveted a brigadier general by the President. New Mexicans, who had served under him in the late war and those who still occupied the ranks in his regiment, were filled with pride. Thereafter, for them he was always, "the General." Someone soon after the announcement made a forgetful slip and addressed him as colonel, then profusely apologized. Characteristically, the ever modest Carson drawled, "Oh, call me Kit . . . and be done with it."[60] The mindset of the professional military man never fastened its hold upon him.

A new order that Kit Carson had been hoping for reached him while on a home visit to Taos in the final week of April 1866. It directed him to proceed at once to Fort Garland in the Colorado Territory and assume command of the post. Its location on the eastern edge of the San Luis Valley, not far north of the New Mexico line, made it easily accessible from Taos. So this time, Josefa, the five children, and some of the servants were going along. By May 3, they had reached the fort and taken up quarters in the commander's residence, a log building described as rough but comfortable.[61]

Fort Garland, founded in 1858 near the mouth of LaVeta Pass, was in a neglected state when the Carsons arrived. Carleton needed a strong hand there because the Utes had grown restive of late as settlers and miners continued to intrude upon tribal hunting grounds. Kit Carson in his years as their agent had earned the respect and trust of the Utes, so now they streamed in to the fort to plead their grievances to Father Kit, or "Kitty," the names by which they knew him.

Gen. Carson was not so busy with the Indians' problems over the year and a half he remained at Fort Garland that he was prevented from enjoying his youngsters. Indeed, they would be left with cherished memories of that relatively long and happy time spent close to their father. It would be the last such interval.

The biographer Dr. Peters described Kit Carson as "a kind and indulgent father."[62] Anyone seeing him romping on the parade ground with his lively quintet and little Juan, the Navajo boy Josefa had saved, could have borne witness to the accuracy of that simple statement. For a while, Josefa's sister Ignacia and daughter Teresina came up from Taos to lend a hand in caring for the young Carsons. That probably occurred right after Estafanita (the seventh child) was born on December 23, 1866, the day before Kit's own birthday.[63]

Some incidents involving the children at Fort Garland were recorded. After a band of Moache Utes had raided in the area around Trinidad and killed several people, Carson invited their leaders to parley with him at the fort. Young Teresina Carson was assisting at serving food to the Indians when she noticed one of them wearing a pair of store-bought women's shoes. Asking him where they came from, the Ute brazenly replied that he had killed a white squaw and taken her shoes.

Teresina was horrified and refused to serve the man more food, whereupon he became angry and struck her with a heavy rawhide whip. Kit, Jr., who told the story, said that his father "rushed at the fellow and [might] . . . have killed him then and there, but mother [intervened] . . . and begged him to let it go."[64]

During September, prior to the birth of Estafanita (or Stella, as the family called her), Gen. William T. Sherman, then commanding the vast Military Division of the Missouri, came to Fort Garland on an inspection tour. One day he and Carson were seated in a room discussing military business, when the children ran in, as Sherman remembered it, "half clad and boistrous . . . [both] boys and girls as wild and untrained as a brood of Mexican mustangs."

When he expressed his concern for the over-indulged miscreants, Kit admitted that they were a source of great anxiety to him and went so far as to say, "I fear I have not done right by my children." He was especially worried about the skimpiness of their education.[65]

The problem of their future care had taken on new meaning over the past year or so, owing to Kit's rapid physical decline. Carter contends that Carson gave little thought to making provision for his family before it was too late.[66] While that may be true, we have to wonder how he could have fitted in any serious money-making enterprise during his unflagging years in military service. Unfortunately, the volunteer army, unlike the regular army, was not entitled to retirement pay.

While Carson was still at Fort Union, Gen. Carleton had suggested that upon leaving the service, he apply for a sutlership, as a way of supporting his family. The sutler, a civilian merchant, operated a store at isolated garrisons for the benefit of men under arms. During the war, the army had authorized one sutler per volunteer regiment.[67]

Soon after reaching Fort Garland, Kit sent a letter to Sen. Lafayette Foster, who as a member of the Doolittle Commission had enjoyed the hospitality of the Carson home. He told the senator that after five years in the service, he was poorer than when he enlisted. And he asked for help in securing the sutler's position at Fort Garland, for as he explained, it would "comfortably support myself and family." His request could not be acted upon, however, because of a new ruling that separated sutlerships from the military.[68]

Following that disappointment, Kit learned that consideration was being given to separating the Indian Superintendency in the Colorado Territory from the office of governor. Believing that his long experience with Indians would help his case, he applied for the superintendent's job, in the event that it became available. The proposed severance, in fact, did not take place before Carson's untimely death, and anyway his illiteracy would probably have disqualified him from acquiring that high office.[69]

He also asked to have his old job back as Indian agent for the Moache Utes and Jicarilla Apaches, now served by an agency in Cimarron rather than Taos. However, the office was occupied, with no prospect of a vacancy in the near future. Hence, Carson abandoned any hope of employment in that quarter.[70]

As early as 1865, he had developed an interest in prospecting and mining speculation. Carleton may have led him in that direction, for he assisted the general in locating and recording several mining claims.[71] For his help, he was possibly handed a few of what proved to be worthless mining shares issued by Carleton.

While at Fort Union in 1866, Carson on the side joined with nine other men to form the Kit Carson Mining Company, with the purpose of filing a claim to exploit a copper deposit not far from the garrison. As nothing more has been learned of this venture, it is safe to assume that it suffered a quiet death.[72]

A U.S. Geological Survey of the Territories (1867) reported that, "In 1865 and 1866, Kit Carson with a party prospected in Colorado's San Juan Mountains . . . and took up many valuable claims." If so, Kit failed to profit from his efforts, since his will makes no reference to these or any other mineral holdings of value.[73]

The stray mentions of his prospecting together with his attempts to secure a sutlership or a position in the Indian Service can be taken as a measure of Kit's desperate bid to find some remunerative work that might allow him to support his family after discharge from the army.

At the time of Sherman's visit in 1866, he had learned that the general was planning to phase out the few volunteer regiments still serving in the West, and replace them with regular army troops.[74] That news fueled Kit's worries about the status of his own future. Of Daniel Boone in his last difficult years, a friend had said: "He seemed to feel his poverty quite keenly."[75] Those words equally described Kit Carson's mood as he contemplated the pending termination of his military career.

After Sherman's departure, Kit escorted his family back to Taos where Josefa was to place the children in schools that now existed there. During the heavy winter of 1866–1867, between quick visits home from Fort

Garland, he carried on with the niggling details of post administration and with keeping a watchful eye on the Utes. In spring and early summer, he could have easily gone west a short distance on his recreation time to prospect in the San Juans.

The long-expected mustering out of Carson's First Regiment finally came in the fall of 1867. Kit saw to that, then he rode down to Santa Fe in the second week of November for his own formal separation from the service. Of that newsworthy event, the press there reported that Gen. Kit Carson had come into District Headquarters to be mustered out, having joined the New Mexico Volunteers at the beginning of the war in 1861.[76]

He was the last man to leave the regiment, which was now completely dissolved and henceforward would exist only in the pages of history books. The poignancy of that moment did not escape Gen. Carson's notice.

Conclusion

In 1859, while Kit Carson was serving as Taos agent for the Utes, a small problem developed over his distribution of grain, beef, and blankets to the Indians. In a letter to Superintendent Collins in Santa Fe, he defended himself, saying: "I don't know whether I done rite or wrong, but I done what I thought was best."[1]

That brief statement, so typical of the man, could well have applied to every one of the challenges he faced in life. In each, the historical evidence suggests that he "done what he thought was best," although in some cases his best proved insufficient to deal with the matter at hand. Carson seemingly explained his own occasional failures in an off-hand remark attributed to him: "My damn luck—thar's the difficulty! It always places me in positions I am no more fit to fill than I am fit to fill a pulpit."[2] Such an observation illustrates his natural humility, a trait regularly noted by those close to him, but is also an example of his habitual hard-headed, no-nonsense facing of reality.

That being so, we cannot help but wonder how Kit rated his success as a husband and father in his third marriage. The regret he so often expressed during his army years over his inability to be with his young children, who were at an age when they most needed him, and the paltry financial resources he was able to provide for their support caused him as much pain as his physical injuries.

At Kit's death, Tom Boggs, administrator of his estate, lamented that he had left his three boys and four girls in almost destitute circumstances.[3] Any self-doubts Carson may have entertained about his fitness as a father, could only have been partially offset by the warm affection and devotion he always showed toward his children.

Promptly upon reverting to civilian status, Carson hastened to Taos where he and Josefa, pregnant now for the eighth time, gathered up their youngsters and a few possessions for a trip over the eastern mountains. They were joining Tom and Rumalda Boggs who had been developing a new ranch on a part of the old Vigil and St. Vrain land grant. The site was on the lower Purgatory River, not far above its junction with the Arkansas, and some five miles west of Fort Lyon in the Colorado Territory.

In 1865 Kit had purchased from Cerán St. Vrain two parcels of land farther up the Purgatory, with the intent of settling there some day to raise livestock and farm as he had once done at Rayado. Tom Boggs was constructing a number of adobe buildings, and as other settlers clustered around him, his ranch headquarters took the name Boggsville. Generously, he offered his in-laws, the Carsons, use of three rooms that were attached to another apartment occupied by storekeeper John Hough. The crowded lodgings were meant to be temporary, until Kit was able to see to the raising of a suitable house on his own land.[4]

In fact, his health was failing so rapidly there appeared little chance that he would ever build anything on his property. Soon after arrival, he went to visit his friend of old, William Bent, who had a ranch nearby at the mouth of the Purgatory.

Dr. Henry R. Tilton, the army surgeon from Fort Lyon, also happened to be present at Bent's when he mentioned to Carson that he was an amateur trapper. Kit, according to the doctor, "threw off all reserve . . . , saying, the happiest days of his life were spent trapping. He gave me many practical hints on trapping and hunting."[5]

It is perhaps significant that Carson more than once in his later years made a similar assertion to other men, concerning the joys of his trapper era.[6] So far as can be learned, he never made any particular claim to unbounded happiness deriving from staying at home with his family.

At that initial meeting, Dr. Tilton was struck by Carson's debilitated look. "He was then complaining of a pain in his chest, the origin of which he attributed to a fall received in 1860. It happened while he was descending a mountain," recorded the physician.

"The General, as Carson was popularly and officially known," says Sabin, "now was a sick man, without long-assured income, was the sole support of a goodly family, and was facing evil days."[7]

Kit's neighbor John Hough recalled later: "Carson's health at that time was very bad. Not being able to ride about, he spent most of his time keeping me company, my trading store being only a few feet away from our quarters."[8]

Hough was referring to his friend's inability any longer to mount a horse. But the general several times was driven in his own carriage to Fort Lyon for medical consultation with Dr. Tilton. The soldiers at the post always made a great fuss over him, and Kit enjoyed a renewal of the military camaraderie that had been such a large part of his life since 1861.

Josefa struggled to keep the family in good spirits, even while the dark shadow hovered over them all. She was grateful for the help and companionship of her niece Rumalda Boggs, and the several other women in the little tight-knit community. But she looked frail and wan, burdened as she was by worries over her husband and by having to deal with the prospect of another child to care for. Dr. Tilton spoke of her as "evidently having been a very handsome woman," his words indicating that now at age 39, she had lost much of her beauty.[9]

The new year, 1868, had hardly begun when the government imposed upon Kit Carson once more. On November 12, the previous year, Commissioner of Indian Affairs N. G. Taylor had announced that a delegation of Ute leaders would be brought to Washington to air their litany of grievances and more significantly to negotiate a treaty that would cede much of their vast territorial claims, while establishing for them a sizeable reservation in western Colorado. An unspoken purpose of the trip was to dazzle the Indians with the numerical superiority and power of the whiteman.[10]

The task of assembling a delegation of ten Ute chiefs and an equal number of support personnel, including two of the tribe's far-flung Indian agents, clerks, and interpreters, was handed to Colorado governor Alexander G. Hunt, who still held the office ex officio of Indian superintendent for the territory. Not until the second half of December was he able to devote his full attention to recruitment, and mid January had arrived before he strongly urged Kit Carson to participate.[11]

The appeal caused a stir in the Carson household. Kit doubted he was physically up to the long, arduous journey. Moreover, the possibility existed that he would miss the birth of their last child, even though Josefa was not due until April. But in the end, against his will, he answered the call to duty, as he had done so often in the past. Gov. Hunt indicated that Carson's presence would instill confidence in the chiefs who trusted him implicitly, and might spell the difference in obtaining a treaty. Josefa probably helped her husband make the hard decision by pointing out that he could seize the opportunity to visit doctors in the East who might be able to alleviate his medical condition.[12]

In late January, Kit parted with his loved ones and was driven to Fort Lyon where he caught the stagecoach for the railhead, then at Fort Hays in western Kansas. From there it was a comfortable train ride to Washington, via St. Louis. He reached the capital on February 2, to join the rest of the delegation, which had taken the Union Pacific from Cheyenne.

Over the ensuing weeks, the Utes were wined, dined, entertained, given suitcases full of candy and cigarettes, and allowed to take a prodigious number of Turkish baths, all designed to keep them in a mellow mood, while the treaty talks were proceeding.

Carson, when he felt up to it, made a round of personal visits to the Secretary of Interior, the Commissioner of Indian Affairs, the headquarters of Gen. Ulysses S. Grant, and the War Department, where he conferred with generals Phil Sheridan and William T. Sherman, who happened to be in town on official military business.[13]

The 5th of February, 1868, the entire 21-man delegation from Colorado visited the Executive Mansion to exchange pleasantries and receive a guided tour conducted by President Andrew Johnson. Carson was delighted to be back in the historic building, which he had last seen in 1847, when upon delivering his California dispatches, he was received by President Polk.[14]

Some days later, John C. Frémont came down from New York to see his old friend. He was distressed to find Carson looking so ill and in pain. Thus, he wrote to his wife Jessie that he had advised Kit, when he went next with the delegation to New York, he ought to consult a good physician there. Carson listened and took the advice.[15]

On March 2 a treaty with the Utes was concluded, granting them a huge slice of western Colorado and various concessions they had requested. Kit felt only relief when the deed was done, not only because it brought the day closer when he could start for home, but also owing to the realization that his quiet diplomacy in support of the document had contributed to the success of the trip, or as his biographer Peters defined it, "his mission of charity in behalf of the Indians."[16]

On February 25, a week before the signing, Kit had replied to a letter, forwarded to him, from his grandniece in Missouri, Fannie O. Avery. She had learned from the papers that he was in Washington. Kit told her in words that still resonate with pathos that, "I am now quite old and worn out and hardly my own master on account of my faithful services when younger to the government. They now still claim that I should serve in some capacity." Those remarks show that he was ruefully aware of the price he had paid for his diligence in pursuing his perceived public duty.[17]

When Kit Carson came to Washington, he possessed no official office or standing, as he had in 1865 when he carried a federal appointment as commissioner to assist in making the Indian treaties on the Little Arkansas. During the six weeks he was in the capital, neither government documents nor the media referred to him by any title other than "General."

At the end of the negotiations, when ways of executing the pending treaty were under consideration, Gov. Hunt petitioned Indian Commissioner Nathaniel G. Taylor to recommend that Carson be made a Special Agent, so that he could attend to the settling of the Utes on their new reservation. (Kit had already served in a similar capacity for the Navajos at Bosque Redondo.) Hunt added: "I expect much from Gen. Carson, . . . but he is in feeble health, and his long service, and great usefulness both as a soldier and citizen demands at least this recognition from a generous government." Commissioner Taylor, however, was unable to make any appointment until the senate ratified the treaty.[18]

Before leaving Washington, Carson and three other members of the party went to the studio of renowned Civil War photographer Mathew Brady and sat for pictures. The image of Kit seems drawn and haggard, the physical decline plainly evident in his hollow cheeks and troubled expression.

With the official aim of the trip accomplished, the delegation moved on to New York, where the leading papers, March 16, noted its arrival on the previous day.[19] They were lodged at government expense in the Metropolitan Hotel, 582 Broadway. On the 16th the *Times* carried an item of entertainment news, saying that "the famous Kit Carson and a group of Indian chiefs from Colorado will visit the New York Circus this evening."

During the three days the party was resident in the city, the Indians were constantly entertained. Carson, ailing and exhausted, spent much of the time "confined in his hotel room on account of heart disease."[20] His quarters were shared with two of the chiefs.

He did manage the first day to visit Dr. Lewis Albert Sayre, prominent physician and orthopedic surgeon, probably recommended to him by Frémont in Washington. Kit gave details of his accident and underwent a brief physical examination. The verdict was what he had expected: nothing could be done and he might die at any moment.

Dr. Sayre thought the patient might extend his time a bit by avoiding fatigue, excitement, and alcohol, the last of which Carson seldom touched anyway.

He replied solemnly: "I must take the chiefs to see Boston. They depend on me. I told them I would. Then we go home, straight. My wife must see me. If I . . . died out here, it would kill her. I must get home, and I think I can do it."[21]

Jessie Frémont who had heard from her husband, still in Washington, that Kit Carson was to be in New York City, came down from their home on the Hudson River. She arranged to meet him at the house of a personal friend of hers, located on Madison Square.

When he entered the room, she was appalled at his appearance, so different from the way she remembered him in Washington twenty years earlier. In describing that moment long afterward, Jessie wrote, "He was already stricken with death."[22]

Kit felt so weak, he cut the visit short. It was incomparably sad. When they parted, both knew it would be for the last time. Later, still depressed, Jessie arranged to send him violets at the Metropolitan.[23]

If Washington, accustomed to seeing such people, had taken the colorful Utes in stride, and New York had shown them mild but courteous interest, Boston by contrast pulled out all the stops in scheduling diversions for the Indians.

The first day of the Boston tour, they and their western escorts were whisked away by carriage to view tourist "sights of the Hub," including Bunker Hill. Accompanied by the mayor and city aldermen, the exotic guests spent the afternoon at the State House where they were greeted by the governor and introduced to the legislature, then in session. Gov. Hunt made a slight speech. "Gen. Carson was also invited to speak," stated a newspaper reporter, "but was obliged to decline on account of his feeble health."

A banquet followed that evening at the fashionable Parker House and concluded with additional perorations, among them a warm thank you from one of the chiefs who expressed the hope that peace would continue between his nation and the United States. According to the *Daily Journal*, the entire party, with the exception of Gen. Carson, then adjourned to the Boston Theater and enjoyed a performance of the "White Fawn," a wildly popular ballet.[24]

Had he been in fit condition, Kit would have delighted in the day's events. But with his ebbing strength and his memory of Dr. Sayre's grim diagnosis, all of his thoughts now turned toward Josefa and his children. "My wife must see me," he had said in New York. Before leaving Boston, he and Gov. Hunt visited the studio of J. W. Black and had their pictures taken. Not surprisingly, it proved to be the last photograph made of Kit Carson.[25]

After that, he was done with Boston and finished with government business that separated him from his family. With one of the Ute agents, Daniel C. Oakes, as his attendant, Kit boarded a train for Colorado. Returning, he took the northern route through Chicago and Omaha to Cheyenne. There he and Oakes climbed aboard a stagecoach for Denver.[26]

By the time they reached there, Kit was utterly exhausted and feeling terrible. Chronic pain in his chest and neck, which had afflicted him throughout the journey, was becoming more intense. In addition, he had caught a severe cold in Washington, further aggravating his discomfort. Necessity forced him to check into the Planter's House where he took to his bed for two or three days.

The enforced rest restored some of his strength and high spirits. Sabin declares that concerned Denverites gathered daily in front of his hotel seeking news of his condition. The last day, Kit emerged and standing on a dry goods box delivered a few encouraging words to the crowd.[27]

Shortly, Carson climbed in an open wagon and with Oakes driving, they started south down the eastern skirt of the Front Range to Pueblo on the Arkansas River. Still weak, Kit rode most of the way lying on a bed of blankets in the back, and sleeping there under the stars at night. Oakes's daughter, Mrs. W. A. Bennett, in a 1924 interview said that the pair had left Denver late in the afternoon and gone only eight miles to the Bennett ranch, where they stopped overnight. "At this time," she noted, "Carson was much distressed by severe coughing spells, and declined to sleep in the house, saying he would only keep everybody awake."[28]

About the second of April, Daniel Oakes drove his wagon and team into Pueblo. He tied up at a local hotel where he and his ailing passenger could get a midday meal. While eating, Kit sent a runner to notify the town physician, Dr. Michael Beshoar, that he was sick and needed to see him right away.

Beshoar, who doubled as the editor and publisher of the *Colorado Chieftain*, happened to be working at the newspaper when he received the surprise message from Gen. Kit Carson. He hurried over to his medical office, arriving just a couple of minutes before the general, who appeared tired and drawn.

Upon examination, Dr. Beshoar found that Kit had an aneurysm of the carotid artery. The condition, a bulge in the weakened wall of the artery, was prominent enough to be seen and could break at any time. The heartbeat was abnormally rapid. The patient spoke of the constant pain he had been experiencing in the chest and neck, and complained, "I can hardly breathe."[29]

Beshoar advised the general to stay over in Pueblo for a couple of days' bedrest before continuing on to Boggsville. Carson refused, saying that his wife was expecting a child and he needed to be with her at the birth. As he was leaving, the doctor handed him a bottle of wild cherry syrup laced with opium for his cough, and tincture of veratrium to slow his heart action. For these and the office visit, Kit paid a fee of three silver dollars.[30]

Either here or earlier in Denver, he had managed to send ahead to Josefa a notice informing her of his schedule and the day of his arrival in Boggsville. She had been looking for him on the stagecoaches coming from Fort Hays, since that was how he had gone. News that he would be returning from the west by way of Pueblo surprised her.

As Carson emerged from Dr. Beshoar's office, he was confronted by a small crowd of curious residents who had gathered to have a look at the renowned frontiersman. Without lingering, he and Oakes mounted the wagon and entered upon the last leg of the journey, down the Arkansas River 85 miles to Boggsville.

Overcome with impatience to see her beloved Cristóbal, Josefa persuaded Tom Boggs to drive her in the Carson carriage up the river to intercept him. On April 11, near La Junta some 20 miles west of Boggsville, they met the Oakes wagon. It could only have been a touching reunion. Kit transferred to the carriage and the reunited couple returned home to their children.

As a forty-year-old woman in the final stage of her eighth pregnancy, Josefa Carson could scarcely have fared well in making a round trip of two score miles over a badly rutted road. Whether the experience in any way contributed to what followed cannot be determined now. In any event, two days after seeing her husband home, she bore a tiny daughter, Josefita, named after herself. Kit was no doubt grateful that he had lived to see this child, and he must have been the one who decided on her name.

No sooner was Carson back from Washington than his health rallied a bit, helped quite likely by a return to the warm embrace of his family. Shortly after Josefita's birth, he dictated a letter to an admirer he had met in New York City, Andrew Leckler, saying: "I arrived home on the 11th inst. and found my family all well. I was very sick but since my arrival home I have improved some & hope it will continue."[31] In fact, he was beginning to think again about developing his land and even building a house.

Then the world fell in on Christopher Carson! After her baby was born on April 13, Josefa did not recover. Instead, day by day she grew weaker and more sickly. Still, her family supposed the setback was temporary. She had always seemed so resilient.

At 8 o'clock in the evening of April 27, Josefa was sitting upon a pallet on the dirt floor of their three-room apartment. Kit was reclining on his own pallet in the adjoining room, no bedsteads having been brought up from Taos.

As she was combing the hair of her thirteen-year-old daughter Teresina, Josefa suddenly stopped and called out in Spanish, "Kit. Come here!"

Sensing the urgency in his wife's voice, he hurried to her side and supported her in his arms. Her last words were these: "Kit, I'm very sick." Then she died.

The tight little community of Boggsville was staggered by the suddenness of Josefa Carson's unexpected death, and none more so than her husband and children. Burial took place the following afternoon, in a garden 500 yards from the house where she had died. Kit stood at graveside utterly benumbed by the loss. Fear for his soon to be orphaned brood, now numbering seven with the addition of two-week-old Josefita, compounded his misery.

The cause of Josefa's death is usually listed as complications from childbirth. Historian Dale Morgan referred to it specifically as puerperal fever, or "childbed fever," essentially the same malady that, as suggested earlier in this book, may have claimed the life of Kit's first wife, Waa-nibe. If so, it could have occurred to him in his new sadness that fate had twice dealt him tragedies almost unbearable.[33]

According to the youngest son Charles, remembering the aftermath of his mother's passing: "That was a terrible time. Father was sick and we children didn't know what would become of us. He just seemed to pine away after mother died."[34] Dr. Tilton said a grieving Carson informed him that he and Josefa had been married for twenty-five years. "Her sudden death had a very depressing effect upon him," wrote the doctor.[35]

Be that as it may, necessity forced Carson to move beyond his grief. On May 5, a week after burying Josefa, he got off a letter to Taos for Aloys Scheurich, Teresina Bent's husband, with whom he had developed a close friendship. Kit said that he had been sick upon arriving back from Washington, but began to improve immediately. "I would [now] be comparatively healthy," he guessed, "if the misfortune [of] losing my wife hadn't happened. Those were trying days for me."

"I have given the necessary orders to have my own body, if I should die, and that of my wife's, sent together to Taos, to be buried in our graveyard," adding, "as soon as the weather is cool enough to do so." And, finally, he got to the real purpose of the letter, stating: "Please tell the old lady [that is, Josefa's older sister Ignacia] that there is nobody in the world who can take care of my children but her, and she must know that it would be the greatest of favors to me, if she would come and stay until I am healthier. . . ."[36] This would prove to be Kit's final letter.

In response, Ignacia and her daughter Teresina and husband Aloys began packing up and within three days they set out on the more than 200-mile trip to Boggsville. They reached there on May 15, to find that Kit had been moved to Fort Lyon only the day before. Tom Boggs took Aloys Scheurich there "to see the general," as Teresina related it. And she reported that Carson asked Mr. Scheurich not to leave but to stay, and he sent word back with Tom Boggs that Ignacia and Teresina should take care of his children.[37]

a

Kit Carson (seated, hands joined), with three members of the Ute delegation, Washington, D.C., posing at the Mathew Brady studio. (Kansas State Historical Society, Topeka)

The "Washington House," hotel across the street from the Indian Bureau in Washington, D.C., where Kit Carson and the Ute delegation were lodged during their stay in the capital, 1868. (National Archive Photo)

b

Dr. Michael Beshoar who treated Kit Carson at Pueblo, Colorado in April 1868. (Colorado Historical Society photo, negative number 24,683)

Surgeon's quarters at Ft. Lyon, Colorado, where Kit Carson died in 1868. (Rio Grande Historical Collections photo)

C

Kit and Josefa's youngest son,
Charles, as an adult. (Photo
courtesy of Bill Zwerner)

d

A portion of the building that served as the last home of Kit and Josefa Carson at Boggsville, Colorado, as it looked about 1908. The structure was later washed away by the flooding Purgatory River. (Marc Simmons Collection)

Army surgeon Dr. Henry Remsen Tilton, thirty-five years after he attended Kit Carson at Fort Lyon. (National Archive Photo)

It had been Dr. Tilton's idea to bring Gen. Carson to Fort Lyon. His "improvement" that Kit mentioned in the letters to Leckler and Scheurich, proved fleeting. The doctor described the decline in these terms: "His disease, aneurysm of the aorta, had progressed rapidly; and the tumor pressing on the pneumo-gastric nerves and trachea caused frequent spasms of the bronchial tubes which were exceedingly distressing."[38]

On one of his house calls to Boggsville, Tilton had urged his patient to come to the fort where, in the physician's own quarters, he could have around-the-clock care. A swift move was imperative because the spring snow melt in the Rocky Mountains was swelling the currents in the Arkansas and Purgatory rivers, both of which had to be forded between the Carson home and Fort Lyon. Kit agreed and on May 14 a mule-drawn army ambulance had conveyed him to Dr. Tilton's small stone residence at the east end of the fort's parade ground.

Kit's presence, the doctor reflected, "enabled me to make his condition much more comfortable." Over the next week, he administered chloroform to relieve the pain and coughing spasms, whenever his patient requested it. Carson, at his own request, lay propped up atop a bed of blankets and buffalo robes placed on the floor. That was the only position that seemed to ease his breathing, he claimed.[39]

The day after his arrival, May 15, Dr. Tilton persuaded him to make his will. The document is in the hand of the surgeon, and closes with the distinctive signature of "C. Carson." In it, Thomas O. Boggs is named executor of Kit's estate. The will was subsequently filed in the County Courthouse at Pueblo, Colorado.[40]

In the long hours of the day while he sat with Kit, Tilton read aloud Dr. Peters's biography and, prompted by the stirrings of memory, Carson from time to time would comment on the incidents of his eventful life.[41]

How distant it all must have seemed now: The family farm in Missouri and the faint image of a boy in his teens, sweating away at a saddler's workbench, just before his flight over the Santa Fe Trail that launched a long career in the Far West. Surely, as Kit contemplated his imminent demise, pictures of the three women with whom he had shared his adult life crowded his recollections. The submissive doe-like Waa-nibe, who was prepared to follow him wherever he roamed. The proud and assertive Making Out Road, who needed him less than he needed a surrogate mother for his two daughters. And finally, the light-hearted, faithful Josefa, whose love and devotion had sustained him for a quarter of a century.

Teresina Bent Scheurich says that when she and her mother Ignacia reached Boggsville from Taos, Tom Boggs brought word that Kit was so weak he was not up to seeing them, or his own children for that matter, as it would be too painful to think they were soon to be orphans.[42]

Toward the end, however, he partially relented and requested that eldest son William and youngest son Charles be brought to the fort to see him. The boys had a brief but memorable visit, during which their father sent out to the post sutler and bought them each a new hat. When the two parted with him, it was for the last time.

Fording the swollen Purgatory River on the way back to Boggsville, little Charles on a wagon seat in the wind saw his treasured gift fly off his head and into the water. Loss of that hat remained a source of sorrow as long as he lived.[43]

It is clear that Carson recognized the origin of his infirmity, as tracing back to the 1860 accident. His physician remembered that he said several times, pointing to his chest, "If it was not for this, I might live to be a hundred years old."[44]

The end of it all came dramatically, late in the day. Dr. Tilton was resting in the sick room. Aloys Scheurich, whom Kit always called affectionately, *compadre*, sat next to him, speaking quietly about something. Suddenly, the patient called out. "I sprang to him," Tilton stated, "and seeing a gush of blood from his mouth, remarked, 'This is the last of the general.' I supported his forehead on my hand, while death speedily closed the scene." The aneurysm had ruptured into the trachea. Death took place at 4:25 P.M., May 23, 1868.

Kit Carson's final exclamation, addressing his pair of companions, had been, "Doctor, compadre, adios!" His last two words on earth were in Spanish.[45]

The flag floating over the Fort Lyon parade ground was immediately lowered to half-staff and a messenger mounted a horse to carry the sad tidings to family and friends at Boggsville. The body of Kit Carson was laid in state in the office of the post adjutant. The following morning at 10 a.m., army chaplain, Rev. Gameliel Collins conducted a service attended by the troops and their families. At its conclusion, three rifle volleys were fired in the air, taps sounded, and as a procession carrying the casket started for Boggsville, the post artillery thundered a prolonged salute.[46]

Kit received temporary burial next to Josefa. In accord with his stated wish, the two caskets were raised within a year and transported to Taos for re-interment behind their own home. A Colorado newspaper perhaps provided the most fitting tribute, among the many, to Kit Carson. In announcing his death, it described him simply as "an American citizen of preeminent worth and usefulness."[47] Those unvarnished words would have immensely pleased the old soldier.

As observed at the beginning of this book, various impediments stand in the way of properly assessing Kit Carson's personal history as a family man. Prominent among the difficulties in that regard is the paucity of hard information about the private lives of his three wives. Even after assembling all available fragments from the documentary record, the researcher is still left with frustratingly weak profiles of these women.

That Waa-nibe, Making Out Road, and Josefa appear in history at all is owing almost entirely to the happenstance of their marriages to a frontier hero and national celebrity. In the absence of that association, they would now be completely forgotten.

These women moved in and out of Carson's life, like fillers between the episodic adventures that studded his career. That was true even of Josefa, who in her quarter century of wedlock knew months-long and even years-long periods in which she did not see her husband. No wonder then that Kit's family history tends to get lost in the narration of seemingly more exciting sides of his story.

Yet, it is well to remember that his marriage partners each exercised influence over his behavior and attitudes at particular moments in his life. Since the content of his inner world remains largely unknown to us, it is impossible to declare with any precision just how their influence might have shaped his decisions and performance while engaged in public service.

One thing we can say with fair certainty is that despite their father's best intentions, the Carson children keenly felt the strain of frequent partings with him, and the added anxiety in the 1860s over deterioration of his health. When within a matter of weeks, they lost both of their parents, the shock and psychological trauma must have been overwhelming. Confirmation is implicit in the painful recollection of an elderly Charles Carson: "That was a terrible time . . . and we children didn't know what would become of us."[48]

In point of fact, the Carson brood collectively seemed fated for misfortune. Four of them died tragically, and two others experienced major upheavals in their lives. To what degree those outcomes can be linked to the children's orphaning in 1868 remains a matter for speculation. The full history of Kit and Josefa's heirs is yet to be written.

So too is the final judgment on Kit Carson's place in history. The sullying of his once proud reputation that began in the late 1960s was a phenomenon coinciding with the rise of postmodernist thought, which drove the last nails in the coffin of nineteenth-century individualism, and which disavowed respect, or even recognition, for the time-honored concept of the heroic exemplar.

Although an independent, confident, self-motivated man, Carson had his flaws, and instances can be singled out in which he made serious errors of judgment. Nevertheless, on the whole he showed himself to be a moral person of firm character and expansive courage, attributes often recognized and acknowledged by his contemporaries. His life can be seen, therefore, as confirmation of the psychological truism that in the final analysis everything depends on the quality of the individual.

The closing words of the original biographer, Dr. DeWitt Clinton Peters, accurately sum up the authentic Kit. The physician and author wrote: "General Carson was a man of singularly striking virtues, for one who led such a rough kind of life. His gentleness of heart was shown in his love for his friends, and in his domestic inclination, for over and above all desire for adventure, he loved home!"[49]

Notes

Preface

1. Patricia Nelson Limerick, *The Legacy of Conquest: The Unbroken Past of the American West* (New York: W.W. Norton, 1987), 291.

2. Marc Simmons, "Kit and the Indians," in R. C. Gordon-McCutchan, ed., *Kit Carson: Indian Fighter or Indian Killer?* (Niwot: University Press of Colorado, 1996), 73–75.

3. September 18, 1857.

4. Letter of O. P. Byers to L. S. Hungerford, vice president, Pullman Co., Chicago, Dec. 11, 1923, Ms. Div., Kansas State Historical Society, Topeka.

5. Carter, *Dear Old Kit* (Norman: University of Oklahoma Press, 1968). Dunlay, *Kit Carson & the Indians* (Lincoln: University of Nebraska Press, 2000). Utley, *A Life Wild and Perilous* (New York: Henry Holt, 1997). Roberts, *A Newer World* (New York: Simon & Schuster, 2000).

6. DeWitt C. Peters to Kit Carson, Mar. 7, 1859, New York City, Carson Papers, Bancroft Library, University of California, Berkeley. (Hereinafter: BL, UC)

7. The most useful edition of the memoirs is included in Carter, *Dear Old Kit*, 37–150.

8. Dunlay, *Kit Carson & the Indians*, 142.

Introduction

1. Carter, '*Dear Old Kit*,' 42, 44.

2. Carter, '*Dear Old Kit*,' 50.

3. Thomasson, "Recollections of Kit Carson," printed speech delivered to the Military Order of the Loyal Legion of the United States, Chicago, March 1, 1928. Copy in Library of Congress, Washington, D.C.

4. Jerry Thompson, ed., *Civil War in the Southwest, Recollections of the Sibley Brigade* (College Station: Texas A&M University Press, 2001), 36.

5. Pamela Herr and Mary Lee Spence, eds., *The Letters of Jessie Benton Frémont* (Urbana: University of Illinois Press, 1993), 479.

6. Coulter interview, "With Kit Carson," *Rocky Mountain News*, Jan. 16, 1893.

7. Wynkoop, unpublished "Manuscript, 1876," 20. Colls. of the Colorado Historical Society, Denver. See also, *Daily New Mexican*, Feb. 24, 1886, Santa Fe, N.Mex.

Waa-Nibe

1. Rev. Samuel Parker, *Journal of an Exploring Tour Beyond the Rocky Mountains* (repr. ed. of 1838; Minneapolis: Ross and Haines, 1967), 75.

2. David J. Wishart, *The Fur Trade of the American West* (Lincoln: University of Nebraska Press, 1979), 191–93.

3. Philander Simmons, "Reminiscences of Kit Carson," Ms. 657, n.d., Harold B. Lee

Library, Brigham Young University, Provo, Utah. (Hereinafter: Lee, BYU)

4. Parker, *Journal*, 77.

5. Jeanette Hussey, *The Code Duello in America* (Washington, D.C.: Smithsonian Institution, 1980), 5, 7.

6. Parker, *Journal*, 79.

7. Carter, 'Dear Old Kit,' 63.

8. De Witt Clinton Peters, *The Life of Kit Carson, The Nestor of the Rocky Mountains* (1st ed.; New York: W. R. C. Clark, 1858), 92–94. Carter, 'Dear Old Kit,' 63.

9. Carter, 'Dear Old Kit,' 64, n. 73.

10. Leroy R. Hafen, *The Mountain Men and the Fur Trade of the Far West* (10 vols.; Glendale, Calif.: Arthur H. Clark Co., 1965–1972), 1:146.

11. Pay order of Lucien Fontenelle on Pratte, Chouteau & Co., to Joseph Chouinard, Sept. 17, 1834, Bellevue, P. Chouteau-Moffitt Coll., Missouri Historical Society, St. Louis. (Hereinafter: MHS)

12. Pay order of Lucien Fontenelle on Pratte, Chouteau & Co., to Kit Carson, July 8, 1834, Blackfork of Green River, P. Chouteau-Moffitt Coll., MHS. Dale L. Morgan and Eleanor Towless Harris, eds., *The Rocky Mountain Journals of William Marshall Anderson* (Lincoln: University of Nebraska Press, 1987), 277.

13. Cyprien Tanguay, comp., *Dictionaire Genealogique des Familles Canadiennes* (8 vols.; Montreal: Eusébe Senécal & Fils, 1887), 3:76–79. And personal interview with Dr. E. G. Chuinard, Independence, Mo., August 7, 1983.

14. Brown, "Three Years in the Rocky Mountains," (first published in 1845), reprinted in David A. White, ed., *News of the Plains and the Rockies, 1803–1865* (8 vols.; Spokane, Wash.: Arthur H. Clark Co., 1996), 1:396. DeVoto, "The Great Medicine Road," *American Mercury*, 11 (May 1927) 104.

15. Stewart, *Edward Warren* (repr. ed. of 1854; Missoula, Mont.: Mountain Press Publ. Co., 1986), 147–48. This book is "an autobiographical novel" based on the author's experiences with the mountain men. He attended more than one rendezvous, becoming quite well acquainted with Carson, Bridger, and others. Carson's quote from his memoirs appears in Carter, 'Dear Old Kit,' 63.

16. David Brown in his "Three Years in the Rocky Mountains," 396, establishes that Chouinard had been drinking before the duel.

17. Brown, "Three Years in the Rocky Mountains," 396, speaks of Kit bridling his horse. But from the circumstances he describes, it appears that Kit did not take time to go for a saddle.

18. Bil Gilbert, *Westering Man, The Life of Joseph Walker* (New York: Atheneum, 1983), 21. Carter has a different view, saying that Carson tended to be hot-headed in a fight. 'Dear Old Kit,' 197.

19. Carter, 'Dear Old Kit,' 65.

20. Carter, 'Dear Old Kit,' 65.

21. Parker, *Journal*, 79. Brown, "Three Years in the Rocky Mountains," 396. Kit provided some small details about the fight, not included in his memoirs, that appeared in an unsigned article in the Washington *Daily Union*, June 15, 1847, titled "Kit Carson of the

West." Jessie Benton Frémont's biographer, Pamela Herr, thinks that Jessie, a warm friend of Carson's, probably wrote the article. Herr and Spence, *Letters of Jessie Benton Frémont*, 105, n. 3. However, an introductory note in the original issue of the *Union* makes clear that the anonymous author was "a gentleman." Harvey Carter included a somewhat abbreviated version of the article (omitting, for example, the introductory note) as an appendix in his *'Dear Old Kit,'* 222–30. On Shunar's wound, also see Dale L. Morgan's "Notes on the Fur Trade, David L. Brown," n.d., microfilm ed., reel 79, BL, UC.

22. Henry Inman, *The Old Santa Fe Trail* (Topeka: Crane & Co., 1899), 385. The only writer to take note of Inman's reference to the horse "rearing" at the moment of fire was Edwin L. Sabin, who failed to draw any conclusion. *Kit Carson Days* (Chicago: A. C. McClurg, 1914; and 2nd expanded ed., 2 vols.; New York: Press of the Pioneers, 1935), 1:260.

23. Inman, *Tales of the Trail* (Topeka: Crane & Co., 1898), 261. Jessie Benton Frémont also claimed to have seen the scar, and said it was on the collar bone. "Kit Carson," *Land of Sunshine*, 6 (February 1897), 101. So despite some reports that Kit escaped the duel unscathed, he evidently received a superficial wound.

24. Morgan and Harris, *Journals of William Marshall Anderson*, 277.

25. Carter, *'Dear Old Kit,'* 65.

26. Parker, *Journal*, 79–80.

27. Carter, *'Dear Old Kit,'* 65, n. 75.

28. Brown, "Three Years in the Rocky Mountains," 396.

29. Tom Dunlay in his monumental *Kit Carson & The Indians*, 73, suggests convincingly that the Rev. Parker's companion, missionary-physician Dr. Marcus Whitman, probably was summoned to tend the wounded "Shunar," if the Frenchman in fact remained among the living, or if not, to conduct a post-mortem examination. That would explain Parker's very precise description of the wound in his *Journal*, 79. This theory was first floated in Personal Correspondence, Dunlay to Marc Simmons, July 31, 1995.

30. This Peters quote appears in the second edition, retitled, *Kit Carson's Life and Adventures* (Hartford, Conn.: Dustin Gilman & Co., 1873), 112.

31. Peters, *Kit Carson* (1873), 115–16.

32. Smith H. Simpson to Edwin L. Sabin, Nov. 10, 1911, Christopher Carson Coll., Lee, BYU. Sabin's letter of inquiry to Simpson, dated Nov. 8, 1911, is preserved in the Smith Simpson Papers, Kit Carson Archive, Southwest Research Center of Northern New Mexico, Taos. (Hereinafter: KC, SRC)

33. Quaife, Milo Milton, ed., *Kit Carson's Autobiography* (Chicago: Lakeside Press, 1935), 44, n. 33. Carter, *'Dear Old Kit,'* 65, n. 75.

34. June 15, 1847.

35. Simpson to Sabin, Nov. 10, 1911, Lee, BYU.

36. Brown, "Three Years in the Rocky Mountains," 396.

37. Stanley Vestal, *Kit Carson, The Happy Warrior of the Old West* (Boston: Houghton Mifflin Co., 1928), 126–27. For Bent's comments about Carson, see George E. Hyde, *A Life of George Bent, Written From His Letters* (Norman: University of Oklahoma Press, 1967), 62–68. And, Quaife, *Kit Carson's Autobiography*, 44, n. 3. This is an early, thinly edited

version of the Carson memoirs. In the note, Quaife quotes from a personal letter to him, undated, written by Vestal, referring to the "Arapaho Watan, now deceased."

38. Vestal, *Kit Carson*, 126. And, John R. Swanton, *The Indian Tribes of North America* (BAE Bull. 145; Washington, D.C.: Smithsonian Institution, 1953), 389.

39. Vestal, *Kit Carson*, 119.

40. Bernice Blackwelder in her biography, *Great Westerner, The Story of Kit Carson* (Caldwell, Idaho: Caxton Printers, 1962), 61, proposes that such was the case.

41. Vestal, *Kit Carson*, 115–25. Peters, *Kit Carson's Life and Adventures* (1873), 115.

42. Vestal, *Kit Carson*, 125. The author kept records of his interviews with the Indians, but as he reported in 1935: "Unhappily my notes were destroyed by a flood which filled the basement of the [university] building where my boxes were stored when I was on leave." W. S. Campbell (a.k.a. Stanley Vestal) to Milo M. Quaife, Detroit, February 28, 1935, W. S. Campbell Coll., box 71, f. 2. Western History Colls., University of Oklahoma Library, Norman.

43. See, e.g., Ann Hafen, "Campfire Frontier," *Rocky Mountain Empire Magazine* (September 1, 1946), 5–6.

44. Morgan, "The Fur Trade and Its Historians," *The American West*, 3 (spring 1966), 31. Camp, "Review of Kit Carson, The Happy Warrior of the Old West," *California Historical Society Quarterly*, 7 (September, 1928), 194–95.

45. Tassin, *Stanley Vestal, Champion of the Old West* (Glendale, Calif.: Arthur H. Clark Co., 1973), 16–17.

46. Vestal, *Kit Carson*, 115. M. Morgan Estergreen, in her *Kit Carson, A Portrait in Courage* (Norman: University of Oklahoma Press, 1962), 69, declares: "Camped a short distance from the trappers' lodge was a band of Arapaho Indians who had come to the rendezvous to trade." On this question, see the doubts expressed by Carter, 'Dear Old Kit,' 64, n. 74. And, Dunlay, *Kit Carson & The Indians*, 71.

47. Dodge, *Our Wild Indians*, 597.

48. Jacqueline Peterson, "Prelude to Red River: A Social Portrait of the Great Lakes Métis," *Ethnohistory*, 25 (winter 1978), 47.

49. Quoted by Dunlay, *Kit Carson & The Indians*, 79.

50. Swagerty, "Indian Trade in the Trans Mississippi West to 1870," in Wilcomb E. Washburn, ed., *History of Indian-White Relations*, vol. 4 of William C. Sturtevant, gen. ed., *Handbook of North American Indians* (Washington, D.C.: Smithsonian Institution, 1988), 367–68.

51. Walter O'Meara, *Daughters of the Country, The Women of the Fur Traders and Mountain Men* (New York: Harcourt, Brace & World, 1968), 55–56.

52. Sister M. Inez Higer, *Arapaho Child Life and Its Cultural Background* (BAE Bull. 148; Washington, D.C.: Smithsonian Institution, 1952), 212. Virginia Cole Trenholm, *The Arapahoes, Our People* (Norman: University of Oklahoma Press, 1970), 58–59. Photos from several tribes show adulterous women with the tips of their noses missing. For a published example, see H. Henrietta Stockel, *Women of the Apache Nation* (Reno: University of Nevada Press, 1991), 20.

53. O'Meara, *Daughters of the Country,* 47. And, Gilbert, *Westering Man,* 165.

54. William R. Swagerty, "Marriage and Settlement Patterns of Rocky Mountain Trappers and Traders," *Western Historical Quarterly,* 11 (April 1980), 164.

55. Gilbert, *Westering Man,* 164. Standard works on the life of Meek, who was associated with Carson in various adventures, are Frances Fuller Victor, *The River of the West* (Hartford, Conn.: Columbian Book Co., 1870); and, Harvey Tobie, *No Man Like Joe. The Life and Times of Joseph L. Meek* (Portland, Ore.: Binfords & Mort, 1949).

56. Col. Dodge in *Our Wild Indians,* 218, states that an Indian father could get a bride price from a whiteman twice the amount he could expect from an Indian. He adds: "Having sold and got his price, he feels relieved of all responsibility regarding her."

57. Dr. Peters's revised biography refers to Kit's first wife only as "an Indian girl." *Kit Carson's Life and Adventures* (1873), 174. Sabin's first edition of his *Kit Carson Days* (1914), 201, likewise, uses "Arapaho girl," and in his pages she remains unnamed. Unfortunately, the name Waa-nibe, with its spelling and translation, appears initially in Vestal, *Kit Carson* (1928), 118–19, spreading from there widely throughout the Carson literature during the remainder of the twentieth century. Vestal's source was his elderly Arapaho informant, Watan, and since names are more apt to stick in the memory than anything else, the accuracy of the name Waa-nibe can probably be accepted with a fair amount of confidence. Still, because it is Vestal derived, the shadow of doubt cannot be entirely lifted.

58. Sabin, *Kit Carson Days* (1914), 201.

59. Dr. LeRoy R. Hafen, State Historian of Colorado, first waved a red flag when he, rather mildly, referred to the Wiggins material as "a line of questionable stories," in his "Fort Davy Crockett, Its Fur Men and Visitors," *The Colorado Magazine,* 29 (January 1952), 27. The definitive dethroning of Wiggins was accomplished by Lorene and Kenny Englert, "Oliver Perry Wiggins, Fantastic, Bombastic, Frontiersman," *The Denver Westerners Monthly Roundup,* 20 (February 1964), 3–14. The authors strengthened their case in a monograph, with the same title (Palmer Lake, Colo.: Filter Press, 1968). Harvey Carter in his widely respected *'Dear Old Kit,'* 20–22, commented upon the Englert findings at length and concluded, "I am prepared to state that nothing Wiggins said of his relations with Carson was true." For a brief summary of Wiggins as "the source of much misinformation about Kit Carson and mountain man frontier days," consult Dan L. Thrapp, *Encyclopedia of Frontier Biography* (3 vols.; Glendale, Calif.: Arthur H. Clark Co., 1988), 3:1563.

60. Oliver P. Wiggins, "How I First Met Kit Carson," *The Garden of the Gods Magazine,* 1 (Part 1, June 1902), 19. And 1 (Part 2, October 1902), 31–34. Although Wiggins is credited as the author, it is apparent that an anonymous interviewer was recording his oral statement and adding explanatory text.

61. Sabin, *Kit Carson Days* (1914), 201.

62. Carter, *'Dear Old Kit,'* 65.

63. Frank C. Robertson, *Fort Hall, Gateway to the Oregon Country* (New York: Hastings House, 1963), 65–68.

64. Blackwelder, *Great Westerner,* 65.

65. Carter, *'Dear Old Kit,'* 65.

66. For an overview of the tragedy, see, Clyde D. Dollar, "The High Plains Smallpox Epidemic of 1837–38," *Western Historical Quarterly*, 8 (January 1977), 13–18. The devastating effects on the Blackfeet are described by John C. Ewers, *The Blackfeet, Raiders of the Northwestern Plains* (Norman: University of Oklahoma Press, 1958), 65–66.

67. Carter, '*Dear Old Kit*,' 76, n. 108. Sabin, *Kit Carson Days* (1935), 2:150.

68. Beale communicated Kit's words to John Charles Frémont who included them in his *Memoirs of My Life* (Chicago: Belford, Clarke & Co., 1887), 74. Regarding the circumstances that led Beale to obtain that quote, see Gerald Thompson, *Edward F. Beale & The American West* (Albuquerque: University of New Mexico Press, 1983), 24.

69. Carter, '*Dear Old Kit*,' 70–71.

70. Hilger, *Arapaho Child Life*, 16–17. Alfred E. Kroeber, *The Arapaho* (Bull. 18; New York: American Museum of Natural History, 1902), 54–58.

71. Quantrille D. McClung, comp., *Carson-Bent-Boggs Genealogy* (Denver: Denver Public Library, 1962), 18. And, *Carson-Bent-Boggs Genealogy, Supplement* (1973), 195. Arapaho children were given names in a special naming ceremony, but they could be changed later in life. See Jeffrey Anderson, *The Four Hills of Life: Northern Arapaho Knowledge and Life Movement* (Lincoln: University of Nebraska Press, 2001), 131.

72. Pioneer freighter Alexander Majors remarked in his memoirs that, "The Cheyenne and Arapahoes were especially noted for their skill in sign language." *Seventy Years on the Frontier* (repr. ed. of 1893; Minneapolis: Ross & Haines, Inc., 1965), 121.

73. Carter, '*Dear Old Kit*,' 71.

74. Wishart, *The Fur Trade*, 185.

75. Hafen, "Fort Davy Crockett," 19. Osborne Russell, who attended the 1838 rendezvous, stated that it ended on July 20. Aubrey L. Haines, ed., *Journal of a Trapper* (Lincoln: University of Nebraska Press, 1955), 90.

76. Carter, '*Dear Old Kit*,' 71.

77. Hafen, "Fort Davy Crockett," 18.

78. Sabin, *Kit Carson Days* (1914), 177. Carter, '*Dear Old Kit*,' 71.

79. LeRoy R. Hafen and Ann W. Hafen, eds., *To The Rockies and Oregon, 1839–1842* (Glendale, Calif.: Arthur H. Clark Co., 1955), 174.

80. The existence of this daughter was long unknown to Carson biographers. Reference to her was buried in the interview notebooks compiled by Colorado avocational historian Francis W. Cragin between 1903 and 1910. From Kit Carson's nephew-in-law, Jesse Nelson, Cragin obtained his information on this subject. See Francis W. Cragin's unpublished "Early Far West Notebooks," VIII, no. 75, The Colorado Springs Pioneers Museum, Colorado Springs, Colo. (Hereinafter: CSPM) For background, consult, Dorothy Price Shaw, "The Cragin Collection," *Colorado Magazine*, 25 (July 1948), 166–78.

81. Peters, *Kit Carson's Life and Adventures* (1873), 174.

82. See e.g. Estergreen, *Kit Carson*, 71.

83. For my narrative, I have accepted this time frame, proposed by Thelma S. Guild and Harvey L. Carter, *Kit Carson, A Pattern for Heroes* (Lincoln: University of Nebraska Press, 1984), 92, but with reservations. David Lavender has Kit moving to Bent's Fort in

1839, with Waa-nibe and Adaline in tow, and Waa-nibe dying there. *Bent's Fort* (Garden City, N.Y.: Doubleday & Co., 1954), 184. He may have been following the shaky lead of Vestal, *Kit Carson*, 153; 178–79, who presents a fanciful death scene for Waa-nibe at Bent's Fort. Both authors could have been misled by Oliver P. Wiggins, whose "recollections" they accepted as valid.

84. Carter, *'Dear Old Kit,'* 71–72.

85. Blackwelder, (*Great Westerner*, 80–81) was the first writer to suggest that Kit had his daughters baptized at the 1840 rendezvous. Although no contemporary source confirms it, her speculation seems warranted.

86. Quoted in Forbes Parkhill, *The Blazed Trail of Antoine Leroux* (Los Angeles: Westernlore Press, 1965), 75.

87. Carter, *'Dear Old Kit,'* 78–79.

88. William Swilling Wallace, *Antoine Robidiux, 1794–1860* (Los Angeles: Glen Dawson, 1953), 14–17. And John D. Barton, *Buckskin Entrepreneur: Antoine Robioux and the Fur Trade of the Uinta Basin, 1824–1844* (Vernal, Utah: Oakfield Publishing Co., 1996), 89.

89. Guild and Carter, *Kit Carson*, 92.

90. Peters, *Kit Carson's Life and Adventures* (1873), 74.

91. Carter, *'Dear Old Kit,'* 77.

92. Dodge, *Our Wild Indians*, 245.

Making Out Road

1. T. Lindsey Baker and Billy R. Harrison, *Adobe Walls* (College Station: Texas A&M University Press, 1986), 3–4. And, *Missouri Republican*, July 3, 1840.

2. McClung, *Carson-Bent-Boggs Genealogy*, 98. Lavender, *Bent's Fort*, 174, gives the probable marriage year as 1837.

3. Mark L. Gardner, "The Bent Brothers and the Call of the West," *Russell's West* [The C. M. Russell Museum Magazine], 6 (autumn 1998), 13. David Greco, "The Legend of Little Whiteman," *Persimmon Hill*, 17 (winter 1990), 37. Since William was from an upper-class St. Louis family, his taking an Indian wife must have raised eyebrows.

4. Carter, *'Dear Old Kit,'* 79.

5. The epistolary argumentation was published together under the title, "An Informative Dialogue-by-Letter About Kit Carson's Early, Uncertain Chronology," *Montana Magazine*, 16 (July 1968), 86–90.

6. Peters, *The Life of Kit Carson* (1858), 129. Sabin, *Kit Carson Days* (1914), 179–80.

7. Sabin, *Kit Carson Days* (1935), 1:280. Lavender, *Bent's Fort*, 184, written in 1954 accepts Sabin's 1838–1842 inclusive dates for Kit's presence there, and states, as have some other modern writers, that Waa-nibe accompanied him and died at the fort. No published mention of Waa-nibe dying at Bent's Fort, seen by this writer, traces back to a reliable source.

8. A brief summary of Charlotte Green's personal history appears in Marc Simmons, "Servant Couple Created a Legacy at Bent's Fort," *New Mexican* (Santa Fe), January 12, 2002. [Reprinted in *Wagon Tracks*, 16 (February 2002), 7]. Western author Ralph Moody

in an undated [ca. 1963] letter to Charles Wood (grandson of Kit Carson), states: "All of the sources with which I am familiar say that . . . Kit placed Adaline under the care of William Bent's Negro slave, Charlotte, who mothered her until he took her to St. Louis." Copy of the letter courtesy of John Pimm of Bristol, England, in possession of the present author. On Charlotte Green, see also Estergreen, *Kit Carson*, 84.

9. The battle, which took place on Wolf Creek, a tributary of the North Canadian River, is described in detail by George Bird Grinnell, *The Fighting Cheyennes* (repr. ed. of 1945; Norman: University of Oklahoma Press, 1956), 45–62.

10. Donald J. Berthrong, *The Southern Cheyennes* (Norman: University of Oklahoma Press, 1963), 83.

11. Lavender, *Bent's Fort*, 188.

12. Vestal, *Kit Carson*, 181. The author's description of Kit's first meeting with Making Out Road, whom he claims was riding around the encampment with a chum, is extraordinarily similar to the initial meeting between Kit and Waa-nibe at the Green River rendezvous that Vestal told about earlier in his book. Very little that he relates in his detailed chapter on Making Out Road can be accepted unconditionally.

13. For a sketch of Grinnell's varied career, consult, Thrapp, *Encyclopedia of Frontier Biography*, 2:590–91.

14. Grinnell, "Bent's Old Fort and Its Builders," *Collections of the Kansas State Historical Society, 1919–1922*, 15 (Topeka, 1923), 37.

15. Vestal, *Kit Carson*, 181.

16. Ida Ellen Rath, *The Rath Trail* (Wichita, Kans.: McCormick-Armstrong Co., 1961), 11–12. The author was a daughter-in-law of Charles Rath, who was briefly married to Making Out Road in the early 1860s.

17. Grinnell, *The Fighting Cheyennes*, 46.

18. This information derives from Making Out Road's daughter by a later husband. Rath, *The Rath Trail*, 18.

19. Grinnell, *The Cheyenne Indians, Their History and Ways of Life* (2 vols.; New Haven, Conn.: Yale University Press, 1923), 1:90–91. Rath, *The Rath Trail*, 11.

20. Rath, *The Rath Trail*, 12.

21. O'Meara, *Daughters of the Country*, 58, 190–91.

22. Simpson to Sabin, Nov. 10, 1911, Christopher Carson Coll., Lee, BYU.

23. Frémont, *Memoirs*, 74. Jessie Frémont, "Kit Carson," 98.

24. Estergreen, *Kit Carson*, 77.

25. For Blackwelder's view on this question, see her *Great Westerner*, 62–63.

26. Carter, "Kit Carson," in Hafen, *The Mountain Men*, 6:116, n. 26.

27. Hyde, *A Life of George Bent*, 67.

28. Gregg, *Commerce of the Prairies* (repr. ed. of 1844; Norman: University of Oklahoma Press, 1990), 104.

29. Historian Fray Angélico Chávez, studying the Taos parish registers that show baptisms and marriages, observed the unexpected explosion of population after 1826 and its steady growth over the next two decades. See his *But Time and Chance, The Story of Padre*

Martínez of Taos, 1793–1867 (Santa Fe: Sunstone Press, 1981), 27.

30. Allen H. Bent, *The Bent Family in America* (Boston: David Clapp & Son, 1900), 123. Lavender, *Bent's Fort*, 165, 393.

31. Cragin, "Early Far West Notebooks," VIII, no. 51, and, XII, no. 15. Janet Lecompte, *Pueblo, Hardscrabble, Greenhorn, The Upper Arkansas, 1832–1856* (Norman: University of Oklahoma Press, 1978), 72–73.

32. Estergreen, *Kit Carson*, 86.

33. Garrard, *Wah-to-yah and the Taos Trail* (repr. ed. of 1850; Norman: University of Oklahoma Press, 1955), 181.

34. For the interpretation of Making Out Road's state of mind as a result of this marital incident, I am relying on her behavior at a later date during a similar episode, when she believed that her then husband Charles Rath had left her for another woman. Rath, *The Rath Trail*, 177.

35. Robert H. Lowie, *Indians of the Plains* (New York: McGraw Hill Book Co., 1954), 80.

36. O'Meara, *Daughters of the Country*, 62–63. Grinnell, *The Cheyenne Indians*, 1:53.

37. Vestal, *Kit Carson*, 184.

38. Sabin, *Kit Carson Days* (1935), 1:312. Grinnell, *Bent's Old Fort*, 37.

39. The phrasing here is Lavender's, *Bent's Fort*, 206; but for other examples that make the point, see, O'Meara, *Daughters of the Country*, 201; Dunlay, *Kit Carson*, 60; and Roberts, *A Newer World*, 100. That Making Out Road followed standard native procedure for a divorce would confirm, in Indian eyes at least, that they had, indeed, been husband and wife.

40. Vestal, *Kit Carson*, 185.

41. Grinnell, "Bent's Old Fort," 37.

42. Sabin, *Kit Carson Days* (1935), 1:312.

43. Sabin's source for this, he claims inexactly, was "letters from Carson descendants." *Kit Carson Days* (1935), 2:936, n. 261. This collection, of his own personal correspondence with Carson family members, he sold in the mid 1930s to Denver Americana dealer Fred Rosenstock, and it was eventually acquired by the Harold B. Lee Library, Brigham Young University, Provo, Utah. Donald E. Bower, *Fred Rosenstock, A Legend in Books and Art* (Flagstaff, Ariz.: Northland Press, 1976), 124.

44. Roberts, *A Newer World*, 100.

45. Lavender, *Bent's Fort*, 206.

46. Copies in Spanish of both the baptismal and marriage certificates are on file in the KC, SRC, and in Collections of the Manuscript Division, Library of Congress, Washington, D.C. (Hereinafter: LCMD) An English translation of the baptismal certificate is given in Sabin, *Kit Carson Days* (1935), 1:313–14. See also, Brother Claudius Antony, "Kit Carson, Catholic," *New Mexico Historical Review*, 10 (October 1935), 323–36. (Hereinafter: *NMHR*) The actual date written out in the baptismal book is January 28, 1842. However, surrounding dates on the page are all for documents dated 1843. Genealogist Fray Angélico Chávez concluded that the copyist probably made an error in setting down the year (easily done in January) and Kit was actually baptized January 28, 1843. See his *Origins of New Mexico Families* (revision of 1954 ed.; Santa Fe: Museum of New Mexico Press, 1992), 410. However, it

seems just as likely that the 1842 record through an oversight had not been entered in the baptismal book and its omission, discovered prior to Kit and Josefa's wedding, was corrected by placing it among the current 1843 entries, but with the accurate original date. Kit's age given in the certificate seems to confirm 1842 as the correct year of his baptism.

47. Correspondence, Margaret S. McGuinn, Spartanberg, N.C., January 31, 1942, to Q. D. McClung, Genealogical Dept., Denver Public Library. A copy of this letter is in the Carson File, Colorado Historical Society, Denver.

48. Carter, '*Dear Old Kit*,' 81.

49. *Missouri Republican*, May 19, 1842.

50. Cragin, "Early Far West Notebooks," XII, no. 21. Cragin's information in this matter came from an interview with Kit's daughter Teresina Carson Allen at her home in Raton, N.Mex., March 18, 1908.

51. For this information, I am indebted to historian Mark L. Gardner, who also advised me, Nov. 17, 2001, that owing to the lack of surviving business records, as well as personal correspondence of Charles and William Bent, the commercial arrangements between Bent, St. Vrain & Co. and others are murky.

52. Ledger book CC, p. 359, Chouteau-Moffitt Coll., MHS, as cited by Lecompte, *Pueblo, Hardscrabble, Greenhorn*, 278, n. 14.

53. Ida Ellen Rath reported that Making Out Road also had three boys, but their names and who their fathers were are unknown. *The Rath Trail*, 12. Also, Grinnell, "Bent's Old Fort," 37.

54. Thrapp, "Charles Rath," in *Encyclopedia of Frontier Biography*, 3:1192.

55. Rath, *The Rath Trail*, 12.

56. Rath, *The Rath Trail*, 24–25. C. Robert Haywood, *The Merchant Prince of Dodge City, The Life and Times of Robert M. Wright* (Norman: University of Oklahoma Press, 1998), 39–43, and 201, n. 2.

57. Rath, *The Rath Trail*, 12, 132.

58. Grinnell, "Bent's Old Fort," 37. Rath, *The Rath Trail*, 13.

59. Adrienne Christopher, "Daniel Yoacham, Pioneer Innkeeper of Westport," *Westport Historical Quarterly*, 1 (November 1965), 3–7.

60. Adrienne Christopher, ed., "Recollections of Susannah Yoacham Dillon," *Westport Historical Quarterly*, 1 (November 1965), 11.

61. The U.S. Census, 1840, Howard County, Missouri, includes Rebecca Carson Martin as the wife of Joseph Martin, Kit's step-father. Joseph remarried during May, 1842, suggesting that Rebecca had died sometime during the previous year, the exact date as yet undetermined. McClung, *Carson-Bent-Boggs Genealogy*, 16.

62. Quoted in Sabin, *Kit Carson Days* (1935), 1:314–15. See also, Blackwelder, *Great Westerner*, 99–100. H. Denny Davis, "Kit Carson Brought Daughter Here For Schooling," *Fayette Advertiser* (Missouri), October 1, 1986.

63. Carter, '*Dear Old Kit*,' 81.

64. William M. Lytle and Forest R. Holdcamper, comps., *Merchant Steam Vessels of the United States, 1790–1868* (New York: Steamship Historical Society of America, 1975), 189,

294. In 1844 the Rowena burned to its waterline.

65. Carter, *'Dear Old Kit,'* 81.

66. Frémont, *Memoirs*, 74.

67. Blackwelder, *Great Westerner*, 100, n. 13.

68. Peters, *Kit Carson's Life and Adventures* (1873), 174.

69. The tradition is described in a small religious pamphlet by Eugene P. Murphy, S.J., *Blessed Philippine Duchesne—Pioneer Apostle of the Sacred Heart* (St. Louis: Radio League of the Sacred Heart, 1940). See, Father Frank N. Schepers, Sacred Heart Church, to Jack Boyer, Dir., Kit Carson Museum, Nov. 13, 1961, in Carson File, KC, SRC.

70. On Maxwell's possible role, see Lawrence R. Murphy, *Lucien Bonaparte Maxwell, Napoleon of the Southwest* (Norman: University of Oklahoma Press, 1983), 39. Also, Lavender, *Bent's Fort*, 211–12.

71. Of the many editions of Frémont's official reports, the best, containing much ancillary documentation and excellent annotations, is Donald Jackson and Mary Lee Spence, eds., *The Expeditions of John Charles Frémont* (3 vols.; Urbana: University of Illinois Press, 1970–1984). Steckmesser, *The Western Hero in History and Legend* (Norman: University of Oklahoma Press, 1965), 17.

72. The power of attorney document is preserved in the Howard County Deed Book U, p. 244, Fayette, Mo. In the same book, p. 230, is a deed for the sale of Kit's land, dated June 5, 1842 and signed Linsey Carson, Agent for Christopher Carson. These documents were discovered by H. Denny Davis who supplied copies to the author.

73. Carter, *'Dear Old Kit,'* 81.

74. Carter, *'Dear Old Kit,'* 84–85.

75. Carter, *'Dear Old Kit,'* 85–86, n. 133.

76. Jackson and Spence, *Expeditions of Frémont*, 1:151. Although Carson had been hired as a guide only, he seems to have been pressed into service as hunter along the way, when Maxwell did not prove entirely satisfactory in that role.

77. McClung, *Carson-Bent-Boggs Genealogy*, 71. The marriage date is also recorded among hand-written entries in the Bent Family Bible, preserved in the Fray Angélico Chávez History Library, Museum of New Mexico, Santa Fe. (Hereinafter: FACHL)

Josefa, Chapter 1

1. Cather, *Death Comes for the Archbishop* (New York: Alfred A. Knopf, 1955), 154. Journalist Albert D. Richardson in 1859, for example, after a stay at the Carson house, referred to Josefa as "an intelligent Spanish lady." *Beyond the Mississippi* (Hartford, Conn.: American Publishing Co., 1867), 260. And Army surgeon Dr. George Gwyther, who knew the Carsons at Fort Garland, Colorado, in 1866, called Josefa, "a most amiable and graceful lady." Others too used the description "lady" with some regularity. "A Frontier Post and Country," *Overland Monthly*, 5 (December 1870), 526.

2. On this subject see the comments of Harvard-educated O. W. Williams, who first came to the Southwest for his health in the latter 1870s. Printed letter, Williams, Fort Stockton, Texas, March 8, 1931, to Capt. Jesse C. Williams, in the Albright Coll., KC, SRC.

The common practice of referring to one's Indian grandmother as "a Cherokee princess," in the bid to improve her social status, can still be found in some quarters.

3. Chávez, *Origins of New Mexico Families*, 199. José Antonio Esquibel and John B. Colligan, *The Spanish Recolonization of New Mexico, An Account of the Families Recruited at Mexico City*, 1693 (Albuquerque: Hispanic Genealogical Research Center of New Mexico, 1999), 225–26. Chuck Chapman, comp., "Jaramillo Family: A Colonial Family of New Mexico," unpublished, unpaginated typescript, Carson Coll., KC, SRC. Roque shortened the family surname Jaramillo Negrete, using simply Jaramillo.

4. Chapman, "Jaramillo Family." For official grant papers see, Roque Jacinto Jaramillo Grant, case no. 228, Records of the U.S. Court of Private Land Claims, reel no. 52, NMSRCA.

5. Santa Cruz de la Cañada Baptisms, Archives of the Archdiocese of Santa Fe, microfilm edition, reel 13 (1795–1819) and reel 14 (1820–1833). Place of baptism is not listed for the first two children, possibly just an oversight on the part of the Potrero priest.

6. Louis F. Serna, "Descendants of Francisco Estavan Jaramillo," unpublished manuscript, copy in possession of the author.

7. Seventh Census of the United States, 1850, New Mexico, sheet 162, reel 3, Taos County, NMSRCA.

8. Chávez, *Origins of New Mexico Families*, 311–12. John B. Colligan, *The Juan Paéz Hurtado Expedition of* 1695 (Albuquerque: University of New Mexico Press, 1995), 39–40.

9. F. Stanley, *Giant in Lilliput, The Story of Donaciano Vigil* (Pampa, Tex.: Pampa Print Shop, 1963), 129. Estergreen, *Kit Carson*, 125, no. 2.

10. "Cornelio B. Vigil," biographical typescript, Carson Coll., KC, SRC.

11. Herbert O. Brayer, *William Blackmore: The Spanish-Mexican Land Grants of New Mexico and Colorado*, 1863–1878 (2 vols.; Denver: Bradford-Robinson, 1949), 1:127–32. Leroy R. Hafen, "Mexican Land Grants in Colorado," *The Colorado Magazine*, 4 (May 1927), 87–88.

12. Serna, "Descendants of Francisco Estevan Jaramillo," 1. Santa Cruz de la Cañada Baptisms, reel 13 (1820–1833), NMSRCA.

13. Richard D. Woods, comp., *Hispanic First Names* (Westport, Conn.: Greenwood Press, 1984), 107.

14. Jacqueline Dorgan Meketa, *Legacy of Honor, The Life of Rafael Chacón* (Albuquerque: University of New Mexico Press, 1986), 123.

15. Personal correspondence, Prof. Nasario Gracía, Las Vegas, N.Mex., to Marc Simmons, December 10, 2001.

16. Correspondence, Joseph Beuthner to Christopher Carson, Fernando de Taos, January 6, 1864, Christopher Carson Coll., doc. #28, Lee, BYU.

17. Mrs. Hal Russell, comp., *Land of Enchantment, Memoirs of Marian Russell on the Santa Fe Trail* (repr. of 1954 ed.; Albuquerque: University of New Mexico Press, 1984), 51.

18. Antony, "Kit Carson, Catholic," 326. McClung, *Carson-Bent-Boggs Genealogy*, 84.

19. McClung, *Carson-Bent-Boggs Genealogy*, 177–78. Lecompte, *Pueblo, Hardscrabble, Greenhorn*, 72.

20. Lecompte, *Pueblo, Hardscrabble, Greenhorn*, 72. Rebecca McDowell Craver, *The*

Notes

Impact of Intimacy, Mexican-Anglo Intermarriage in New Mexico, 1821–1846 (El Paso: Texas Western Press, 1982), 11.

21. Gutiérrez, *When Jesus Came, The Corn Mothers Went Away: Marriage, Sexuality, and Power in New Mexico, 1500–1846* (Stanford, Calif.: Stanford University Press, 1991), 271–72. Beatrice Gottlieb, *The Family in the Western World* (New York: Oxford University Press, 1995), 60.

22. O'Meara, *Daughters of the Country*, 285.

23. On the subject of parental consent in marriage among the New Mexicans, see Gutiérrez, *When Jesus Came*, 248–55; and Craver, *The Impact of Intimacy*, 14–15. Some of the contradictions surrounding the topic are explored in Asunción Lavrin, ed., *Sexuality and Marriage in Colonial Latin America* (Lincoln: University of Nebraska Press, 1992), 209–13.

24. Albert H. Schroeder, "Kit Carson House," *La Gaceta* [El Corral de Santa Fe Westerners], 5 (1970), 21. Also see promotional literature, "Kit Carson Home and Museum," on file, KC, SRC.

25. Personal correspondence, Jerry Padilla, Taos, N.Mex., to Marc Simmons, January 27, 1992.

26. Gutiérrez, *When Jesus Came*, 231.

27. The foregoing summary of Kit's movements is expanded in Lavender's *Bent's Fort*, 224–26.

28. Carter, *'Dear Old Kit,'* 87–88.

29. Carter, *'Dear Old Kit,'* 88ff.

30. For example, in the last letter dictated by Carson, May 5, 1868, from Boggsville, Colorado, he spoke of Ignacia as "the Old Lady." Letter printed in William A. Keleher, *Turmoil in New Mexico, 1846–1868* (Santa Fe: Rydal Press, 1952), 136.

31. Frank D. Reeve, ed., "The Charles Bent Papers," *NMHR*, 30 (July 1955), 254.

32. Among hand-written inscriptions in the Bent Family Bible, Alfredo Bent is referred to uniformly as Elfego Bent. The Bible is in the FACHL. Another Bent Bible is in possession of the Colorado Historical Society, Denver. The most complete genealogical table for the Charles Bent children appears in Serna, "Descendants of Francisco Esteban Jaramillo," 2–3. But see also, McClung, *Carson-Bent-Boggs Genealogy*, 91–92. And, Allen H. Bent, *The Bent Family in America*, 123.

33. Serna, "Descendants of Francisco Esteban Jaramillo," 7. McClung, *Carson-Bent-Boggs Genealogy*, 84.

34. James Josiah Webb, *Adventures in the Santa Fe Trade* (Glendale, Calif.: Arthur H. Clark Co., 1931), 63–64.

35. Carter, *'Dear Old Kit,'* 95.

36. Harvey L. Carter, "The Divergent Paths of Frémont's 'Three Marshalls,'" *NMHR*, 48 (January 1973), 13–14.

37. Peters, *The Life of Kit Carson*, 182. Carter, "Frémont's 'Three Marshalls,'" 14.

38. Carter, *'Dear Old Kit,'* 95.

39. Peters, *The Life of Kit Carson*, 195.

40. Lavender, *Bent's Fort*, 252–55.

41. On Tom Boggs, see McClung, *Carson-Bent-Boggs Genealogy*, 106–8. Also, F. Stanley, *Thomas Oliver Boggs Story* (Nazareth, Tex.: privately printed, 1982), 45.

42. Cragin, "Early Far West Notebooks," VIII, nos. 4 & 5.

43. Lavender, *Bent's Fort*, 256.

44. The full text of Kearny's letter is printed in Edwin Bryant, *What I Saw in California, Being the Journal of a Tour in the Years* 1846, 1847 (repr. of 1848 ed.: Minneapolis: Ross & Haines, 1967), 295–96. For official notice of the meeting with Carson, refer to the Expedition's log, October 6, 1846, in Letters Received by the Office of Adjutant General, Main Series, 1822–1860, National Archives Microfilm M567, reel 319, fr. 280. And, Hans von Sachsen-Altenberg and Laura Gabiger, eds., *Winning the West: General Stephen Watts Kearny's Letter Book, 1846–1847* (Booneville, Mo.: Pekitanoui Publications, 1998), 171. The letter of an anonymous soldier with Kearny, describing the encounter with "Mr. Christopher Carson" on the Rio Grande, appeared in the *Jefferson Inquirer* (Jefferson City, Mo.), December 1, 1846, being the first reference published.

45. Thomas H. Benton, *Thirty Years View* (2 vols.; New York: D. Appleton Co., 1854–1856), 2:718.

46. Historian William S. Wallace suggests another reason for Carson's displeasure: that he resented the lost opportunity to visit Washington and have a personal interview with the president. *Antoine Robidoux,* 35. Given Carson's character and his proverbial uneasiness in formal society, that explanation seems less tenable.

47. Frémont, *Memoirs*, 586.

48. Hughes, *Doniphan's Expedition* (repr. of 1847 ed.; College Station: Texas A&M University Press, 1997), 106. Cooke, *The Conquest of New Mexico and California* (New York: G. P. Putnam's Sons, 1878), 85.

49. Senate Exec. Docs., 1st sess., 31st Congr., 1850 (Ser. Set #557), 183–86.

50. Interview with Rumalda Luna Boggs by Albert W. Thompson, ca. 1897, Clayton, N.Mex., in an unidentified, undated Clayton newspaper clipping in the Bent File, FACHL. A different R. L. Boggs interview by Thompson with variance in some details, is "Insurrection at Taos," *New Mexico Magazine*, 20 (April 1942), 18. Teresina Bent, as an adult, gave several versions of her recollections of the killing of her father. Most accessible is the one printed in Ralph Emerson Twitchell, *Leading Facts of New Mexican History* (5 vols.; Cedar Rapids, Iowa: The Torch Press, 1911–1917), 2:235. Ignacia's version of her husband's death was given "in a most graphic manner and in very pure Spanish" to Lt. John G. Bourke at her home in Taos during July 1881, two years before her death. Lansing B. Bloom, ed., "Burke on the Southwest," *NMHR*, 12 (January 1937), 51.

51. E. Bennett Burton, "The Taos Rebellion," *Old Santa Fe*, 1 (October 1913), 182.

52. Sena de Luna later petitioned Congress to indemnify him for his losses in the 1847 revolt. Serna, "Descendants of Francisco Esteban Jaramillo," 2.

53. *Washington Daily Union*, June 15, 1847. Richardson, *Beyond the Mississippi*, 262.

54. Diario de la Corte de Pruebas, 1847–1855, March term, 1847, transcription in KC, SRC. The first paragraph of the Diario refers to destruction of all previous documents.

55. Mark L. Gardner, "Tragedy in Taos," *New Mexico Magazine*, 78 (October 2000), 34.

56. Luís Martínez, "The Taos Massacre, 1847," WPA typescript (1936), no. 233, NMSRCA.

57. Teresina's account in Twitchell, *Leading Facts*, 2:235. Burton, "The Taos Rebellion," 182.

58. Gardner, "Tragedy in Taos," 37. The *Santa Fe New Mexican Review*, July 22, 1883, printed a roster of the Avengers.

59. Sabin, *Kit Carson Days* (1935), 2:561.

60. Garrard, *Wah-to-yah and the Taos Trail*, 181–82.

61. Bloom, "Bourke on the Southwest," 51.

Josefa, Chapter 2

1. Sánchez, *Memorias Sobre la Vida del Presbitero Don Antonio José Martínez*, trans. by Ray John de Aragón (Santa Fe: The Lightning Tree, 1978), 72, 74. For background on Sánchez and the "eulogistic recollection" of the life of Padre Martínez, see David J. Weber, ed., *Northern Mexico on the Eve of the United States Invasion* (New York: Arno Press, 1976), 21.

2. Twitchell, *Leading Facts*, 2:235n.

3. Twitchell, *The Military Occupation of New Mexico, 1846–1851* (Denver: Smith-Brooks Co., 1909), 133. Howard Roberts Lamar, *The Far Southwest, 1846–1912* (New Haven, Conn.: Yale University Press, 1966), 70. Sabin, *Kit Carson Days* (1935), 2:563, says that "Carson could not pardon this treachery of Martínez."

4. Sánchez, *Memorias*, 74.

5. See Carson's remarks in 1858 upon the excommunication of Padre Martínez. W. J. Howlett, *Life of the Right Reverend Joseph P. Machebeuf* (repr. of 1908 ed.; Denver: Register College, 1954), 231–32.

6. Carter, '*Dear Old Kit*,' 116.

7. Contemporary accounts indicated that most American houses were torched. A story in the *Taos News*, February 15, 1996, Rick Romancito, "Where Did Kit Carson Live?" reported that recent removal of plaster in one room of the Carson house revealed burned adobe bricks and above them scorched *vigas* (roof beams).

8. Allan Nevins, *Polk, The Diary of a President* (London: Longmans, Green and Co., 1929), 241.

9. A facsimile of Carson's commission from Polk can be seen in the Kit Carson File, NM-SRCA. By passage of a bill, May 19, 1846, Congress provided for the raising of a Regiment of Mounted Volunteer Riflemen. Albert G. Brackett, *History of the United States Cavalry* (New York: Harper & Brothers, 1865), 60.

10. Sabin, *Kit Carson Days* (1935), 2:573. Sabin cites no source for "the swathing" of Kit, but his assumption may not be unwarranted. Carson's courier instructions from the War Department dated June 14, 1847, appear in Letters Received by the Sec. of War, Registered Series, 1801–1870, National Archives Microfilm, M 221, reel 139, fr. 0152.

11. Sabin, *Kit Carson Days* (1935), 2:575.

12. Estergreen, *Kit Carson*, 184. Guild and Carter, *Kit Carson*, 171, suggest that Kit and Josefa's meeting in Santa Fe was "unexpected." But an accidental reunion seems highly implausible.

13. George Douglas Brewerton, *Overland With Kit Carson* (repr. of 1930 ed.; Lincoln: University of Nebraska Press, 1993), 143.

14. The arrival date was reported by the *Santa Fe Republican*, June 27, 1848.

15. Ralph Moody in his *Kit Carson and the Wild Frontier* (New York: Random House, 1955), 133, states without citing a source that the Senate also failed to approve payment of the men who had been in Frémont's service. This may not have referred to the membership of his Third Expedition, but to his local Battalion of California Volunteers to whose men he had pledged $25 per month salary. Spence and Jacson, *The Expeditions of Frémont*, 2:334.

16. Carter, *'Dear Old Kit,'* 121.

17. Lecompte, *Pueblo, Hardscrabble, Greenhorn*, 217. Guild and Carter, *Kit Carson*, 178.

18. The full story of the Apache attack is provided by Janet Lecompte, "The Manco Burro Pass Massacre," *NMHR*, 41 (October 1966), 305–18.

19. Blackwelder, *Great Westerner*, 235. Sabin provides the 16,000 miles figure. *Kit Carson Days* (1914), 271.

20. Leroy R. Hafen and Ann W. Hafen, eds., *Frémont's Fourth Expedition* (Glendale, Calif.: Arthur H. Clark Co., 1960), 199. For a more recent analysis of the expedition, consult, Patricia Joy Richmond, *Trail to Disaster* (Niwot, Colo.: University Press of Colorado, 1990).

21. Hafen and Hafen, *Frémont's Fourth Expedition*, 208.

22. In mid October 1848, Albert N. Powell, traveling west on the Santa Fe Trail, noted that Kit Carson and his brother Lindsey caught up with his own party at Diamond Spring, west of Council Grove. "Carson came up and shook hands with all of us. He always was the very soul of politeness and wellbred courtesy." See, "Rev. A. N. Powell on Early Days," *Colorado Springs Gazette*, January 19, 1902.

23. The original undated letter is in the archive of the Newberry Library, Chicago. It has been transcribed and published by Janet Lecompte, "A Letter from Jessie to Kit," *Bulletin of the Missouri Historical Society*, 29 (July 1973), 260–63.

24. Charles Wentworth Upham, *Life, Explorations, and Public Services of John Charles Frémont* (Boston: Ticknor and Fields, 1856), 189.

25. Frémont to Carson, New York City, March 2, 1857, in Beinecke Rare Book and Manuscript Library, Yale University, New Haven, Conn.

26. Carter, *'Dear Old Kit,'* 123.

27. Lecompte, "The Manco Burro Pass Massacre," 308. And, Robert W. Frazer, *Forts and Supplies, The Role of the Army in the Economy of the Southwest, 1846–1861* (Albuquerque: University of New Mexico Press, 1983), 51. For Quinn land transactions, see Ralph L. Hayes, comp., *Taos County, New Mexico [Genealogy]* (Albuquerque: New Mexico Genealogical Society, 1989), 116.

28. *Santa Fe New Mexican Review*, July 22, 1883, and, Muster Roll, St. Vrain's Company, January 23, 1847, Territorial Archives of New Mexico, reel 85, frs. 5–7, NMSRCA. Cragin, "Early Far West Notebooks," VIII, no. 6.

29. Lawrence R. Murphy, "Rayado: Pioneer Settlement in Northeastern New Mexico, 1848–1857," *NMHR*, 46 (January 1971), 39. See, for the origin of the $1,000 loan, Cragin, "Early Far West Notebooks," VIII, no. 69.

30. A news story in the *New York Daily Tribune*, March 17, 1853, referred to "Kit Carson and Mr. Maxwell, his partner in business." But an earlier document mentioned "Mr.

Carson and his two associates." Col. John Monroe, Santa Fe, N.Mex., April 15, 1850, to Maj. Gen. R. Johns. Report of the Sec. of War, House Exec. Doc. 1, 31st Congr., 2nd sess. (Serial Set #594).

31. Carter, *'Dear Old Kit,'* 181.

32. Murphy, "Rayado," 38–39.

33. Capt. Henry B. Judd, Las Vegas, June 11, 1849 to Lt. John H. Dickerson (assistant adjutant), Letters Received, 9th Military Dept., Record Group 393, NA, M1102, reel 1, fr. 0706.

34. María E. Montoya, *Translating Property, The Maxwell Land Grant in the American West, 1840–1900* (Berkeley: University of California Press, 2002), 51.

35. Judd to Dickerson, June 1, 1849, NA M1102, reel 1, fr. 0696.

36. Carter, *'Dear Old Kit,'* 123–24.

37. Judd to Dickerson, June 1, 1849, NA, M1102, reel 1, fr. 0696.

38. Pancoast, *A Quaker Forty-niner* (Philadelphia: University of Pennsylvania Press, 1930), 208–9.

39. Harry C. Myers, "Massacre on the Santa Fe Trail: Mr. White's Company of Unfortunates," *Wagon Tracks* [Santa Fe Trail Ass'n. Quarterly], 6 (February 1992), 23.

40. Carter, *'Dear Old Kit,'* 124–26. Murphy, "Rayado," 43.

41. On Holland, see Jim Berry Pearson, *The Maxwell Land Grant* (Norman: University of Oklahoma Press, 1961), 11. Father Stanley Crocchiola (F. Stanley) in an article published in the *Raton Range*, November 13, 1948, claims that John Holland was actually a soldier, "handy as a builder." The 1850 Census listed him as a native of New York, age 42.

42. Blackwelder, *Great Westerner*, 244; and, Edmunds Claussen, "Rayado Rancho," *New Mexico Magazine*, 24 (March 1946), 37.

43. Sabin, *Kit Carson Days* (1935), 2:618.

44. Baptismal Register, 1847–1850, Nuestra Señora de Guadalupe Parish, from a copy in the KC, SRC. The Seventh U.S. Census, 1850, Taos County, N.Mex., identifies the first Carson son as Charles B. Carson, the B possibly standing for Bent. Thus, the true middle name remains uncertain.

45. Guild and Carter, *Kit Carson*, 185, state that Charles was born prematurely.

46. Carter, *'Dear Old Kit,'* 128.

47. Carter, *'Dear Old Kit,'* 129.

48. Maurine Nelson Bradshaw, *Pioneer Parade* (New York: Vantage Press, 1966), 10–11. The author is a direct descendant of Susan Carson Nelson.

49. For example, Francis W. Cragin interviewed Jesse Nelson on his Colorado ranch, July 9, 1908. For the results, see Cragin's "Early Far West Notebooks," VIII, *passim.*

50. McClung, *Carson, Bent, Boggs Genealogy*, 75.

51. Leo E. Oliva, *Fort Union and the Frontier Army in the Southwest*, Professional Papers no. 41 (Santa Fe: National Park Service, 1995), 56.

52. Cragin, "Early Far West Notebooks," VIII, no. 49.

53. Robert W. Frazer, ed., *New Mexico in 1850, A Military View* (Norman: University of Oklahoma Press, 1968), 147.

54. Historian Ralph Emerson Twitchell, in his *The Military Occupation of New Mexico,*

279, in 1909 briefly sketched the episode. He gives no source, but his information probably came from a Carson family member. Edwin L. Sabin interviewed Teresina Bent, but her version differs in some details and was also incomplete. *Kit Carson Days* (1935), 2:632–33. For another instance in the Far West of a frontiersman preparing to kill his family during an Indian emergency (in Montana, 1863), see Walt Coburn, *Stirrup High* (Lincoln: University of Nebraska Press, 1997), 78–79.

55. Sabin's complete interview with Teresina concerning this event appears in his *Kit Carson Days* (1935), 2:633.

56. Carter, '*Dear Old Kit*,' 132.

57. McClung, *Carson, Bent, Boggs Genealogy*, 74–75. William Carson was named for William Bent.

58. LeRoy R. Hafen, "Louy Simmons," in Hafen, *The Mountain Men*, 5:319.

59. *The California State Journal*, September 5, 1853, from a copy in KC, SRC. This is the only source indicating that Carson's herd contained goats as well as sheep. On the background of Mercure and Bernavette (or Bernadet), see Carter, '*Dear Old Kit*,' 134, n. 284.

60. The presence of the cousin from Missouri is cited only by Blackwelder, *Great Westerner*, 263.

61. Issue of September 5, 1853, KC, SRC.

62. John O. Baxter, *Las Carneradas, Sheep Trade in New Mexico, 1700–1860* (Albuquerque: University of New Mexico Press, 1987), 126. The figure of 5,000 sheep that reached Sacramento is given in *The California State Journal*, Sept. 5, 1853, KC, SRC. In the Southwest, an aggregate of sheep was commonly referred to as a herd rather than a flock.

63. Carter, '*Dear Old Kit*,' 133.

64. LeRoy R. Hafen, "The W. M. Boggs Manuscript," *The Colorado Magazine*, 7 (March 1930), 60.

65. Original of the Lindsey Carson, Jr. letter in the Carson Correspondence and Papers, BL, UC.

66. Hobbs, *Wild Life in the Far West* (repr. of 1872 ed.; Glorieta, N.Mex.: Rio Grande Press, 1969), 448.

67. William F. Switzler, "Kit Carson," *Missouri Historical Society Collections*, 2 (January 1900), 38.

68. Hobbs, *Wild Life in the Far West*, 448.

69. Cragin, "Early Far West Notebooks," VIII, no. 75.

70. Hobbs, *Wild Life in the Far West*, 63.

71. Hobbs, *Wild Life in the Far West*, 447. Trees, known locally by the name Balm of Gilead, were cut for the fence's corner posts. "As in the nature of this tree, [the posts] took root and grew, marking the site with four large trees in the form of a square." Wallis R. McPherson, "Resting Place of Carson's Daughter," *Mono Inn News*, undated but ca. 1955. Copy in possession of the author.

The square presumably was used to establish the site in 1930 when a grave monument to replace the lost headboard was proposed. Edwin L. Sabin searched for such a monument in 1933 without success, and it may have never been built. McClung, *Carson, Bent, Boggs Genealogy*, 172. In 1973 a historical plaque was placed on a public road next to the Mono Inn. Titled "Grave of Adaline Carson Stilts," the plaque text is confusing and inaccurate. For example, she was never called Prairie Flower by her father, and her death was not in 1859. The plaque, as the text indicates, is not actually on the grave site.

Sabin, *Kit Carson Days* (1935), 2:955, said that Adaline died at Mono Lake "about 1860." Most subsequent writers dispensed with Sabin's qualifier, "about," and stated simply that Adaline's death occurred in 1860, except for Estergreen, *Kit Carson*, 208, who gives 1861.

In reality, she was still living on January 20,1862, when Records of the Mono County Clerk, Book A, 307, show that Adaline Carson received $100 from B. F. Snyder of nearby Aurora, Nevada. See also, Frank S. Wedertz, *Mono Diggings* (Bishop, Calif.: Chalfant Press, 1978), 35, 40.

Louy Simmons briefly turned up in New Mexico during the winter of 1857–1858. Stray accounts have him trapping thereafter in the northern Rockies. At some point, he was struck by lightning while carrying steel traps over his shoulder. He survived but remained mentally unbalanced. In March 1894, he was committed to the state hospital at Provo, Utah, where he died six months later at age 77. Hafen, "Louy Simmons," *The Mountain Men*, 5:321–24.

72. Davis, *El Gringo or, New Mexico and Her People* (repr. of 1857 ed.; Santa Fe: The Rydal Press, 1938), 125. And, *Santa Fe Weekly Gazette*, December 31, 1853.

73. After noting that Sen. Benton's and Frémont's influence had waned, Dunlay, *Kit Carson & the Indians*, 146–47, suggests that: "Perhaps Edward Beale brought up Kit's name in the right places."

74. Taos became a permanent site for the Ute (or Utah) Agency earlier in 1853. Some Jicarilla Apaches and the Indians of Taos Pueblo also used its services on occasion. The first agent, and Kit's predecessor, E. A. Graves, had been transferred to Doña Ana in lower New Mexico, to serve the southern Apaches. E. A. Graves to George W. Manypenny, Comm. of Indian Affairs, Washington, November 29, 1853, Letters Received by Office of Indian Affairs, 1849–1853, M 234, reel 547, NA.

Josefa, Chapter 3

1. Jack K. Boyer, Taos, undated interview with Mrs. Charles Carson (ca. 1939), typescript in KC, SRC. Mitchell Wilson, *American Science and Invention* (New York: Bonanza Books, 1960), 134–35.

2. Cragin, "Early Far West Notebooks," VIII, no. 83. McClung, *Carson-Bent-Boggs Supplement*, 26. Charles W. Bowman, "History of Bent County," in O. L. Bashin, comp., *History of the Arkansas Valley, Colorado* (Chicago: Bashin & Co., 1881), 876. According to Sabin, Kit sold his Rayado interests (probably in the latter 1850s) to one Pedro Neares [Narváez?]. *Kit Carson Days* (1935), 2:649.

3. Sabin, *Kit Carson Days* (1914), 336. Estergreen, *Kit Carson*, 210, asserts that the agency was on the west, not the south, side of the plaza and that Kit moved his family into the building. She cites no source for the statement, but it probably derived from Teresina Bent.

4. By the end of 1854, the amount of the bond demanded of new agents was $10,000. Alban W. Hooper, ed., "Letters To and From Abraham G. Mayers, 1854–1857," *NMHR*, 9 (July 1934), 291.

5. Donald Warrin and Geoffrey L. Gomes, *Land As Far As the Eye Can See: Portuguese in the Old West* (Spokane, Wash.: Arthur H. Clark Co., 2001), 55–75. Marc Simmons interview with Judge Ben Hernández, Albuquerque, November 7, 1996. Hernández's father knew Antonio Joseph, who died in 1910. Hayes, *Taos County, New Mexico [Genealogy]*, 122–23. *Santa Fe New Mexican Review*, July 22, 1883. In his will, Peter Joseph named Kit Carson as one of the executors of his estate.

6. Addendum to: Meriwether to George W. Manypenny, Comm. of Indian Affairs, March 31, 1857, Letters Received, New Mexico Superintendency, (NMS), 547, N.A. From a copy in the Frank McNitt Coll., NMSRCA.

7. Charles E. Mix, acting Comm. of Indian Affairs, to Christopher Carson, August 4, 1855, Carson Coll., Lee, BYU. Manypenny to W. W. H. Davis, Acting Governor of N.M., January 3, 1856, Letters Received Relating to Kit Carson, 1854–1856, NMS, Microcopy T-21, NA. [Hereinafter: Carson Agency Correspondence]. Guild and Carter, *Kit Carson*, 322, n. 3. A voucher for the Taos Agency, March 31, 1859, is in the sum of $45 paid as three-months rent on office and quarters for Indians when visiting. Lee, BYU. Other Indian agents in New Mexico received a salary of $1,500.

8. George H. Pettis to Smith Simpson, May 15, 1908, Simpson Papers, KC, SRC.

9. Meriwether to Manypenny, March 31, 1857, NMS, 548, McNitt Coll., NMSRCA.

10. Warrin and Gomes, *Land As Far As The Eye Can See*, 71.

11. Dunlay, *Kit Carson*, 178. John Greiner to Manypenny, February 20, 1855, NMS, 547, McNitt Coll., NMSRCA. Marshall D. Moody, "Kit Carson, Indian Agent to the Indians in New Mexico, 1853–1861," *NMHR*, 28 (January 1953), 8–9.

12. Sabin, *Kit Carson Days* (1935), 2:649. *Santa Fe Gazette*, April 1, 1854.

13. Sabin, *Kit Carson Days* (1935), 2:649–50.

14. Sherman to Edward S. Ellis, June 25, 1884, printed in Ellis, *The Life of Kit Carson* (Chicago: M. A. Donohue & Co., 1889), 249.

15. For a representative pay order to Solomon Beuthner, see Carson to Collins, April 20, 1857, Carson Agency Correspondence. For related documents, see Christopher Carson Coll., PE-64, Box 3, BL, UC. And also, Peter Joseph, Taos, January 20, 1859 to firm of Webb & Kingsbury, regarding drafts drawn on Supt. Collins by C. Carson, James J. Webb Coll., MHS. William J. Parish, *The Charles Ilfeld Company* (Cambridge, Mass.: Harvard University Press, 1961), 16.

16. Carter, *'Dear Old Kit,'* 180.

17. Cragin, "Early Far West Notebooks," VIII, no. 80.

18. Murphy, *Maxwell*, 96.

19. Brewerton, *The War in Kansas, A Rough Trip to the Border* (New York: Derby & Jackson, 1856), 122–23.

20. Ferdinand Maxwell, Lucien's younger brother, reached Taos in 1859 and opened his own store. According to Skip Keith Miller, "He went into partnership with his brother,

Thomas Boggs, and possibly Kit Carson, raising horses, mules and sheep for the government contracts Lucien always seemed to win." "Ferdinand Maxwell: The Other Maxwell," *Taos Lightnin'* [Taos Historic Museums News], 3 (fall 1997), 4. The stock raising refers to the Rayado operation.

21. "Daughter of Kit Carson," interview, *Raton Range* (New Mexico), April 27, 1907.

22. Janet Lecompte and Lester F. Turley, "The Turleys from Booneslick," *The Bulletin of the Missouri Historical Society*, 27 (April 1972), 190. Charles B. Churchill, *Adventurers and Prophets, American Autobiographers in Mexican California, 1828–1847* (Spokane, Wash.: Arthur H. Clark Co., 1995), 159–60.

23. Carter, *'Dear Old Kit,'* 148–50, n. 32.

24. Peters to Turley, March 11, 1858, Turley Papers, MHS.

25. Peters to Carson, March 7, 1859, Christopher Carson Coll., BL,UC.

26. Gwyther, "A Frontier Post and Country," 521. In a letter printed in the *Army and Navy Journal*, Dr. Peters in 1870 claimed that, "[Kit] even dictated his life to me." Reprinted in Blanche C. Grant, ed., *Kit Carson's Own Story of his Life* (Taos, N.Mex.: privately printed, 1926), 136. In reviewing Grant's publication, Charles L. Camp wrote: "Comparison of some of Mrs. Peters [*sic*] letters with the MS. [of Kit's original memoirs preserved in the Newberry Library, Chicago] shows that she took the dictation." The review appears in the *California Historical Society Quarterly*, 5 (December 1926), 408–9. This assumption challenges Carter's conclusion, cited above, concerning who actually wrote down Carson's memoirs.

27. McClung, *Carson, Bent, Boggs Genealogy*, 74. One finds a number of spelling variations for "Estafana," and several for "Josefita," who when grown was addressed as Josephine.

28. A. B. Sanford, "Reminiscences of Kit Carson Jr.," *The Colorado Magazine*, 6 (September 1929), 179–84. Russell, *Land of Enchantment*, 51–52.

29. Stevenson, "Following the Trail, Or Scouts of the Plains," undated holograph manuscript of personal recollections, John C. Stevenson Coll., Milwaukee County Historical Society, Wisconsin.

30. Richardson, *Beyond the Mississippi*, 260.

31. Meketa, *Legacy of Honor*, 123.

32. Russell, *Land of Enchantment*, 52.

33. Jessie Frémont, "Kit Carson," 100–101.

34. Blackwelder, *Great Westerner*,

35. George Bent's obituary appeared in the *Santa Fe Republican*, November 13, 1847. Alfredo (or Elfego) Bent's departure east from the fort is noted in an inscription in the Bent Family Bible, FACHL. See also, Lavender, *Bent's Fort*, 303–4; Mark L. Gardner, *Bent's Fort on the Santa Fe Trail* (draft manuscript of forthcoming publication by the National Park Service).

36. McClung, *Carson, Bent, Boggs Genealogy*, 89.

37. Sabin, *Kit Carson Days* (1935), 2:783.

38. Sabin, *Kit Carson Days* (1935), 2:783. Both the statement by Charles and Nicanor's letter, in translation, appear here. The original Nicanor letter in Spanish is in the Christopher Carson Coll., BL, UC.

39. Beuthner to Carson, Taos, Christopher Carson Coll., doc. 28, Lee, BYU.

40. Gottlieb, *Family in the Western World*, 7.

41. Sabin, *Kit Carson Days* (1935), 2:783.

42. Taos Book of Baptisms, Archives of the Archdiocese of Santa Fe, microfilm ed., NMSRCA.

43. Sanford, "Reminiscences of Kit Carson, Jr.," 130.

44. Sanford, "Reminiscences of Kit Carson, Jr.," 131.

45. Carson to Supt. Collins, November 30, 1858, Carson Agency Correspondence.

46. Carson to Supt. Collins, November 30, 1858, Carson Agency Correspondence.

47. Taos Book of Baptisms, Archives of the Archdiocese of Santa Fe, microfilm ed., NMSRCA. At Boggsville, Colorado, to which the Carsons moved in 1867, Dolores may have served in the house of Tom Boggs, as the small three-room residence where Kit, Josefa, and their children stayed could not have easily accommodated her. Afterward, she married Louis Domingo who was killed by the Leyba brothers in 1876. The following year Dolores Carson died of severe burns after falling into a fire. It was supposed that she was intoxicated at the time. *Las Animas Leader* [Colorado], December 7, 1877. Copy in the Don Cline Papers, KC, SRC. Like Dolores, a woman from Ranchos de Taos, Gavina García, seems to have accompanied the Carsons to Boggsville near Las Animas. Before her death there in 1963 at age 113, she claimed to have been their housekeeper, although no corroboratory source confirms that. Unidentified newspaper clipping, Januray 24, 1963, titled, "Kit Carson's Housekeeper Dies," KC, SRC.

48. James F. Brooks, *Captives & Cousins, Slavery, Kinship, and Community in the Southwest Borderlands* (Chapel Hill: University of North Carolina Press, 2002), 327–30.

49. See especially, David M. Brugge's chapter, "Conditions of Life for Navajo Captives," in his *Navajos in the Catholic Records of New Mexico, 1694–1875* (Tsaile, Ariz.: Navajo Community College, 1985), 109–25.

50. Carson to Supt. Collins, January 12, 1859, Carson Agency Correspondence.

51. On the Hoerster case, see run of correspondence beginning December 28, 1859, in Carson Agency Correspondence. Also, James M. Day and Norman Winfrey, eds., *Texas Indian Papers*, 1860–1916 (Austin: Texas State Library, 1961), 1. And, *San Antonio Herald*, December 17, 1859. For locating the elusive *Herald* reference, the author is indebted to Carson scholar John M. Pimm of Bristol, England.

52. Susan M. Yohn, *A Contest of Faiths, Missionary Women and Pluralism in the American Southwest* (Ithaca, N.Y.: Cornell University Press, 1995), 51. John M. Ingham, *Mary, Michael and Lucifer, Folk Catholicism in Central Mexico* (Austin: University of Texas Press, 1986), 82.

53. Paul Horgan, *Lamy of Santa Fe* (New York: Farrar, Straus and Giroux, 1975), 504. García lived to be 102. "Longevity Formula," *The [Franciscan] Provincial Chronicle*, 34 (winter 1962), 250.

54. Sabin, *Kit Carson Days* (1935), 2:773.

55. Richardson, "A Visit To Kit Carson," *Frank Leslie's Illustrated Newspaper* (December 8, 1860), 37. Gwyther, "A Frontier Post and Country," 524.

56. Sen. James Doolittle to Gen. Carleton, Taos, July 11, 1865, Record Army Command (RAC), Box 2, McNitt Coll., NMSRCA. Also, Carleton to Carson, Santa Fe, August 6, 1865, Christopher Carson Coll., doc. 38, Lee, BYU.

57. For a general description of upper-class life in the region, consult Manuel G. González, *The Hispanic Elite of the Southwest* (El Paso: Texas Western Press, 1989).

58. Long after the dinner at the Carson home, R. J. Alexander published his recollections of it, "Talks with Kit Carson," in *The National Tribune* [periodical of the Grand Army of the Republic], Washington, D.C., August 21, 1902, p. 2. The author, Simmons, acknowledges John P. Wilson for calling this fugitive reference to his attention.

59. These letters, in translation, are printed in Sabin, *Kit Carson Days* (1935), 2:772–74. They were once in the Thomas Boggs Papers of the Bancroft Library, University of California, but the originals today cannot be located.

60. Teresina and Estafina Bent's initial enrollment is noted in Our Lady of Light school register, preserved in the Archives, Loretto Motherhouse, Nerinx, Ky. A copy can be seen in the Teresina Bent Scheurich Papers, NMSRCA. The Bent Family Bible in FACHL contains an inscription regarding the girls' first departure from Taos to attend the Santa Fe school. For Carson's comment on the Loretto Sisters, see Russell, *Land of Enchantment*, 51.

61. The report card is preserved in the Thomas Boggs Papers, BL, UC.

62. Sabin, *Kit Carson Days* (1935), 2:774.

63. Beuthner to Carson, Taos, January 6, 1864, Christopher Carson Coll., doc. 18, Lee, BYU. Theodore D. Wheaton was the U.S. attorney general for the territory.

64. John Schock to Kit Carson, Taos, August 5, 1865 Christopher Carson Coll., doc. 37, Lee, BYU.

65. Robert G. Athearn, "The Education of Kit Carson's Son," *NMHR*, 31 (April 1956), 137.

66. McClung, *Carson, Bent, Boggs Genealogy*, 90. Ruth Fish, "The Life Story of Teresina Bent Scheurich, Daughter of Governor Charles Bent," *Ayer y Hoy*, 21 (winter 1997), 14. Aloys Scheurich's obituary appears in the *Denver Republican*, November 17, 1907. On Lux's desertion, see Case of Teresina B. Scheurich, Record of Bureau of Pensions, November 23, 1908, Dept. of Interior, Washington, D.C., NA.

67. On the anti-Masonic movement in the United States, 1826–1840, see Steven C. Bullock, *Revolutionary Brotherhood* (Chapel Hill: University of North Carolina Press, 1996), chap. 10.

68. Ernle Bradford, *The Shield and the Sword, The Knights of St. John, Jerusalem, Rhodes and Malta* (New York: E. P. Dutton, & Co., 1973), 25. John J. Robinson, *Born in Blood, The Lost Secrets of Freemasonry* (New York: M. Evans & Co., 1989), xvi, 67.

69. James Valentine, Sec. of Bent Lodge No. 42, Taos, to John J. McCurdy, Lincoln, Kans., August 26, 1949, Masonic File, KC, SRC. Anonymous, "A Brief Story of Freemasonry in New Mexico," *The New Mexico Freemason*, 3 (October 1938), 4. Ray V. Denslow, "Kit Carson, Freemason," *Missouri Grand Lodge Bulletin*, 1 (February 1924), 22–23. Several of Kit's brothers were also Masons, including his half-brother Moses and youngest brother Lindsey, Jr., a charter member of the lodge in Lakeport, Calif. McClung, *Carson, Bent, Boggs Supplement*, 44. Carson's certificate showing his Degree of Master Mason, Montezuma Lodge, Santa Fe, and dated December 27, 1859, is contained in the Christopher Carson Coll, BL, UC. Also in the same collection can be seen a printed receipt issued by the Montezuma Lodge to Carson for payment of $12 annual dues, December 27, 1859.

70. *Santa Fe Weekly Gazette*, December 30, 1854.

71. *Santa Fe Weekly Gazette*, December 30, 1854.

72. Peters to his father (unnamed), Fort Massachusetts, N.M., January 18, 1856, De Witt Clinton Peters Papers, KC, SRC. *Santa Fe Weekly Gazette*, December 29, 1855.

73. LaMoine Langston, *A History of Masonry in New Mexico* (Roswell, N.Mex.: Hall-Poorbaugh Press [1978]), 230. Jack K. Boyer, *A History of Freemasonry in Taos, New Mexico: Bent Lodge No. 42* (Taos: The Lodge of Research, 1971), 2–3.

74. For an account of traditional Christmas observances in the Taos Valley, see Cleofas M. Jaramillo, *Shadows of the Past* (Santa Fe: Ancient City Press, 1972), 77–80.

75. Sabin, *Kit Carson Days* (1935), 951, n. 472.

76. Howlett, *Life of Joseph P. Machebeuf*, 232.

77. Thomasson, "Recollections of Kit Carson," 3.

78. For a survey of the traditional status of female Southerners, see Bertram Wyatt-Brown, *Southern Honor, Ethics and Behavior in the Old South* (New York: Oxford University Press, 1982), 226–53.

79. Janet Lecompte, "The Independent Women of Hispanic New Mexico, 1821–1864," *Western Historical Quarterly*, 12 (January 1981), 19.

80. Last Will and Testament of Kit Carson, May 15, 1868; and, Carson Estate Inventory (undated), both in the Thomas Boggs Papers, BL, UC.

81. Misc. Accounts, Col. C. Carson's wife, Bought of Peter Joseph, 1860–1862, PE-64, Christopher Carson Coll., BL, UC.

Josefa, Chapter 4

1. Baskin, *History of the Arkansas Valley, Colorado*, 836. Parkman, *The Oregon Trail*, E. N. Feltskog, ed. (Madison: University of Wisconsin Press, 1969), 359.

2. Jessie B. Frémont, *The Will and the Way Stories* (Boston: D. Lothrop Co., 1891), 43–44.

3. The letter, Tilton to Abbott, is printed in the second edition of John S. C. Abbott, *Christopher Carson, Known As Kit Carson* (New York, Dodd, Mead and Co., 1901), 343–48. The quote appears on p. 344.

4. Quoted in the *Santa Fe New Mexican*, October 27, 1868.

5. For examples, see Carter, '*Dear Old Kit*,' 154; and Sabin, *Kit Carson Days* (1935), 2:673. On trapper Old Bill Williams suffering a similar accident, with a horse, see Lavender, *Bent's Fort*, 69.

6. Sabin, *Kit Carson Days*, (1914), 492.

7. McClung, *Carson, Bent, Boggs Genealogy, Supplement*, 44. Thompson, *Civil War in the Southwest*, 36.

8. Roberts, *A Newer World*, 254. *The Missouri Statesman*, September 18, 1857. Dunlay, *Kit Carson & the Indians*, 434, suggests that Carson simply "never addressed the problem in the abstract."

9. *New York Daily Herald*, June 6, 1861. Blackwelder, *Great Westerner*, 301. Beuthner letter, doc. 21, Christopher Carson Coll., Lee, BYU. A copy of Kit's oath is in Compiled Military Service Record, Retired Service Records, NA. A facsimile is available in KC, SRC.

Commissioner of Indian Affairs Dole to Supt. Collins, May 27, 1861, states: "... on the 24th instant, the President ... appointed Agent Carson Lieut. Colonel." Office of Indian Affairs, New Mexico Superintendency, T21-5, NA. By that date, Kit had already resigned as agent.

10. Kit's mustering in occurred on July 25, 1861, as stated by E. T. Ladd, Military Secretary, letter to Charles C. Carson, May 2, 1906, War Department, Washington, D.C., NA.

11. Chris Emmett, *Fort Union and the Winning of the Southwest* (Norman: University of Oklahoma, 1965), 239, 251.

12. Oliva, *Fort Union and the Frontier Army*, 256–59.

13. Emmett, *Fort Union*, 249, quoting St. Vrain's letter, from a copy in the Arrott Coll., New Mexico Highlands University, Las Vegas. Lavender, *Bent's Fort*, 347.

14. "Office Muster-in," October 30, 1861, Kit Carson Military Service Record, NA, indicates that he was entitled to colonel's pay beginning September 20, 1861. Copy in Don Cline Coll., KC, SRC. And, Executive Record Book 21, 1851–1882, p. 269, Territorial Archives of New Mexico, NMSRCA. Reference courtesy of E. Donald Kaye.

15. Field and Staff Muster Roll, September/October, 1861, Kit Carson Military Service Record, NA. Copy in Don Cline Coll., KC, SRC.

16. Col. Carson to Lt. Nicodemus, November 28, 1861, Albuquerque, Letters Received, Department of New Mexico, M1120, reel 13, NA.

17. Col. Carson to Col. Canby, December 14, 1861, Albuquerque, Letters Received, Department of New Mexico, M1120, reel 13, NA.

18. Marc Simmons, "Kit Carson at Fort Craig," in Charles Carroll and Lynn Sebastian, eds., *Fort Craig, The United States Fort on the Camino Real* (Socorro: New Mexico Bureau of Land Mangement, 2000), 151.

19. Estergreen, *Kit Carson*, 231.

20. A full account of the engagement is provided in John Taylor, *Bloody Valverde* (Albuquerque: University of New Mexico Press, 1995).

21. Quoted in Ralph Emerson Twitchell, *Old Santa Fe* (Santa Fe: New Mexican Publishing Co., 1925), 378.

22. "Edward W. Wynkoop's Unfinished Colorado History, 1876," MSS Coll. no. 695, FF2, Colorado Historical Society, Denver.

23. The Chaves recollections of Valverde were published in the *Albuquerque Daily Citizen*, June 21, 1890.

24. Report of Col. C. Carson, April 3, 1862, Fort Craig, Letters Received, Department of New Mexico, Record Group 98, NA.

25. The original of the Santistevan letter is in the Christopher Carson Coll., BL, UC, and is printed in "Notes and Documents," *NMHR*, 23 (July 1948), 240–45.

26. Capt. Edward Wynkoop, serving with Col. Carson, recorded several anecdotes regarding the commander's casual, even innocent, way of enforcing regulations and dealing with daily problems. See his "Unfinished Colorado History, 1876," MSS Coll. no. 695, FF2, Colorado Historical Society, Denver.

27. Sabin, *Kit Carson Days* (1935), 2:701.

28. Carson to Canby, Los Lunas, September 21, 1862, Military Department of New

Mexico, Compiled Service Records, M-427, reel no. 4, NA. Printed in Lawrence C. Kelly, *Navajo Roundup, Selected Correspondence of Kit Carson's Expedition Against the Navajo, 1863–1865* (Boulder, Colo.: Pruett Publishing Co., 1970), 4.

29. Gen. Carleton's order, sent by his adjutant, Ben C. Cutler, September 27, 1862, is printed in Sabin, *Kit Carson Days* (1935), 2:701.

30. Sanford, "Reminiscences of Kit Carson, Jr.," 179–80.

31. Carson to Nicodemus, Christopher Carson Coll., Lee, BYU. Canby's response was written on the back of Carson's letter and returned to him.

32. C. L. Sonnichsen, *The Mescalero Apaches* (Norman: University of Oklahoma Press, 1958), 98–103.

33. Carson to Carleton, Fort Stanton, February 3, 1863, Christopher Carson Compiled Military Service Record, Retired Service Records, NA. (Hereinafter: CMSR, NA)

34. Sabin, *Kit Carson Days* (1935), 2:706.

35. Carson to Carleton, November 1, 1863, and the response, Carleton to Carson, December 5, 1863, both appear in Kelly, *Navajo Roundup*, 68–69.

36. Regimental Returns, First New Mexico Cavalry, January/February, 1864, CMSR, NA.

37. Kelly, *Navajo Roundup*, 133. McClung, *Carson, Bent, Boggs Genealogy*, 74.

38. Kelly, *Navajo Roundup*, 147.

39. Guild and Carter, *Kit Carson*, 250.

40. Carleton to Carson, September 18, 1864, Letters Sent, Department of New Mexico, NA, from a copy in Blackwelder Papers, KC, SRC.

41. Utley, "Kit Carson and the Adobe Walls Campaign," *American West*, 2 (winter, 1965), 4.

42. *The War of the Rebellion: A Compilation of the Official Records of the Union and Confederate Armies* (70 vols. in 128; Washington, D.C.: GPO, 1880–1901), ser. 1, vol. 41, p. 944. (Hereinafter: OR)

43. The entire letter, translated from the Spanish, appears in Sabin, *Kit Carson Days* (1935), 2:772–73.

44. Beuthner to Carson, Taos, January 6, 1864, Christopher Carson Coll., doc. 28, Lee, BYU.

45. Richardson, *Beyond the Mississippi*, 260.

46. A receipt from the U.S. Internal Revenue Collector's Office, May 1, 1866, shows that Col. C. Carson paid excise tax of $2.00 on one carriage. Christopher Carson Coll., BL, UC.

47. Enos to Capt. Lawrence G. Murphy, May 20, 1864, RAC, Carson Correspondence, McNitt Coll., NMSRCA.

48. A firsthand description of the building of Camp Nichols is provided in Russell, *Land of Enchantment*, 101–2.

49. Special Order no. 22, August 5, 1865, Department of New Mexico, CMSR, NA.

50. The military ambulance was used not only for moving the wounded and sick, but also as a general transportation vehicle, particularly for families of service men. For a detailed account of the Little Arkansas Council of 1865, see Dunaly, *Kit Carson & the Indians*, 360–67.

51. James R. Mead, *Hunting and Trading on the Great Plains, 1859–1875* (Norman: University of Oklahoma Press, 1986), 176–77.

52. Special Order, no. 87, October 30, 1865, St. Louis, Department of the Missouri, CMSR, NA. Guild and Carter, *Kit Carson*, 259.

53. Carson to Carleton, Taos, November 29, 1865, CMSR, NA.

54. Sabin, *Kit Carson Days* (1935), 2:697.

55. Special Order no. 18, December 8, 1865, District of New Mexico, CMSR, NA.

56. Carleton to Carson, Santa Fe, January 30, 1865, OR, ser. 1, vol. 48, pt. 1, p. 689.

57. Oliva, *Fort Union and the Frontier Army*, 326–27.

58. James B. Fry, "The Brevet System in the United States Army," in Francis B. Taunton, ed., *The English Westerns' Brand Book*, 1971–72 (London: English Westerners' Society, 1972), 6–7. Guild and Carter, *Kit Carson*, 256. March 13, 1865 was the date of brevet promotion of almost every Union officer who served honorably in the Civil War. Personal correspondence, E. Donald Kaye to Marc Simmons, Santa Fe, October 27, 2002.

59. Carson to Sec. Stanton, Fort Union, January 2, 1866, District of New Mexico, CMSR, NA. As required by his brevet appointment, Kit took an Oath of Allegiance on November 10, 1866. Military Service Record, Blackwelder Papers, KC, SRC.

60. James F. Meline, *Two Thousand Miles on Horseback*, 1866 (repr. of 1867 ed.; Albuquerque: Horn & Wallace, 1966), 250.

61. Special Order no. 12, April 21, 1866, District of New Mexico, CMSR, NA. James F. Rusling, *Across America, Or the Great West* (New York: Sheldon & Co., 1875), 135.

62. Peters, *Kit Carson's Life and Adventures* (1873), 541.

63. McClung, *Carson, Bent, Boggs Genealogy*, 74–75.

64. Sanford, "Reminiscences of Kit Carson, Jr.," 181.

65. Sherman to Edward S. Ellis, St. Louis, June 25, 1884, printed in Ellis, *The Life of Kit Carson*, 248–49.

66. Carter, '*Dear Old Kit*,' 212.

67. David Michael Delo, *Peddlers and Post Traders, The Army Sutler on the Frontier* (Salt Lake City: University of Utah Press, 1992), 107.

68. Blackwelder, *Great Westerner*, 315.

69. Guild and Carter in their *Kit Carson*, 278, without citing a source, inexplicably claim that in January 1868 Carson received the appointment. In no correspondence nor in any newspaper account related to Kit's subsequent trip to Washington with a Ute delegation is he referred to by the title "Superintendent," whereas Colorado Governor Hunt, also a member, was consistently so designated.

70. The N.M. Supt. A. B. Norton to Comm. of Indian Affairs N. G. Taylor, Santa Fe, July 27, 1867, New Mexico Superintendency of Indian Affairs, Letters Sent, Microcopy no. 234, reel 554, NA.

71. Carson to Carleton, May 1, 1865, Letters Received, Department of New Mexico, RAC, Record Group 98, NA.

72. Claim Record, Kit Carson Mining Company, May 23, 1866, Mora, N.Mex., First County Record, Justice of the Peace Book, 1:229. Also a copy in KC, SRC.

73. Typescript, undated, from a geological survey by F. V. Hayden, in KC, SRC.

74. Carleton to Carson, Santa Fe, October 1, 1866, Letters Received, Department of New

Mexico, RAC, Record Group 98, NA. Copy from McNitt Coll., NMSRCA.

75. John Mack Faragher, *Daniel Boone, The Life and Legend of an American Pioneer* (New York: Henry Holt & Co., 1992), 293.

76. *Santa Fe Gazette*, November 16, 1867.

Conclusion

1. Carson to Collins, Taos, September 20, 1859, Carson Agency Correspondence, NA. Tom Dunlay in his *Kit Carson & the Indians*, 148, uses that line by Carson as a subheading for his Chapter 5 on the Ute Agency.

2. *Farm and Field*, 5 (March 31, 1888), 6.

3. Quoted in Sabin, *Kit Carson Days* (1935), 2:800. Roughly five years after Kit's death Boggs stated in an accounting of the children's inheritance that, "The means left by Gen. Carson were inadequate to the rearing of so large a family." Account Book, Carson Estate, n.d., Thomas O. Boggs Papers, BL, UC.

4. Blackwelder, *Great Westerner*, 356. Phil Petersen, "Boggsville: A Trail Settlement," *Wagon Tracks*, 6 (November 1992), 7–11.

5. Abbott, *Christopher Carson*, 343–44.

6. This view was common among mountain men in their later years.

7. Sabin, *Kit Carson Days* (1935), 2:792.

8. Hough to Sabin, Lake City, Colo., November 17, 1901, Sabin Papers, Lee, BYU.

9. Abbot, *Christopher Carson*, 345.

10. Hunt to Nathaniel G. Taylor, December 17, 1867, Letters Received by the Office of Indian Affairs, Colorado Superintendency, 1867–1868, Microcopy 234, reel 199, NA. The practice of bringing Indians to eastern cities in an attempt to awe them dated back to the presidency of George Washington. Katherine C. Turner, *Red Men Calling on the Great White Father* (Norman: University of Oklahoma Press, 1951), xiv. See also, Nathaniel G. Taylor, *Report of the Commissioner of Indian Affairs* (Washington: GPO, 1868), 182.

11. Boskin, *History of the Arkansas Valley, Colorado*, 836.

12. Carter, *'Dear Old Kit,'* 174.

13. Associated Press report on the Washington activities of Kit Carson, printed in the *Boston Daily Journal*, February 4, 1868.

14. *Daily National Intelligencer*, February 6, 1868.

15. Jessie Benton Frémont, *The Will and the Way Stories*, 43.

16. For the hard bargaining of head chief Ouray and the eventual disintegration of the treaty, see Marshall Sprague, *Massacre, The Tragedy at White River* (repr. of 1957 ed.; Lincoln: University of Nebraska Press, 1980), 92–93. Peters's quote in Grant, *Kit Carson's Own Story*, 137.

17. Paul I. Wellman, "Kit Carson's Letter in an Old Trunk," in *Kansas City Star*, September 20, 1942.

18. Hunt to Taylor, February 29 and March 12, 1868; and Sec. Browning to Taylor, March 17, 1868. Evidently, Carson received no pay for his work on behalf of the treaty, although his travel expenses were covered. Hunt to Taylor, February 12, 1868 [delegation expenses]. All

in Letters Received by the Office of Indian Affairs, Colorado Superintendency, 1867–1868, Microcopy 234, reel 199, NA. (Reference courtesy of Lee Burke) On the government's method of financing Indian delegations to Washington, see Herman J. Viola, *Diplomats in Buckskin* (Washington, D.C.: Smithsonian Institution Press, 1981), 54–68.

19. The papers were the *New York Times*, the *Evening Telegram*, and the *New York Tribune*.

20. The *Boston Daily Journal*, March 19, 2002.

21. Jessie Benton Frémont, *The Will and the Way Stories*, 46–47.

22. Jessie Benton Frémont, "Kit Carson," 102.

23. Herr, *Jessie Benton Frémont*, 386.

24. The *Boston Daily Journal*, March 20, 1868. (Reference courtesy of Mel and Mary Cottom) All preceding quotes about the tour are from this source.

25. Notice of the Carson-Hunt photographic session at the Black Studio appeared in the *Boston Daily Evening Transcript*, March 21, 1868.

26. After Carson left the group, Gov. Hunt led the Utes on an excursion to Niagara Falls. Guild and Carter, *Kit Carson*, 281, claim that Oakes returned to Denver before Carson. However, the *Boston Daily Journal*, March 19, still listed him among the members of the delegation, as of that date. Since Kit himself departed for Colorado a few days later, and needed assistance while traveling, it seems highly probable that the two men went together.

27. Sabin, *Kit Carson Days* (1935), 2:798.

28. Mrs. Bennett, whose husband had been a clerk with the Ute delegation to Washington, granted an interview to Albert B. Sanford of the Colorado Historical Society. Portions of it appeared in the *Rocky Mountain News*, August 1, 1924. See also, Marita Hayes, "D. C. Oakes, Early Colorado Booster," *Colorado Magazine*, 31 (July 1954), 224.

29. Barron B. Beshoar, *Hippocrates in a Red Vest, The Biography of a Frontier Doctor* (Palo Alto, Calif.: American West Publ. Co., 1973), 106.

30. Beshoar, *Hippocrates*, 107.

31. Carson to Leckler, Boggs Ranch [April 16, 1868], original now in a private collection; copy in possession of the author.

32. Raymond W. Settle, "The Twilight Days of Kit Carson," *The West*, (March 1969), 70. For these details, Settle interviewed the widow of Kit Carson, Jr., and also Charles Carson, before his death in 1938. Another version of Josefa's death, by L. A. Allen, a rancher at Boggsville, varies in some particulars. Internal evidence disqualifies it as a reliable source. "Old Cattleman's Tales." An undated newspaper clipping in a supplementary bundle of documents associated with a manuscript by Col. Calvin D. Cowles, "Genealogy of Five Allied Families," Library of Congress, Rare Books Division, Washington, D.C. Allen's brother, DeWitt F. Allen, married Teresina Carson at Boggsville in 1871. McClung, *Carson, Bent, Boggs Genealogy*, 79. Col. Cowles was descended from Kit's uncle, Andrew Carson, of North Carolina. Also see, Guild and Carter, *Kit Carson*, 333, n. 18.

33. Morgan and Harris, *Anderson's Rocky Mountain Journals*, 281. Judith Hanneman, "Doctor, compadre, adios!" *Rocky Mountain Medical Journal*, 8 (April 1968), 37.

34. Settle, "Twilight Days," 70.

35. Abbott, *Christopher Carson*, 345.

36. The entire letter to Aloys Scheurich from Carson is printed in Estergreen, *Kit Carson*, 274–75.

37. Teresina Bent Scheurich's statement on this matter appears in Sabin, *Kit Carson Days* (1935), 2:799–800.

38. Abbott, *Christopher Carson*, 344. Thoracic aneurysms through the nineteenth century were not uncommon, and sometimes expanded to enormous size. Robert H. Shikes, M.D., *Rocky Mountain Medicine* (Boulder, Colo.: Johnson Books, 1986), 236, n. 41. The contemporary press often referred to Carson's malady as "heart disease."

39. Abbott, *Christopher Carson*, 345.

40. Albert W. Thompson, "The Death and the Last Will of Kit Carson," *Colorado Magazine*, 5 (1928), 186.

41. Abbott, *Christopher Carson*, 345. During the Navajo campaign, his quartermaster, Capt. Asa B. Carey, had read the Peters book to Kit, who responded with criticisms and corrections, which the captain had entered on the interleaves. That copy belonging to Carey has long since disappeared, a major loss, since the notes, if available now, might reveal useful insights into Kit Carson's thinking and sentiments. Carey to Sabin, Fort Sam Houston, Texas, January 13, 1909, MSS/sc 1972, Lee, BYU.

42. Sabin, *Kit Carson Days* (1935), 2:800.

43. Settle, "Twilight Days," 70. The present writer in an address to the Santa Fe Trail Association Symposium, September 26, 1993 at La Junta, Colorado referred to the "lost hat incident" as having occurred while the Carson boys were crossing the Arkansas. Charles's son, the late Jess Carson, was in the audience and afterward let it be known that the small mishap actually took place at the fording of the Purgatory.

44. Abbott, *Christopher Carson*, 346.

45. Abbott, *Christopher Carson*, 347.

46. *Santa Fe Gazette*, June 12, 1868. Sabin, *Kit Carson Days* (1935), 2:803–4.

47. The *Colorado Transcipt* (Golden City), June 3, 1868.

48. Settle, "Twilight Days," 70.

49. Peters, *Kit Carson's Life and Adventures* (1873), 566.

Bibliography

Notes
Abbreviations

BL, UC Bancroft Library, University of California, Berkeley
CMSR Combined Military Service Records, NA.
FACHL Fray Angélico Chávez History Library, Museum of New Mexico, Santa Fe
KC, SRC Kit Carson Historic Museums, Southwest Research Center
Lee, BYU Harold B. Lee Library, Brigham Young University, Provo, Utah
MHS Missouri Historical Society, St. Louis
NA National Archives, Washington, D.C.
NMHR *New Mexico Historical Review*
NMS New Mexico Superintendency
NMSRCA New Mexico State Records Center and Archives, Santa Fe
OR *The War of the Rebellion: A Compilation of the Official Records of the Union and Confederate Armies*, Washington: Government Printing Office, 1880–1901
RAC Record Army Command, NA

Archival Materials
California

Bancroft Library, University of California, Berkeley
    Thomas Boggs Papers
    Christopher Carson Collection

Connecticut

Beinecke Rare Book and Manuscript Library, Yale University, New Haven
    John C. Frémont Letters

Colorado

Colorado Historical Society Archives, Denver
    Kit Carson File
    Edward W. Wynkoop, "Colorado History Manuscript, 1876"
Colorado Springs Pioneers Museum, Starsmore Center for Local History
    V. F. K. Carson Collection
Francis W. Cragin Collection: Early Far West Notebooks

178

Kansas
Kansas State Historical Society, Manuscript Division, Topeka
    Kit Carson Papers

Missouri
Howard County Courthouse, Office of the County Clerk, Fayette
    Deed Records

Missouri Historical Society, Archives, St. Louis
    Christopher Carson Collection
    P. Chouteau-Moffitt Collection
    Turley Family Papers
    James J. Webb Collection

New Mexico
Archives of the Archdiocese of Santa Fe
    Baptisms
    Marriage Registers
Kit Carson Historic Museums, Southwest Research Center, Taos
    Albright Collection
    Blackwelder Collection: Carson Military Service Records
    Kit Carson Files
    Don Cline Collection
    DeWitt Clinton Peters Papers
    Smith Simpson Papers
Fray Angélico Chávez History Library, Archives, Santa Fe
    Bent Family Bible
    Kit Carson File
Highlands University Library, Las Vegas
    Arrott Collection: Fort Union
New Mexico State Records Center and Archives, Santa Fe
    Kit Carson File
    Frank McNitt Collection
    Records of the U.S. Court of Private Land Claims
    Teresina Bent Scheurich Collection
    Territorial Archives of New Mexico

Oklahoma
Western History Collection, University of Oklahoma Library, Norman
    W. S. Campbell (Stanley Vestal) Collection

Utah

Harold B. Lee Library, Brigham Young University, Provo
    Christopher Carson Collection
    Edwin L. Sabin Papers
    Philander Simmons, "Reminiscences of Kit Carson," Manuscript 657

Washington, D.C.

Library of Congress, Manuscript Division
    Col. Calvin D. Cowles Collection
    Navajo Campaign Letterbook, 1863–1864
    Capt. Nelson Thomasson, "Recollections of Kit Carson," Printed Speech,
        delivered March 1, 1928, Chicago
National Archives
    Office of Adjutant General, Letter Received, 1822–1860
    Bureau of Indian Affairs:
        Colorado Superintendency, 1867–1868
        New Mexico Superintendency, 1849–1853
        Carson Agency Correspondence
    Bureau of Pension Records
    Compiled Military Service Records
    Military Department of New Mexico
        Letters Sent and Received, 1851–1868
    Secretary of War
        Letters Received, 1801–1870

Wisconsin

Milwaukee County Historical Society, Archives
    John C. Stevenson Collection

Newspapers

Albuquerque Daily Citizen
Boston Daily Journal
Boston Evening Journal
California State Journal (Sacramento)
Colorado Springs Gazette
Colorado Transcript (Golden City)
Daily National Intelligencer (Washington, D.C.)
Daily New Mexican (Santa Fe)
Denver Republican
Fayette Advertiser (Missouri)
Jefferson Inquirer (Missouri)
Kansas City Star

Las Animal Leader (Colorado)
Missouri Republican (St. Louis)
National Tribune (Washington, D.C.)
New York Daily Herald
New York Daily Tribune
New York Evening Telegram
New York Times
Raton Range (New Mexico)
Rocky Mountain News (Denver)
San Antonio Herald (Texas)
Santa Fe Gazette
Santa Fe New Mexican Review
Taos News (New Mexico)

Books

Abbott, John S. C. *Christopher Carson, Known as Kit Carson*. New York: Dodd, Mead,and Co., 1901.

Anderson, Jeffrey. *The Four Hills of Life: Arapaho Knowledge and Life Movement*. Lincoln: University of Nebraska Press, 2001.

Baker, T. Lindsey and Billy R. Harrison. *Adobe Walls*. College Station: Texas A&M University Press, 1986.

Barton, John D. *Buckskin Entrepreneur: Antoine Robidoux and the Fur Trade of the Uinta Basin, 1824–1844*. Vernal, Utah: Oakfield Publishing Co., 1996.

Bashin, O. L. *History of the Arkansas Valley, Colorado*. Chicago, Bashin & Co., 1881.

Baxter, John O. *Las Carneradas: Sheep Trade in New Mexico, 1700–1860*. Albuquerque: University of New Mexico Press, 1987.

Benton, Thomas H. *Thirty Years' View*. 2 vols. New York: D. Appleton Co., 1854–1856.

Beshoar, Barron B. *Hippocrates in a Red Vest: The Biography of a Frontier Doctor*. Palo Alto, California: American West Publishing Co., 1973.

Blackwelder, Bernice. *Great Westerner: The Story of Kit Carson*. Caldwell, Id.: Caxton Publishers, 1962.

Bent, Allen H. *The Bent Family in America*. Boston: David Clapp & Son, 1900.

Berthong, Donald J. *The Southern Cheyennes*. Norman: University of Oklahoma Press, 1963.

Bower, Donald E. *Fred Rosenstock: A Legend in Books and Art*. Flagstaff, Ariz.: Northland Press, 1963.

Boyer, Jack K. *A History of Freemasonry in Taos, New Mexico: Bent Lodge No. 42*. Taos: The Lodge of Research, 1971.

Brackett, Albert G. *History of the United States Cavalry*. New York: Harper & Bros., 1865.

Bradford, Ernle. *The Shield and the Sword: The Knights of St. John, Jerusalem, Rhodes and Malta*. New York: E. P. Dutton & Co., 1973.

Brayer, Herbert O. *William Blackmore: The Spanish and Mexican Land Grants of New Mexico and Colorado, 1863–1878*. 2 vols. Denver: Bradford-Robinson Co., 1949.

Brewerton, George Douglas. *Overland with Kit Carson*. Lincoln: University of Nebraska Press, 1993. Reprint.

———. *The War in Kansas: A Rough Trip to the Border*. New York: Derby and Jackson, 1856.

Brooks, James F. *Captives and Cousins: Slavery, Kinship, and Community in the Southwest Borderlands*. Chapel Hill: University of North Carolina Press, 2002.

Brugge, David M. *Navajos in the Catholic Records of New Mexico: 1694–1875*. Tsaile, Ariz.: Navajo Community College, 1985.

Bryant, Edwin. *What I Saw in California: Being the Journal of a Tour in the Years 1846, 1847*. Minneapolis: Ross & Haines, 1967. Reprint.

Bullock, Steven C. *Revolutionary Brotherhood: Freemasonry and the Transformation of the American Social Order, 1730–1840*. Chapel Hill: University of North Carolina Press, 1996.

Carter, Harvey Lewis. *"Dear Old Kit": The Historical Christopher Carson*. Norman: University of Oklahoma Press, 1968.

Cather, Willa. *Death Comes for the Archbishop*. New York: Alfred A. Knopf, 1955.

Chávez, Fray Angélico. But Time and Chance: The Story of Padre Martínez of Taos, *1793–1867*. Santa Fe: Sunstone Press, 1981.

———. *Origins of New Mexico Families*. Santa Fe: Museum of New Mexico Press, 1992. Reprint.

Churchill, Charles B. *Adventurers and Prophets: American Autobiographies in Mexican California, 1828–1847*. Spokane, Wash.: Arthur H. Clark, Co., 1995.

Coburn, Walt. *Stirrup High*. Lincoln: University of Nebraska Press, 1997. Reprint.

Colligan, John B. *The Juan Páez Hurtado Expedition of 1695*. Albuquerque: University of New Mexico Press.

Cooke, Philip St. George. *The Conquest of New Mexico and California*. New York: G. P. Putnam's Sons, 1878.

Craver, Rebecca McDonald. *The Impact of Intimacy, Mexican-Anglo Intermarriage in New Mexico, 1821–1846*. El Paso: Texas Western Press, 1982.

Davis, William W. H. *El Gringo, or New Mexico and Her People*. Santa Fe: Rydal Press, 1938. Reprint.

Delo, David Michael. *Peddlers and Post Traders: The Army Sutler on the Frontier*. Salt Lake City: University of Utah Press, 1992.

Dodge, Col. Richard Irving. *Our Wild Indians*. New York: Archer House, 1959. Reprint.

Dunlay, Thomas. *Kit Carson and the Indians*. Lincoln: University of Nebraska Press, 2000.

Ellis, Edward S. *The Life of Kit Carson*. Chicago: M. A. Donohue & Co., 1889.

Emmett, Chris. *Fort Union and the Winning of the Southwest*. Norman: University of Oklahoma Press, 1965.

Esquibel, José Antonio and John B. Colligan. *The Spanish Recolonization of New Mexico: An Account of the Families Recruited at Mexico City, 1693.* Albuquerque: Hispanic Genealogical Research Center of New Mexico, 1999.

Estergreen, M. Morgan. *Kit Carson: A Portrait in Courage.* Norman: University of Oklahoma Press, 1962.

Ewers, John C. *The Blackfeet: Raiders of the Northwestern Plains.* Norman: University of Oklahoma Press, 1958.

Faragher, John Mack. *Daniel Boone: The Life and Legend of an American Pioneer.* New York: Henry Holt & Co., 1992.

Frazer, Robert W. *Forts and Supplies: The Role of the Army in the Economy of the Southwest.* Albuquerque: University of New Mexico Press, 1983.

———., ed. *New Mexico in 1850: A Military View.* Norman: University of Oklahoma Press, 1968.

Frémont, Jessie Benton. *The Will and the Way Stories.* Boston: D. Lothrop Co., 1891.

Frémont, John Charles. *Memoirs of My Life.* Chicago: Belford, Clark & Co., 1887.

Garrard, Lewis Hector. *Wah-to-yah and the Taos Trail.* Norman: University of Oklahoma Press, 1955.

Gilbert, Bil. *Westering Man: The Life of Joseph Walker.* New York: Atheneum, 1983.

Gonzalez, Manuel G. *The Hispanic Elite of the Southwest.* El Paso: Texas Western Press, 1989.

Gottlieb, Beatrice. *The Family in the Western World.* New York: Oxford University Press, 1993.

Grant, Blanche, ed. *Kit Carson's Own Story of His Life.* Taos, N.Mex.: Privately printed, 1926.

Gregg, Josiah. *Commerce of the Prairies.* Norman: University of Oklahoma Press, 1990. Reprint.

Grinnell, George Bird. *The Cheyenne Indians.* 2 vols. New Haven, Conn.: Yale University Press, 1923.

———. *The Fighting Cheyennes.* Norman: University of Oklahoma Press, 1956.

Guild, Thelma S. and Harvey L. Carter. *Kit Carson: A Pattern for Heroes.* Lincoln: University of Nebraska Press, 1984.

Gutiérrez, Ramón. *When Jesus Came, the Corn Mothers Went Away: Marriage, Sexuality, and Power in New Mexico, 1500–1846.* Stanford: Stanford University Press, 1991.

Hafen, LeRoy R., ed. *The Mountain Men and the Fur Trade of the Far West.* 10 vols. Glendale, Calif.: Arthur H. Clark Co., 1965–1972.

Hafen, LeRoy R. and Ann Hafen, eds. *Frémont's Fourth Expedition.* Glendale, Calif.: Arthur H. Clark Co., 1960.

———., eds. *To the Rockies and Oregon.* Glendale, Calif.: Arthur H. Clark Co., 1955.

Haines, Aubrey L., ed. *Journal of a Trapper.* Lincoln: University of Nebraska Press, 1955.

Hanson, Charles E. *The Plains Rifle.* New York: Bramhall House, 1960.

Hayes, Ralph L., comp. *Taos County, New Mexico* [Genealogy]. Albuquerque: New Mexico Genealogical Society, 1989.

Haywood, C. Robert. *The Merchant Prince of Dodge City: The Life and Times of Robert M. Wright.* Norman: University of Oklahoma Press, 1998.

Herr, Pamela and Mary Lee Spence, eds. *The Letters of Jessie Benton Frémont.* Urbana: University of Illinois Press, 1993.

Higer, Sister M. Inez. *Arapaho Child Life and Its Cultural Background.* BAE Bulletin 148. Washington, D.C.: Smithsonian Institution Press, 1952.

Horgan, Paul. *Lamy of Santa Fe: His Life and Times.* New York: Farrar, Straus and Giroux, 1975.

Hobbs, James. *Wild Life in the Far West.* Glorieta, N.Mex.: Rio Grande Press, 1969. Reprint.

Howlett, J. W. *Life of the Right Reverend Joseph P. Machebeuf.* Denver: Register College, 1954. Reprint.

Hughes, John T. *Doniphan's Expedition.* College Station: Texas A&M University Press, 1997. Reprint.

Hussey, Jeannette M. *The Code Duello in America: An Exhibition at the National Portrait Gallery, December 18, 1980 to April 19, 1981.* Washington, D.C.: Smithsonian Institution Press, 1980.

Hyde, George E. *Life of George Bent: Written from His Letters.* Norman: University of Oklahoma Press, 1967.

Ingham, John M. *Mary, Michael and Lucifer: Folk Catholicism in Central Mexico.* Austin: University of Texas Press, 1986.

Inman, Henry. *The Old Santa Fe Trail.* Topeka, Kan.: Crane & Co., 1899.

Jackson, Donald and Mary Lee Spence, eds. *The Expeditions of John Charles Frémont.* 3 vols. Urbana: University of Illinois Press, 1970–1984,

Jaramillo, Cleofas M. *Shadows of the Past.* Santa Fe, N.Mex.: Ancient City Press, 1972. Reprint.

Keleher, William A. *Turmoil in New Mexico, 1846–1868.* Santa Fe, N.Mex.: Rydal Press, 1952.

Kelly, Lawrence C. *Navajo Roundup.* Boulder, Colo.: Pruett Publishing Co., 1970.

Kroeber, Alfred L. *The Arapaho.* Bulletin 18. New York: American Museum of Natural History, 1902.

Lamar, Howard Roberts. *The Far Southwest, 1846–1912.* New Haven, Conn.: Yale University Press, 1966.

Langston, LaMoine. *A History of Masonry in New Mexico.* Roswell, N.Mex.: Hall-Poorbaugh Press [1978].

Lavender, David. *Bent's Fort.* Garden City, N.Y.: Doubleday & Co., 1954.

Lavrin, Asunción, ed. *Sexuality and Marriage in Colonial Latin America.* Lincoln: University of Nebraska Press, 1992.

Lecompte, Janet. *Pueblo, Hardscrabble, and Greenhorn: The Upper Arkansas, 1832–1856.* Norman: University of Oklahoma Press, 1978.

Limerick, Patricia Nelson. *The Legacy of Conquest: The Unbroken Past of the American West.* New York: W. W. Norton, 1987.

Lowie, Robert H. *Indians of the Plains.* New York: McGraw-Hill Book Co., 1954.

Lytle, William M. and Forrest R. Holdcamper, comps. *Merchant Steam Vessels of the United States, 1790–1868.* New York: Steamship Historical Society of America, 1975.

Majors, Alexander. *Seventy Years on the Frontier.* Minneapolis: Ross & Haines, 1965. Reprint.

McClung, Quantrille D., comp. *Carson-Bent-Boggs Genealogy.* Denver: Denver Public Library, 1962. And *Carson-Bent-Boggs Genealogy, Supplement.* 1973.

Mead, James R. *Hunting and Trading on the Great Plains, 1859–1875.* Norman: University of Oklahoma Press, 1986.

Meketa, Jacqueline Dorgan. *Legacy of Honor: The Life of Rafael Chacón.* Albuquerque: University of New Mexico Press, 1986.

Meline, James F. *Two Thousand Miles on Horseback, 1866.* Albuquerque: Horn & Wallace, 1966. Reprint.

Montoya, María E. *Translating Property: The Maxwell Land Grant and the Conflict Over Land in the American West, 1840–1900.* Berkeley: University of California Press, 2002.

Moody, Ralph. *Kit Carson and the Wild Frontier.* New York: Random House, 1955.

Morgan, Dale L. and Eleanor T. Harris, eds. *The Rocky Mountain Journals of William Marshall Anderson.* Lincoln: University of Nebraska Press, 1987. Reprint.

Murphy, Eugene P., S. J. *Blessed Philippine Duchesne—Pioneer Apostle of the Sacred Heart.* St Louis: Radio League of the Sacred Heart, 1940.

Murphy, Lawrence R. *Lucien Bonaparte Maxwell: Napoleon of the Southwest.* Norman: University of Oklahoma Press, 1983.

Nevins, Allan. *Polk: The Diary of a President.* London: Longmans, Green & Co., 1929.

Oliva, Leo E. *Fort Union and the Frontier Army in the Southwest.* Professional Papers 41. Santa Fe, N.Mex.: National Park Service, 1993.

O'Meara, Walter. *Daughters of the Country: The Women of the Fur Traders and Mountain Men.* New York: Harcourt, Brace & World, 1968.

Pancoast, Charles E. *A Quaker Forty-niner.* Philadelphia: University of Pennsylvania Press, 1930.

Parish, William J. *The Charles Ilfeld Company.* Cambridge, Mass.: Harvard University Press, 1961.

Parker, Rev. Samuel. *Journal of an Exploring Tour Beyond the Rocky Mountains.* Minneapolis: Ross & Haines, 1967. Reprint.

Parkhill, Forbes. *The Blazed Trail of Antoine Leroux.* Los Angeles: Westernlore Press, 1965.

Parkman, Francis. *The Oregon Trail.* E. N. Feltskog, ed. Madison: University of Wisconsin Press, 1969. Reprint.

Pearson, Jim Berry. *The Maxwell Land Grant.* Norman: University of Oklahoma Press, 1961.

Peters, DeWitt Clinton. *The Life of Kit Carson, The Nestor of the Rocky Mountains.* New York: W. R. C. Clark, 1858.

———. *Kit Carson's Life and Adventures.* Hartford, Conn.: Dustin, Gilman & Co., 1873. [Retitled and expanded edition of *The Life of Kit Carson*, 1858.]

Quaife, Milo Milton, ed. *Kit Carson's Autobiography.* Chicago: Lakeside Press, 1935.

Rath, Ida Ellen. *The Rath Trail.* Wichita, Kan.: McCormick-Armstrong Co., 1961.

Richardson, Albert D. *Beyond the Mississippi.* Hartford, Conn.: American Publishing Co., 1867.

Richmond, Patricia Joy. *Trail to Disaster.* Niwot, Colo.: University Press of Colorado, 1990.

Roberts, David. *A Newer World: Kit Carson, John C. Frémont, and the Claiming of the American West.* New York: Simon Schuster, 2000.

Robertson, Frank C. *Fort Hall: Gateway to the Oregon Country.* New York: Hastings House, 1963.

Robinson, John J. *Born in Blood: The Lost Secrets of Freemasonry.* New York: M. Evans & Co., 1989.

Rusling, James F. *Across America, or The Great West.* New York: Sheldon & Co., 1875.

Russell, Mrs. Hal, comp. *Land of Enchantment: Memoirs of Marian Sloan Russell on the Santa Fe Trail.* Albuquerque: University of New Mexico Press, 1984. Reprint.

Sabin, Edwin L. *Kit Carson Days.* Chicago: A. C. McClurg, 1914; 2nd expanded edition, 2 vols. New York: Press of the Pioneers, 1935.

Sachsen-Attenburg, Hans von, and Laura Gabiger, eds. *Winning the West: General Stephen Watts Kearny's Letter Book, 1846–1847.* Booneville, Mo.: Pekitanoui Publishing, 1998.

Sanchez, Pedro. *Memorias Sobre la Vida del Presbitero Don Antonio José Martínez.* Trans. by Ray John de Aragón. Santa Fe, N.Mex.: The Lightning Tree Press, 1978.

Sonnichsen, C. L. *The Mescalero Apaches.* Norman: University of Oklahoma Press, 1958.

Sprague, Marshall. *Massacre, The Tragedy at White River.* Lincoln: University of Nebraska Press, 1980. Reprint.

Stanley, F. *Giant in Lilliput: The Story of Donaciano Vigil.* Pampa, Tex.: Pampa Print Shop, 1963.

———. *The Thomas Oliver Boggs Story.* Nazareth, Tex.: Privately printed, 1972.

Steckmesser, Kent Ladd. *The Western Hero in History and Legend.* Norman: University of Oklahoma Press, 1965.

Stewart, William Drummond. *Edward Warren.* Missoula, Mont.: Mountain Press Publishing Co., 1986. Reprint.

Stockel, H. Henrietta. *Women of the Apache Nation: Voices of Truth.* Reno: University of Nevada Press, 1991.

Swanton, John R. *The Indian Tribes of North America.* BAE Bulletin 145. Washington, D.C.: Smithsonian Institution Press, 1953.

Tanguay, Cyprien, comp. *Dictionaire Genealogique des Familles Canadiennes.* 8 vols. Montreal, Canada: Eusebe Senécal & Fils, 1887.

Tassin, Ray. *Stanley Vestal: Champion of the Old West.* Glendale, Calif.: Arthur H. Clark Co., 1973.

Taylor, John. *Bloody Valverde: A Civil War Battle on the Rio Grande, February 21, 1862.* Albuquerque: University of New Mexico Press, 1995.

Taylor, N. G., comp. *Annual Report of the Commissioner of Indian Affairs, 1866.*

Washington, D. C.: Government Printing Office, 1868.

Thompson, Gerald. *Edward F. Beale and the American West*. Albuquerque: University of New Mexico Press, 1983.

Thompson, Jerry, D. ed. *Civil War in the Southwest: Recollections of the Sibley Brigade*. College Station: Texas A&M University Press, 2001.

Thrapp, Dan L. *Encyclopedia of Frontier Biography*. 3 vols. Glendale, Calif.: Arthur H. Clark Co., 1988.

Tobie, Harvey. *No Man Like Joe: The Life and Times of Joseph L. Meek*. Portland, Ore.: Binfords & Mort, 1949.

Trenholm, Virginia Cole. *The Arapahoes, Our People*. Norman: University of Oklahoma Press, 1970.

Turner, Kathryn C. *Red Men Calling on the Great White Father*. Norman: University of Oklahoma Press, 1951.

Twitchell, Ralph Emerson. *Leading Facts of New Mexico History*. 5 vols. Cedar Rapids, Iowa: The Torch Press, 1911–1917.

———. *The Military Occupation of New Mexico, 1846–1851*. Denver: Smith-Brooks Co., 1909.

———. *Old Santa Fe*. Santa Fe, N.Mex.: New Mexican Publishing Co., 1925.

Upham, Charles Wentworth. *Life, Explorations and Public Services of John Charles Frémont*. Boston: Ticknor and Fields, 1856.

Utley, Robert M. *A Life Wild and Perilous: Mountain Men and the Paths to the Pacific*. New York: Henry Holt & Co., 1997.

Vestal, Stanley. *Kit Carson, The Happy Warrior of the Old West; A Biography*. Boston: Houghton Mifflin Co., 1928.

Victor, Frances Fuller. *The River of the West*. Hartford, Conn.: Columbian Book Co., 1870.

Viola, Herman J. *Diplomats in Buckskins: A History of Indian Delegations in Washington City*. Washington, D. C.: Smithsonian Institution Press, 1981.

Wallace, William Swilling. *Antoine Robidoux, 1794–1860*. Los Angeles: Glen Dawson, 1953. *The War of the Rebellion: A Compilation of the Union and Confederate Armies*. 70 vols. in 128. Washington, D. C.: Government Printing Office, 1880–1901.

Warrin, Donald and Geoffrey L. Gomes. *Land As Far As the Eye Can See: Portuguese in the Old West*. Spokane, Wash.: Arthur H. Clark Co., 2001.

Webb, James Josiah. *Adventures in the Santa Fe Trade*. Glendale, Calif.: Arthur H. Clark Co., 1931.

Weber, David J., ed. *Northern Mexico on the Eve of the United States Invasion*. New York: Arno Press, 1976.

Wederty, French S. *Mono Diggings*. Bishop, Calif.: Chalfant Press, 1978.

Wilson, Mitchell. *American Science and Invention*. New York: Bonanza Books, 1960.

Winfrey, Norman. *Texas Indian Papers, 1860–1916*. Austin: Texas State Library, 1961.

Wishart, David J. *The Fur Trade of the American West*. Lincoln: University of Nebraska Press, 1979.

Woods, Richard D., comp. *Hispanic First Names*. Westport, Conn.: Greenwood Press,

1984. Reprint.

Wyatt-Brown, Bertram. *Southern Honor: Ethics and Behavior in the Old South.* New York: Oxford University Press, 1982.

Yohn, Susan M. *A Contest of Faiths: Missionary Women and Pluralism in the American Southwest.* Ithaca, N.Y.: Cornell University Press, 1995.

Articles

Anonymous. "A Brief History of Freemasonry in New Mexico." *The New Mexico Freemason* 3(October 1938): 3–7.

Antony, Brother Claudius. "Kit Carson Catholic." *NMHR* 10(October 1935): 323–36.

Athearn, Robert G. "The Education of Kit Carson's Son." *NMHR* 31(April 1956): 133–39.

Bloom, Lansing B., ed. "Bourke on the Southwest." *NMHR* 12(January 1937): 41–77.

Brown, David L. "Three Years in the Rocky Mountains." First published 1845. Reprinted in David A. White, *News of the Plains and the Rockies, 1803–1865.* 8 vols. Spokane, Wash.: Arthur H. Clark Co., 1996. 1:379–96.

Burton, E. Bennett. "The Taos Rebellion." *Old Santa Fe* 1(October 1913): 176–95.

Camp, Charles L. "Review of Kit Carson, The Happy Warrior of the Old West." *California Historical Society Quarterly* 7(September 1928): 92–93.

———. "Review of Kit Carson's Own Story of His Life." *California Historical Society Quarterly* 5(December 1926): 408–9.

Carter, Harvey L. "The Divergent Paths of Frémont's 'Three Marshalls.'" *NMHR* 48(January 1973): 5–25.

Christopher, Adrienne. "Daniel Yoacham, Pioneer Innkeeper of Westport." *Wesport Historical Quarterly* 1(November 1965): 11.

———, ed. "Recollections of Susanna Yoacham Dillon." *Westport Historical Society* 1(November 1965): 3–7.

Claussen, W. Edmunds. "Rayado Rancho." *New Mexico Magazine.* 24(March 1946): 11, 37, 39.

Correll, J. Lee. "Navajos Adopted by Kit Carson at Taos, N.M." *Navajo Times* (April 1, 1965).

Denslow, Ray V. "Kit Carson Freemason." *Missouri Grand Lodge Bulletin* 1(February 1924): 20–25.

DeVoto, Bernard. "The Great Medicine Road." *American Mercury* 11(May 1927): 104–12.

Dollar, Clyde D. "The High Plains Smallpox Epidemic of 1837–38." *Western Historical Quarterly* 8(January 1977): 13–38.

Englert, Lorene and Kenny. "Oliver Perry Wiggins, Fantastic, Bombastic Frontiersman." *The Denver Westerners Monthly Roundup* 20(February 1964): 3–14.

Fish, Rush. "The Life Story of Teresina Bent Scheurich, Daughter of Governor Charles Bent." *Ayer y Hoy.* Periodical of the Taos County Historical Society (Winter 1997): 6–7, 14–15.

Frémont, Jessie Benton. "Kit Carson." *Land of Sunshine* 6(February 1897): 97–103.

Fry, James B. "The Brevet System in the United States Army." In Francis B. Taunton, ed. *The English Westerners' Brand Book, 1971–72*. (London: English Westerners' Society, 1972): 1–19.

Gardner, Mark L. "The Bent Brothers and the Call of the West." *Russell's West* [The C. M. Russell Museum Magazine] 6(Autumn 1998): 10–14.

———. "Tragedy in Taos." *New Mexico Magazine* 78(October 2000): 32–38.

Greco, David. "The Legend of Little Whiteman." *Persimmon Hill* 17(Winter 1990): 35–41.

Grinnell, George Bird. "Bent's Old Fort and Its Builders." *Collections of the Kansas State Historical Society, 1919–1922* 15(Topeka 1923): 28–91.

Gwyther, George. "A Frontier Post and Country." *Overland Monthly* 5(December 1870): 520–26.

Hafen, Ann. "Campfire Frontier." *Rocky Mountain Empire Magazine* (September 1, 1946): 5–6.

Hafen, LeRoy R. "Fort Davy Crockett, Its Fur Men and Visitors." *The Colorado Magazine* 29(January 1952): 17–33.

———. "Mexican Land Grants in Colorado." *The Colorado Magazine* 4(May 1927): 82–83.

———. "The W. M. Boggs Manuscript." *The Colorado Magazine* 7(March 1930): 45–69.

Hanneman, Judith. "Doctor, compadre, adios!" *Rocky Mountain Medical Journal* 8(April 1968): 37–40.

Hayes, Martha. "D. C. Oakes, Early Colorado Booster." *The Colorado Magazine* 31(July 1954): 216–24.

Hooper, Alban W., ed. "Letters to and from Abraham G. Mayers, 1854–1857." *NMHR* 9(July 1934): 290–335.

Lecompte, Janet. "The Independent Women of Hispanic New Mexico, 1821–1846." *Western Historical Quarterly* 12(January 1981): 17–35.

———. "A Letter from Jessie to Kit." *Bulletin of the Missouri Historical Society* 29(July 1973): 260–63.

———. "The Manco Burro Pass Massacre." *NMHR* 41(October 1966): 305–18.

Lecompte, Janet and Lester F. Turley. "The Turleys from Booneslick." *Bulletin of the Missouri Historical Society* 27(April 1972): 178–95.

Miller, Skip Keith. "Ferdinand Maxwell: The Other Maxwell." *Taos Lightning* [Taos Historic Museums] 3(Fall 1997): 1–5.

Moody, Marshall D. "Kit Carson, Indian Agent to the Indians in New Mexico, 1853–1861." *NMHR* 28(January 1953): 1–20.

Morgan, Dale L. "The Fur Trade and Its Historians." *The American West* 3(Spring 1966): 28–35.

Morgan, Dale L. and Harvey L. Carter. "An Informative Dialogue-by-Letter About Kit Carson's Early, Uncertain Chronology." *Montana Magazine* 16(July 1986): 86–90.

Murphy, Lawrence R. "Rayado: Pioneer Settlement in Northeastern New Mexico, 1848–1857." *NMHR* 46(January 1971): 37–56.

Myers, Harry C. "Massacre on the Santa Fe Trail: Mr. White's Company of Unfortunates." *Wagon Tracks* [Santa Fe Trail Association Quarterly] 6(February 1992): 18–25.

Petersen, Phil. "Boggsville: A Trail Settlement." *Wagon Tracks* 6(November 1992): 7–11.

Peterson, Jacqueline. "Prelude to Red River: A Social Portrait of the Great Lakes Métis." *Ethnohistory* 25(Winter 1978): 41–67.

Reeve, Frank D., ed. "The Charles Bent Papers." *NMHR* 30(July 1955): 252–54.

Richardson, Albert D. "A Visit to Kit Carson." *Frank Leslie's Illustrated Newspaper* (December 8, 1860): 37–38.

Sanford, A. B. "Reminiscences of Kit Carson, Jr." *The Colorado Magazine* 6(September 1929): 179–84.

Schroeder, Albert H. "Kit Carson House." *La Gaceta* 5(1970): 21–22.

Settle, Raymond W. "The Twilight Days of Kit Carson." *The West* (March 1969): 14–15, 68–70.

Shaw, Dorothy Price. "The Cragin Collection." *The Colorado Magaine* 25(July 1948): 166–78.

Simmons, Marc. "Kit Carson at Fort Craig." In Charles Carroll and Lynn Sebastian, eds., *Fort Craig, The United States Fort on the Camino Real* (Socorro, N.Mex.: Bureau of Land Management, 2000): 148–53.

———. "Kit and the Indians." In R. C. Gordon-McCutchan, ed., *Kit Carson: Indian Fighter or Indian Killer?* (Niwot: University Press of Colorado, 1996): 73–90.

Swagerty, William. "Indian Trade in the Trans-Mississippi West to 1870." In Wilcomb E. Washburn, ed., *History of Indian-White Relations.* Vol. 4 of William C. Sturtevant, ed., *Handbook of North American Indians* (Series in progress. Washington, D.C.: Smithsonian Institution Press, 1988): 351–74.

———. "Marriage and Settlement Patterns of Rocky Mountain Trappers and Traders." *Western Historical Quarterly* 11(April 1980): 159–80.

Switzler, William F. "Kit Carson." *Missouri Historical Society Collections* 2(January 1900): 35–45.

Thompson, Albert W. "The Death and the Last Will of Kit Carson." *The Colorado Magazine* 5(1928): 183–91.

———. "Insurrection at Taos." *New Mexico Magazine* 20(April 1942): 18–19.

Utley, Robert M. "Kit Carson and the Adobe Walls Campaign." *American West* 2(Winter 1965): 4–11, 73–75.

Wiggins, Oliver P. "How I First Met Kit Carson." *The Garden of the Gods Magazine* 1(Part 1, June 1902): 15–19 and 1(Part 2, October 1902): 31–34.

Index

Leal, James W., 73
Lee, Stephen Louis, 72
Leitensdorfer, Eugene, 58
Lobato, Buenaventura, 73
Luna, Antonia, 40
Lux, John T., 105

Making Out Road, daughters, *40c*, *40d*,
45–46; disposition, 36; her name, 35–
36; later life, 46; marriage to Carson,
37–40, 41–42; and Rath, 45, 155
Martínez, Antonio José, *82a*; and 1847
Taos uprising, 73, 75–76; and Carson,
43, 109
Masons, 107–108, *116c*
Maxwell, Ferdinand, 167
Maxwell, Lucien, *82b*; 1842 caravan, 46;
1844 trip, 65; and Apaches, 79–80;
and Carson, 66, 67, 82–83, 96; and
Frémont, 48; and Indian Agent
business, 94–95
McKay, Thomas, 22
Mercure, Henry, 88, 89
Meriwether, David D., 93
Mescalero Apaches, 118–120
Morgan, Dale L., 32, 42–43
Mostin, John, 97

Navajos, 120–124
Nelson, Jesse, 39, 79–80, 85, 86, 92

Oakes, Daniel C., 139
Owl Woman, 32, 37

Padilla, María de la Cruz, 40, 59
Parker, Rev. Samuel, 8–9, 12–13, *17b*
Peters, DeWitt C., *100a*; on Carson and
Chouinard, 13–14; and Carson's

autobiography, 97, 167; his manu-
script, ix–x
Plains tribes 1865 council, 126
Price, Sterling, 71

Quinn, James H., 82, 94–95

Rath, Charles, 37, *40d*, 45, 126
Rayado, New Mex., 83, 86, *82b*
religion, 43, 102, 108–109
Robertson (Robison), Jack, 27
Romero, Tomasito, 72–75
Running Around, 15

Sabin, Edwin L., 21, 41–42
Santa Fe Trail, 31, 123, 125
Santistevan, Juan, *116c*, 117
Sayre, Dr. Lewis Albert, 138
Scheurich, Aloys, *66d*, 106, 142, 144
Sena de Luna, José Rafael, Sr., 73, 161
Shaking Herself, 45
Sherman, William Tecumseh, 78, 106,
129–130
Shunar (Chouinard), 8–15, *18b*
Simmons, Louis, 79–80, 88, 165
Simpson, Smith H., 14
Sinclair, Prewitt, 25
Sitting-in-the-Lodge, 41
slaves, 101–102
de Smet, Pierre Jean, 27
Stilts, George, 90
St. Louis, Mo., 43–44, 46–48, 85
St. Vrain, Cerán, and the "Avengers", 74;
and Bent, 31, 99; his children, 59; in
Civil War, 113, 114; Las Animas
Grant, 57–58

Taos, New Mex., 39–40, 68, 71–75